SIDEWALKS

URBAN AND INDUSTRIAL ENVIRONMENTS

Series editor: Robert Gottlieb, Henry R. Luce Professor of Urban and Environmental Policy, Occidental College

For a complete list of books in the series, please see the back of the book.

Sidewalks

Conflict and Negotiation over Public Space

———

Anastasia Loukaitou-Sideris and Renia Ehrenfeucht

The MIT Press
Cambridge, Massachusetts
London, England

For information about special quantity discounts, please email special_sales@mitpress.mit.edu.

This book was set in Bembo on 3B2 by Asco Typesetters, Hong Kong.
Printed on recycled paper and bound in the United States of America.

Library of Congress Cataloging-in-Publication Data

Loukaitou-Sideris, Anastasia, 1958–
Sidewalks : conflict and negotiation over public space / Anastasia Loukaitou-Sideris and Renia Ehrenfeucht.
    p.   cm.
Includes bibliographical references and index.
ISBN 978-0-262-12307-5 (hardcover : alk. paper)
1. Public spaces. 2. Sidewalks. I. Ehrenfeucht, Irena. II. Title.
HT153.L67   2009
388.4'11—dc22   2008038553

10   9   8   7   6   5   4   3   2   1

To our families

Contents

ACKNOWLEDGMENTS

The first seeds for the development of this book were planted by our colleague, Evelyn Blumenberg at UCLA. Her interest in the Las Vegas sidewalks kindled our eventual inquiry into sidewalks as distinct urban spaces. We thank her for this and for allowing us to rework a co-authored piece to include it in this book.

We also wish to express our appreciation to Eran Ben-Joseph and Terry Szold of MIT. Their invitation to participate in a colloquium they organized in the fall of 2002 and contribute a chapter for their edited book *Regulating Place*, encouraged us to explore the framework of municipal controls affecting sidewalk uses.

Over the course of fieldwork and archival research we spoke with a multitude of individuals about sidewalks—officials in Public Works Departments and Bureaus of Street Services, representatives of Business Improvement Districts and business associations, homeless service providers, community activists, and members of nonprofit organizations. They are too many to list here, and some would not like to see their names in print, but we wish to thank everyone in Boston, Los Angeles, Miami, New York, and Seattle who took the time to talk with us about sidewalk activities and controls in their cities.

We also wish to extend a special note of thanks to our very able research assistants. Leigha Schmidt was a great help early on. Anne McAuley provided invaluable help throughout the project, digging into municipal ordinances and regulations, conducting some interviews, and taking photographs of sidewalks in Los Angeles. Similarly, Jay Jones and Mike Holland at the Los Angeles City Archive gave immense assistance with Los Angeles historical material.

Almost everyone uses sidewalks, and we have had the pleasure of discussing our topic with countless knowledgeable people; we value their interpretations, challenges, and anecdotes. Renia gives special thanks to Ula and Karol Makowski and, when she moved to New Orleans, to Marla Nelson, Wheeler and Max Moorman, Jennifer Ruley, and Paul Lambert who introduced her to sidewalk life in a unique public city. Our friends, family members and colleagues who have talked with us about sidewalks are too numerous to name but much appreciated.

Finally, our deepest appreciation to our institutions, the Department of Urban Planning in the School of Public Affairs at UCLA and the Department of Planning and Urban Studies at the University of New Orleans for providing resources for this intellectual pursuit, and to the staff at the MIT Press, especially Robert Gottlieb, along with Laura Callen, Deborah Cantor-Adams, Susan Clark, Colleen Lanick, Clay Morgan, Mary Reilly, Megan Schwenke, Sharon Deacon Warne, and Rosemary Winfield for their support and wise counsel.

SIDEWALKS

I

———

HISTORY AND EVOLUTION

INTRODUCTION: THE SOCIAL, ECONOMIC, AND POLITICAL LIFE OF SIDEWALKS

Most of us take sidewalks for granted. An undervalued element of the urban form, this public ground connects points of origin and destination, and few people go through the day without traversing at least one sidewalk. Sidewalks are unassuming, standardized pieces of gray concrete that are placed between roadways and buildings, and their common appearance belies their significance and history as unique but integral parts of the street and urban life. A commercial terrain for merchants and vendors, a place of leisure for flâneurs, a refuge for homeless residents, a place for day-to-day survival for panhandlers, a space for debate and protest for political activists, an urban forest for environmentalists: U.S. sidewalks have hosted a wealth of social, economic, and political uses and have been integral to a contested democracy.

What do we want from sidewalks? Various observers argue that public spaces are becoming less democratic, and they point to the historic uses for public spaces to underscore their argument. Fewer explain the ways that people use sidewalks in cities now and the role that sidewalks play in contemporary urban life. In 1961, Jane Jacobs (1961) called sidewalks "the main public places of the city" and "its most vital organs." For Jacobs, sidewalks were active sites of socialization and pleasure, and this social interaction kept neighborhoods safe and controlled. She demanded a better appreciation of the street in the face of modernist planning that intended to replace its complexity with order. In the 1960s, many white, middle-class residents left the cities and settled in suburbs as massive redevelopment projects restructured central-city neighborhoods, displacing thousands of residents and moving downtown shoppers into mall-like complexes.

In many suburban subdivisions, developers avoided the expense and potential liability that public sidewalks can entail. They provided no sidewalks, and planners failed to require them. Even when sidewalks were built, suburbanites rarely used them because they needed their cars to reach schools, banks, grocery stores, and other everyday destinations. The urban form of the mid-twentieth-century suburb—single-use, low-density houses with individual yards—discouraged walking or socializing on the sidewalks. The private backyard could accommodate family outdoor activities, while the suburban shopping mall replaced the commercial street as a place to shop, socialize, and be entertained.

In recent decades, however, people have been returning to the central city and, in some cases, high-density living. The urban downtown and Main Street "renaissance," as some scholars have called it (Teaford 1990), has brought new attention to downtown public spaces. Cities have revitalized abandoned parts of their downtowns, hoping to attract back to the center not only tourists and conventioneers but also suburban residents. They have allowed historic buildings to be converted into lofts, created outdoor destinations with sidewalk cafés, commercial displays, vendors, and performers, and—with corporate help—have rebuilt historic public markets, town centers, and riverfronts. Similarly, towns have sought to bring back their decayed Main Streets, and suburbs have developed new town centers and destination districts. At the same time, the U.S. Surgeon General has encouraged people to walk more to stay healthy and fight obesity (U.S. Department of Health and Human Services 1996) and generated a renewed interest in walking.

Urbanists, heeding Jane Jacobs's early call for an appreciation of public environments, have helped illuminate the complexities and functions of public spaces and inspired a generation of urban designers and planners to envision a public city. "Public," however, does not mean inclusive of all urban residents or all people who use city sidewalks; it never has. And it certainly does not imply accepting frightening or uncomfortable activities. These planners and urbanists have suggested that vibrant public spaces can control undesirable people and activities (Jacobs 1961; Whyte 1988).

When public spaces are redeveloped, some people are planned for as the target users while others are planned against, and redevelopment projects are meant to exclude as much as attract. Some observers have criticized attempts to fortify the city (Davis 1990; Sorkin 1992; Smith 2001; Mitchell 2003; Smith and Low 2006), but others support efforts to regulate public spaces and exclude disruptions, such as public protests and activities associated with panhandling and homelessness (Ellickson 1996). Comfort and safety are attributes cherished by many who choose to visit only public spaces that can ensure pleasant encounters with others like themselves— sidewalks in homogeneous communities, malls, plazas, and movie theaters.

A favorite public-space myth recalls a time when diversity was accepted on city streets. It speaks to a contemporary desire to accommodate diversity, envisioning what public spaces could be rather than describing what they were. Nineteenth-century streets and sidewalks were crowded and complex, but public-space historians have shown that they were also contested sites where rights and access were not guaranteed. Urban streets and sidewalks also have been locations of intervention for reformers and public-health advocates. Municipal interventions restricted those who worked or played on public sidewalks, widened the streets, and cleaned and greened the sidewalks. Urbanites adapted to these changes, at times disregarded them, and inserted different interpretations and priorities into the ever-changing public realm.

THEMES

This book looks at competing sidewalk uses and claims and evolves around some specific themes—distinctiveness, publicness, diversity and contestation, and regulation.

M| Ideas

5

DISTINCTIVENESS

The relative lack of scholarly work on sidewalks might be explained by their status as an undifferentiated part of the street. Streets and sidewalks compose the public right of way in cities. Like streets, sidewalks are ubiquitous and difficult to avoid. Motorists observe them from their vehicles, and pedestrians walk along them from point of origin to destination or from car to building. But sidewalks differ from the roadbed and have historically accommodated distinct uses. The roadbed is used solely for vehicles, but people have walked and socialized on the sidewalks since sidewalks were first constructed.

Sidewalks also differ from one another based on their location within the city, surrounding demographics, and association with particular uses and buildings. Such differences are more nuanced than the roadbed/sidewalk distinction implies. Sidewalks are closely associated with abutting buildings, and the way that they are perceived and used affects the tenants and users of these buildings. In addition, abutting property owners are responsible for keeping sidewalks free from obstructions and sometimes must keep them in good repair. For this reason, sidewalks are simultaneously public and parochial—open to all and yet a space over which a group feels ownership (Lofland 1998). The book therefore highlights the distinct characteristics of urban sidewalks as small public spaces that wind throughout the city.

PUBLICNESS

The book also examines the flexible and ambiguous boundaries that surround sidewalks' publicness. Many different social groups—municipal bureaucrats, abutting property owners, neighborhood councils, merchants, street vendors, homeless people, labor unions, and political activists—have negotiated public access and activities on the sidewalk. The book's focus on sidewalks continues the work that is being done by public-space scholars who have focused on the spaces of everyday life.

As Neil Smith and Setha Low (2006, 3) have explained, global societies have public spaces that operate at different scales—"the range of social locations offered by the street, the park, the media, and Internet, the shopping mall, the United Nations, national governments, and local neighborhoods. 'Public space' envelops the palpable tension between place, experienced at all scales of daily life, and the seeming spacelessness of the Internet, popular opinion, and global institutions and economy." In exploring sidewalks, we also show how local conflicts are moments where larger institutions and processes "touch down." Indeed, one difficulty in public-space debates is agreeing on the issue that is being debated. A Senegalese street vendor in Harlem and his Guatemalan counterpart in East Los Angeles reflect forces that influence economic restructuring and transnational migrations, and their presence can invoke these concerns, but street vending also represents a contested activity on a local corner.

Access to public spaces also is a mechanism by which urban dwellers assert their right to participate in society, and these struggles over the right to use public spaces take different forms. One distinction can be made between a demand to access a space for its defined uses (as was the case with desegregation movements over public transportation and public facilities) and the right to define a space's use (such as a fight against a public sleeping ban). Both are important.

Public spaces are difficult to characterize because they vary significantly: Access to a governance institution is different from access to a sidewalk. In urban public spaces, a space's publicness can be seen as the extent to which people have access without asking permission, expressed or implied. Although the person or organization that holds the title to a property may influence the activities that occur there, this is not the only or even most important factor that makes a space public.

All spaces have restrictions—physical, legal, and social—and the way that a space functions for a public is evaluated comparatively with other public spaces. A shopping plaza differs from the sidewalk in its design, uses, and hours of operation, but both have public functions. Moreover, because some activities necessarily infringe on others (a sidewalk used for lumber storage may be impassable), a space's publicness is better assessed over time because not all activities happen or need to happen at one time. Although any given space may not always be open or accessible, the right to its use as others use it is a significant part of full societal participation. In addition, as Don Mitchell (2003, 35) has argued, what "makes a space *public* is often not its preordained 'publicness.' Rather, a space is made public when, so as to fulfill a pressing need, one group *takes* space and through its actions *makes* it public."

Margaret Kohn (2004, 11–12) places urban spaces on a continuum of public and private usage that is based on the interplay of ownership, accessibility, and intersubjectivity. The public/private dichotomy is still relevant, but it needs to be defined precisely given the extensive scholarship that highlights privacy in public and the range of public spaces that are privately owned. Most sidewalks are public property, but private-property owners exercise significant control over them and often are held responsible for their maintenance. Businesses also often use sidewalks, which benefits both them and other users.

DIVERSITY AND CONTESTATION

The third theme of this book is the role that sidewalks play as shared spaces that accommodate diverse people. This diversity sometimes leads to contestation. How do people use spaces differently and similarly? In what ways do these activities reflect varying notions and different priorities? What underlies the conflicts that arise? What aspects of activities become incompatible with others? Although municipalities enact ordinances and employ other interventions to limit undesirable public-space activities, such ordinances do not reflect the government's perspective but rather the negotiated interests of constituents who want some degree of order.

Public spaces have multiple functions. They provide sites for people to interact with those who are outside their private circles and allow decision making, the articulation of public concerns, and the resolution of common problems. Usually, however, public spaces are used for daily activities such as transportation, shopping, and recreation. Public spaces host an array of activities that overlap and thereby become sites of conflict.

Various groups have identifiably different interests, but no monolithic middle- or upper-income group controls a homogeneous group of low-income residents. Residents in poor neighborhoods are affected by street prostitution and drug use and may want them eliminated from their sidewalks. Small businesses may compete with street vendors or dislike street trees that block their signage. Pedestrians may object to newspaper boxes or sidewalk displays. One person's sidewalk activity may very well compete for limited space or conflict with another's need for order. The complexity arises because multiple interests of various groups overlap on the same narrow stretches of sidewalk pavement.

Although we emphasize differences and conflict among groups, conflict is not always a negative that should be eliminated. As Rosalyn Deutsche (1996, 278) argues, "urban space is the product of conflict." This differs in two essential ways from Jürgen Habermas's view that civilized discussion between groups that share interests can develop a collective voice. First, it highlights conflict over consensus and difference over commonality. Differences are not more important than commonalities, but commonalities are less likely to require negotiation. Second, these discussions are not only verbal but also play out through practices in public spaces. When people simply take space for a given purpose at a given time, they are demanding public spaces for specific and contingent use. We are no longer faced with a question of how to maintain or establish order in a rapidly changing city but rather how to live with differences and adapt cities to the challenges that differences bring (Sandercock 2003).

Every disruptive or conflictual activity has multiple sides. Dissenters may value the opportunity to block a sidewalk and disrupt a convention because they gain the attention of decision makers or the media. The conventioneers may need to use the sidewalk to reach the convention and conduct their business, while other citizens may need the sidewalk for passage. All strands might be legitimate claims, and the ensuing discussions are fundamental to urban democracy.

REGULATION

Public spaces are contested terrains. Through public struggles, urbanites articulate both diverse and common interests and demand mechanisms for regulating shared aspects of urban life that are flexible and transparent. The final theme of this book explores public-space control and the defining of differences among people and boundaries among spaces.

We examine the legal, regulatory, and policy frameworks that have been employed by municipalities and the courts to prescribe sidewalk form and control sidewalk uses. Because the process of developing public space has simultaneously been a process of controlling it, the regulatory framework is a dimension of public space. As many scholars have documented, design and regulatory strategies have constitutional implications for First Amendment speech and assembly rights. They also have subtler effects when they delineate who is protected and who represents a problem. But frameworks of control that differentiate among spaces and people have been central to any discussion about urban life.

Openness has always been limited, and the struggle over public spaces is about constraints and acceptable activities and users. This negotiation over appropriate uses differentiates among activities (in what context does standing become loitering?), spaces (where does standing become loitering?), and the guidelines for the permissible. Efforts to control public spaces depend on these definitions. Defining who can participate and how they can do so is fundamental. Municipalities enact ordinances and regulations to define acceptable uses of sidewalks, and cities and corporate actors employ design and policy strategies to achieve particular effects. How sidewalks can be used (their "primary purposes") and who can use them (their "publicness") have been debated in council chambers and in court by urban residents, business owners, municipal governments, civil rights advocates, and political activists.

Formalized actions come late in the struggle over access to sidewalks, and they reflect agreements on activities, users, and their relative priorities. Agreements do not imply that all parties believe that an ordinance is fair or necessary but suggest that the situation has been defined adequately for the municipality to take some action. In fact, a tension must be framed in a way that offers a course of action.

Many observers fear that public spaces are becoming less democratic, but we argue that this is not because ordinances have been enacted or other devices deployed to control public spaces. Individual ordinances and public-space regulations may be wrong and should be contested. We caution against defining the ordinances and laws as the problem, however, when it is the agreements that they embody that should be examined and evaluated. As Nancy Fraser (1992, 124) reminds us, "The ideal of participation parity is not fully realizable." In the debate over appropriate public space uses that may precede an ordinance, certain actors are more powerful than others, and their voices are heard louder. In fact, the process of justifying controls can engender fear that leads to withdrawal from those very spaces that we attempt to secure. Focusing on eliminating all disorder fails to adapt and respond to changing urban circumstances and results in an unjust society. Public-space controls are important negotiations, and even our tools to fight injustice are restraints on actors (individuals, corporations, and governments). A just city would have controls that define the parameters of public-space use and access and also processes that enable different voices and interests to help define those controls.

AIMS AND APPROACH

This inquiry into urban sidewalks as contested public spaces has some specific aims. To understand what urbanites might want from public spaces, observers have drawn heavily on historical depictions of street and park life, as well as the sociability of bars, restaurants, bath houses, penny arcades, and destinations like Atlantic City. At times, these invocations are tinged with nostalgia for a seemingly ideal public realm. Historians, however, have painted a complex vision of public sociability that was characterized by diverse contested activities. This book draws from historical and contemporary examples to document the evolution of municipal sidewalks as well as their competing functional, social, political, commercial, and environmental uses. It focuses on how the functions and meanings of street activities in U.S. cities shifted and were negotiated through controls and interventions, how different claims to sidewalks were justified, and how primary uses were defined.

This is complemented by case-study research and collection of information from interviews, archival research, and data and statistics from five cities—Boston, Los Angeles, New York, Miami, and Seattle. These cities represent different geographic regions and different population sizes. New

York has been the largest city in the United States since the late eighteenth century. Los Angeles grew rapidly in the twentieth century and became the second largest city in the 1990 census. Boston (twentieth in the 2000 census) and Seattle (twenty-fourth in the 2000 census) have held more or less similar rankings throughout the last three decades. Miami (ranked forty-seventh in the 2000 census) has always been the smallest of the five in population. All five cities are heterogeneous urban environments, which is a growing trend as well as a source of tension.

Despite these differences, municipal responses are similar as they draw on limited tools and the examples of other cities. Municipal governments in these five cities have instigated regulations seeking to intervene, react, and respond to sidewalk issues and conflicts, and business associations have spearheaded attempts to control sidewalks. In 1993, Seattle prohibited sitting on sidewalks, which led to a sit-in by homeless groups and their advocates and a court challenge. Boston introduced aggressive panhandling legislation. Other cities nationwide also addressed panhandling as well as sleeping and sitting in public. Both New York and Los Angeles had early experiences with street peddling and have proclaimed "vending wars" at different times. Other cities have also witnessed an increase in street vending. Florida cities have actively enacted prostitution-abatement zones, such as Miami's "prostitution mapping" project. Other cities nationwide have also experimented with drug-abatement, gang-abatement, and prostitution-abatement zones. The streets and sidewalks of all five cities have hosted parades, public protests, and overlapping everyday interactions.

Finally, our focus is on urban rather than suburban sidewalks. Our examination of mixed-use urban areas reflects our emphasis on diversity, conflict, and negotiation over sidewalk uses. With their emphasis on separating uses, many suburban subdivisions have little sidewalk activity, and many commercial districts are malls. Suburban sidewalks, when present, have been typically devoid of social activity, with the exception of the occasional pedestrian or jogger. Increasingly, however, the distinction between "the urban" and "the suburban" is blurring as suburbs develop mixed-use districts and destination points. Suburban commercial corridors now have competing sidewalk uses as recent controversies over day-labor sites, street prostitution, and homelessness attest.

A Guide to the Chapters That Follow

Part I of this book outlines the history and evolution of urban sidewalks. Following this introductory chapter, chapter 2 briefly discusses international examples of early sidewalks and uses Los Angeles as a case study to examine the provision of sidewalks and negotiations over sidewalk obstructions in the late nineteenth and early twentieth centuries. At this time, the pedestrian was defined as the primary user of sidewalks, an assumption that operates today. Chapter 2 draws from an article that we previously published in the *Journal of Historical Geography* (Ehrenfeucht and Loukaitou-Sideris 2007) and a book chapter that originally appeared in *Regulating Place*, coauthored with Evelyn Blumenberg (Loukaitou-Sideris, Blumenberg, and Ehrenfeucht 2005).

Part II considers sidewalks as spaces where people display individual and group identities and observe others. Sidewalks allow for open interactions and accidental encounters with different urbanites, and chapter 3 explores the possibilities that arise from interacting with others and from performing ritualized activities (such as promenading) that strengthen intragroup cohesion and intergroup differences. Chapter 4 explores parading as a way for people to insert collective identities into a broader public and for groups to negotiate their social position.

Social encounters can also be disruptive to daily activities or social expectations. Part III explores both small and large political actions on the sidewalks and the ways that they become visible expressions of dissent and claim to the city. Chapter 5 focuses on everyday politics, examining three ways that relative status was established and challenged among different groups of participants—engaging in micropolitics, challenging exclusion from the public realm, and creating a dangerous, adult public realm. Chapter 6 turns to ephemeral protest events that use the visibility of sidewalks to capture national or global audiences.

In part IV, we turn to competing uses and meanings of sidewalks and look at three topics—street vending, homelessness, and urban forestry. Chapter 7 examines the sidewalk as a space of economic survival for street vendors and the conflicts between vendors and established businesses. Chapter 8 examines the public-space debates over sidewalk activities that are associated with homelessness. Efforts to remove people from streets and sidewalks or reduce their impact are simultaneously about confronting poverty, defining sidewalk uses and users, minimizing discomfort, and evaluating rights to choice and access. This chapter ponders some of the ensuing dilemmas. Chapter 9 looks at a seemingly noncontroversial issue—the greening of sidewalks— to show how it can still result in disagreement and conflict. Street trees are generally desirable, but they elicit varied responses from different urbanites who want different things from public space. Competing priorities for urban infrastructure often lead to a neglect of the sidewalk as landscape, particularly in poor neighborhoods.

In part V, we examine the complex regulatory frameworks that manage street life and investigate their tools and effectiveness. In chapter 10, we argue that the process of justifying controls and defining problems might heighten fears and work against making public spaces vibrant. We focus on prostitution-mapping ordinances to discuss larger issues of control, access to the city, and the equation of disorder with danger. In chapter 11, we examine the regulatory role that is played by municipal governments and the ways that administrative bodies negotiate among competing uses and as institutions with their own purposes—to maintain public infrastructure, accommodate diverse residents, and create and promote a city's image. Chapter 11 is drawn from the chapter in *Regulating Place* (Loukaitou-Sideris, Blumenberg, and Ehrenfeucht 2005).

Finally, in the concluding chapter, we ponder about the role that is being played by urban sidewalks in the early twenty-first century—what we want from sidewalk life, who should count as the public, how we can balance competing interests, what design features and policies are fair, and how we can facilitate social encounters and vibrancy.

CONSTRUCTION AND EVOLUTION OF SIDEWALKS

The sidewalk—a designated part of the roadway that separates and protects people from vehicles—has a long but interrupted history. The first sidewalks appeared around 2000 to 1990 B.C. "at the *karum* of Kultepe" in central Anatolia (modern Turkey) (Kostof 1992, 191). Accounts relate that the ancient Greek city of Corinth had sidewalks that were used through the fourth century, but the date of their construction is unclear (Catling 1986–1987). Beginning in the third century B.C., the Romans had a special word for sidewalks, *semita* (Kostof 1992, 209), but sidewalks disappeared when Rome was conquered from the north (Geist 1983). In the medieval streets of Europe, pedestrians did not have a separate space but mingled with horses, carts, and wagons on the roadway (Ford 2000). Sidewalks reappeared in Europe only after London's great fire of 1666, when reconstructed streets had sidewalks, and they became more common in the city by the mid-eighteenth century following the Westminster Paving Act of 1751.[1]

In the middle of the eighteenth century, some exclusive Parisian streets had foot pavements or *trottoirs*, which were "unconnected, protruding limestone curbs, serving to hold off carts" (Geist 1983, 62). A few elevated walkways of the city (*promenades*) became integrated into the general street system in the form of boulevards. Boulevards developed as broad, tree-lined streets that segregated vehicles from pedestrians. French police ordinances of 1763 and 1766 stipulated that pedestrians were allowed on protected sidepaths (*contre allées*), while horses were permitted at the center of the roadway (Jacobs, Macdonald, and Rofé 2002). By 1822, only 876 linear feet of sidewalks lined the streets of Paris, but twenty-five years later, 161 miles of sidewalks had been constructed (Kostof 1992).

Sidewalks developed some distinct meanings when they were constructed. According to James Winter (1993), on London's late eighteenth- and nineteenth-century streets, footpaths preceded street paving. Posts separated some footpaths from the road, and others were paved with egg-shaped stones. The raised curb and sidewalk became common in London after the introduction of macadam paving. This had noteworthy effects. The carriageway became larger proportionately as pedestrians increasingly walked on sidewalks, but the sidewalks also became "more sharply differentiated from the other parts increasing the amount of legal ambiguity about what the term 'street' was meant to convey" (Winter 1993, 100). The sidewalks were cleaner than the streets and also affiliated with abutting businesses, in practice if not by law.

By the late eighteenth century, when sidewalks were increasingly common in London, a "border territory" also developed between the footway and the carriageway. The gutter became a zone where both physically and metaphorically those without respect would end. As Winter (1993, 100) explains:

> As for the border area, there could hardly be a "good" [positive connotation] since one of its components, the "verge," connoted the problematical, and another, the "curb," suggested restraint on unwanted impulse, while a third, the "gutter," brought to mind everything that is vile.... Until the end of the horse-drawn era, men customarily urinated against the curb wheels of standing carts and wagons.... After the 1830s, sandwich-board advertisers, recruited from the old and destitute, were required to walk in the gutter, and drivers thought it amusing now and then to give one of these poor creatures a lash of the whip. Vagabonds, prostitutes, drunks, gambling touts, and beggars sought their livelihood on the pavement but, according to convention, were continually teetering on the verge of a descent into that part of the street where, according to tradition, all immorality and corruption finally end.

By the late nineteenth century, sidewalks were commonly constructed in London, Paris, and most other European cities (Olsen 1986). The grand boulevards that were built in Paris, Vienna, and Barcelona reserved generous sidewalks for the crowds of urban flâneurs—to stroll, look, and hang out (Tester 1994). Immortalized by impressionist painters, these sidewalks epitomized nineteenth-century urbanity in the public imagination.

The United States was urbanizing rapidly during the late nineteenth century, but established Americans and new immigrants were more ambivalent than their European counterparts about urban life. People, goods, and vehicles crowded the American streets and sidewalks, and with growth came an increasingly professionalized municipal government, municipal improvements, and public-space controls. As municipalities began to provide sidewalks, they exerted increasing control over how they were used. And one use, walking for transportation, became the primary purpose for which the sidewalks were constructed. The pedestrian's unobstructed mobility became the justification that underlay other activity restrictions, and the pedestrian became the public for whom the sidewalks were being provided. The assumption that walking is the primary use for sidewalks has carried into the twenty-first century.

For the remainder of this chapter, we look at sidewalk development in the United States, using Los Angeles as a case study. We use four main sources to understand the provision of sidewalks in Los Angeles: (1) the Los Angeles city council minutes, ordinances, and petitions from 1880 to 1920 pertaining to sidewalk uses; (2) lively discussions about the sidewalk's purposes and conditions in *Los Angeles Times* articles from 1882 to 1908; (3) articles in the *American City* trade journal from 1918 and 1919 about U.S. and Canadian practices of constructing and regulating streets; and (4) the Los Angeles Police Department's minutes and reports from 1890 to 1915.

CONSTRUCTING U.S. SIDEWALKS

In 1798, the Common Council of New York City established the first Street Department in the U.S, and in subsequent years, as the duties of the Street Department expanded to encompass numerous bureaus, the agency staff included an inspector of sidewalks (Moehring 1981). By the early half of the nineteenth century, large cities had curbs and sidewalks along their heavily traveled streets (American Public Works Association 1976), and sidewalks often appeared prior to street paving. Nineteenth-century town governments passed bylaws regulating streets and street lighting, which at times included tax assessments for the provision of sidewalks (Bates 1912).

By the nineteenth century, sidewalks had become important elements of the urban infrastructure, and thousands of miles of sidewalks were paved in American cities. Chicago residents, for example, viewed public works such as sidewalks, planked streets, and gas lights as significant urban improvements. In the 1850s, the city built hundreds of miles of sidewalks and planked streets, several new bridges, water works, and a sewerage system (Einhorn 1991).

During this time, other U.S. municipal governments also became purveyors of public goods and services, paving miles of roads and constructing sewers and water systems, libraries, and public institutions (Teaford 1984). Early sidewalks were often constructed of wood or gravel, but as early as the 1820s, American engineers knew of and used natural cement deposits for public works such as street paving. Only in the 1880s did a predictable quality of cheap, manufactured concrete become available (McShane 1979), and it was subsequently used for sidewalks. In Salem, Oregon, for example, sidewalks were ordered along all streets from 1851 onward. They were constructed from wood until 1912, when concrete became standard (Salem n.d.).

Street paving was different than larger public-works projects such as sewer and water systems. City councils were often caught between demands for greater services and unwillingness on the part of property owners to pay higher taxes. Because street improvements increased the value of adjacent properties and were not yet perceived as a public good, nineteenth-century entrepreneurs paid for their construction (Fogelson 1993). Likewise, sidewalks benefited abutting properties. They were constructed in conjunction with other improvements (such as grading and graveling), paid for by the adjacent property owners, but administered through the municipal government. To construct improvements, the property owners petitioned the city council, which accepted requests and ordered work done. The board of public works with its growing staff—superintendent of streets, city surveyor, and engineers—surveyed the city, laid out the street lines, established the grades, and developed construction specifications. In their administrative roles, public-works professionals set development standards, oversaw the improvements, and in the case of the sidewalks, required maintenance.[2] They exercised significant influence over the improvements with an eye toward functionality for the city as a whole rather than for the benefit of the petitioners alone. Once improved, the streets were usually dedicated to the city (Schultz and McShane 1978; Teaford 1984).

Because sidewalks were useful and cheaper than roads to pave, they were surfaced with durable materials at a faster rate than the roadbed. In the late 1870s and early 1880s, sidewalks were primarily surfaced with gravel, but by the 1890s, cement sidewalks became common, although roadbed surfacing was still primarily gravel ("Municipal Improvements for 1915" 1915).[3] Sidewalks became cleaner and better paved than carriageways. Pedestrians used sidewalks to avoid traffic, which undoubtedly influenced their decisions about where to walk, and they also preferred sidewalks because they were less muddy than roadways in wet weather and had more even surfaces. Even though photographs indicate that pedestrians "jaywalked" or could step into the street at any point, they appeared to walk primarily along the sidewalks.

In the nineteenth century, sidewalks were funded by special assessments and installed at the request of abutting property owners. For example, the 1833 town charter of Chicago contained a clause that required the collection of at least half of the cost of sidewalks from abutting property owners. The 1835 charter required owners of two-thirds of a street's real estate to request sidewalks, but few property owners did so (Einhorn 1991). Although property owners paid for the sidewalks, the city of Chicago also collected a sidewalk tax to help finance other street projects (Einhorn 1991). In other cities, property owners also paid for sidewalks and were required to maintain the property frontage (McShane 1994).

Although the decision to pave streets and construct sidewalks fell primarily to property owners until the late nineteenth century, this changed rapidly as urban residents adopted the automobile. With increased automobility, the street changed from a locally oriented public space to an efficient transportation corridor. The process of street paving and sidewalk construction reflected this shift. By the late nineteenth century, cities began to take over some paving functions for health reasons—to reduce standing water and improve drainage—but they continued to assess abutting property owners for a portion or all of the paving cost. By the turn of the century, property owners in some cities still retained veto power over paving and sidewalk decisions. But soon the courts began to emphasize the public aspect of sidewalks over the rights of abutting property owners. With the backing of street users such as bicyclists and later motorists, municipalities developed public works paving projects with traffic movement as their primary goal (McShane 1994).

Street standards were institutionalized in the 1930s through 1950s, and efficient vehicular movement became the overarching goal of street design. Although not universal, specification of sidewalks also became a common feature of street standards (Southworth and Ben-Joseph 1995, 1997; American Society of Civil Engineers 1990). In some cities, such as Salem, Oregon, sidewalks were required prior to World War II, but after the war, new housing subdivisions could omit them. In 1958, sidewalks were once again required in Salem (Salem n.d.).

ELIMINATING OBSTRUCTIONS

The municipal government's involvement in street paving had far-reaching implications. Clay McShane (1979) has traced the revolution in street paving to the changing perception of the street and the role played by municipal engineers in developing the street as a circulation system. Durable paving did not always appeal to residents who wanted the street for local uses, not rapid movement. On the other hand, municipal engineers focusing on efficient transportation stressed the merits of durable paving that benefited those passing through.

Because early sidewalks hosted multiple uses, especially in the downtown areas, they were busy. Sidewalks extended the realm of the adjacent shops: shopkeepers displayed fruit and vegetables, deliveries and overstock were stored on the sidewalks, and bulky goods such as furniture fit poorly in small shops and could be more easily displayed outside. Street peddlers also made a living on the streets. Public orators could highlight the ravages of capitalism or preach salvation. Children played around building stoops, and dandies strolled along the pavement with an eye on the life of the street.

Municipal professionals and business leaders increasingly developed a different vision for the sidewalks. City officials and municipal bureaucrats sought order and defined pedestrian circulation as the purpose for sidewalks. To achieve unobstructed circulation, the city adopted ordinances restricting sidewalk use, and the owners or tenants of abutting commercial establishments saw their claims over sidewalks weaken. Orderly and free-flowing movement on the sidewalk suited the interests of the large merchants and department store owners as well. As early as 1882, the *Los Angeles Times* complained that the downtown sidewalks were impassable because of the clutter amassed there by abutting businesses ("Sauce" 1882):

> [A visitor] leaves the Cosmopolitan; possibly she may get up Main Street opposite the Pico House and not find her progress impeded by anything more than a carriage or two arranged for display on the sidewalk. There she crosses the street, comes down on the other side, threads her way through a collection of second hand furniture, crosses Arcadia street, raises her eyes to admire the magnificent proportions of Baker Block, and tumbles into a pile of orange boxes stacked up four deep on the curb! Recovering her equilibrium she continues her course down Main street, picks her way carefully among some empty dry goods boxes and is soon compelled to turn out into the middle of the street and become sandwiched between a passing street car and sundry piles of lumber, a bed of mortar and a wall of bricks. She turns up Main again at the corner of First Street, hoping to get to the hotel, three blocks away, during the hour that still remains before dinner time.

The *Los Angeles Times* articulated the conflict over sidewalk use as one of individual, private interests (those of the shopkeepers) versus the interests of the public. "Have the merchants who made a specialty of displaying their wares on the sidewalks secured special privileges in that respect, regardless

Crowded sidewalk, Fourth and Spring Streets, Los Angeles, California, c. 1905.
Courtesy of the Los Angeles Public Library.

A hotdog stand, at times considered sidewalk clutter, Los Angeles Fashion District, December 2005. Photograph by Renia Ehrenfeucht.

of public convenience?" wondered a *Times* staff writer ("Merchants Amendable for Allowing Boxes and Bales" 1881). Another noted that clearing the streets of obstructions "seems to incur the active disapproval of certain people whose special privileges of discommoding the public are threatened" ("All Along the Line" 1897).

In 1885, the California Supreme Court held in *Marini v. Graham* that "the sidewalks of the public streets of a city are parts of the street. Any obstruction of the sidewalk is therefore an obstruction of the street and a nuisance."[4] Municipal authority to keep streets free from obstructions had been well established, and linking sidewalks to the street detached it from adjacent properties and extended the city's reach. The Los Angeles city council also restricted abutters' use of the sidewalks. It curtailed the display of wares, prohibited sidewalk storage, and regulated sign and signpost location. From 1880 to the 1910s, almost twenty ordinances and amendments pertaining to sidewalk obstructions went through the council.[5] An 1881 ordinance restricted the abutters' use to a three-foot-wide area that was adjacent to the buildings for the display of wares and a period of twenty-four hours for moving delivered goods. The ordinance was immediately modified to two feet, and the hours for storage after delivery to twelve. Each ordinance elicited discussion about how much space, how much time, and for what purposes abutters could use the sidewalks.[6] And although some council members advocated on behalf of their constituents who were small merchants, none appeared to argue against the regulations entirely. The ordinances became increasingly restrictive. In 1887, the time for storage after delivery was reduced to four hours and moved from the sidewalks to the gutter. All displaying of wares or unpacking of goods in a central commercial core was prohibited.[7] The city also forbade signs and signposts on the sidewalks and defined allowable signage.[8] While public information received more protection than commercial displays, by 1898, all "signs, sign posts, bulletin boards and devices of like character" were declared a nuisance and prohibited outright.[9]

To what extent the obstruction ordinances were enforced is unclear. Occasionally, the sidewalks were at least temporarily cleared. In June 1882, a "critic at large" commended the council for clearing the boxes, barrels, and "usual overstock of store merchandise," and the police "busily" notified businesses that they were required to remove all signs across the sidewalks as well as front awnings at the sidewalks' outer edge ("Advice on the Half Shell" 1882). During the following years, the council continued to receive a steady stream of petitions requesting enforcement of its sidewalk ordinances, but few citations were issued.[10] In 1898, only one of 4,485 police court violations was for sidewalk obstructions. In 1912, of the 30,839 violations, no sidewalk obstructions were listed. In 1913, only sixteen complaints were issued for merchandise on the sidewalks and additional four for sidewalk obstructions. In the years 1913, 1915, and 1916, there were, respectively, forty-four, thirty-three, and twenty-six arrests made for blockading the sidewalks, which could have been groups of people as well as merchandise since these fell under the same ordinance.[11]

Municipal efforts against businesses and vendors who obstructed the sidewalk affected some citizens more than others. Small businesses that were constrained by space used the sidewalk to promote their wares, and the shoeshiners and food vendors leased sidewalk space from abutting businesses. In the name of the public interest, the courts repeatedly upheld municipal regulations that excluded working-class activities, many of which were conducted by people of color or foreign-born residents (Isenberg 2004).

Late nineteenth-century pedestrians grumbled over the hindrances blocking the sidewalks, but by the turn of the century they found themselves in the unenviable position of being perceived as "obstructions" to the automobile. Seeing pedestrians as "encroachers" and the major source of urban congestion and accidents, municipal technical bureaucracy sought to constrain pedestrian activity, restricting pedestrians to crossing at corners and obeying traffic signals (Bernier 2002). As early as 1912, professional magazines such as the *American City* advocated the widening of streets at the expense of urban sidewalks and the pedestrians who used them (Hunt 1912).

In the decades that followed, the assault on pedestrians continued. Pedestrians were often hit, injured, and even killed by automobiles, and newspaper editorials often condemned pedestrians as being negligent, defying the rules of the road, and "walking into moving vehicles" ("Pedestrians Who 'Bump'" 1933). "The dumb pedestrian really is pretty dumb," asserted columnist William Ullman from the pages of *Westways* magazine. "As a pedestrian the average man is not very bright.... As an incorrigible individualist, the pedestrian is intellectually inferior to the motorist in his traffic conduct" (Ullman 1937, 24).

Fines for jaywalking and improper pedestrian behavior appeared during this period. Municipal attempts to regulate pedestrian traffic and behavior were deemed "heroic" ("Heroic Attempts in Detroit" 1929) but often reached unimaginable extremes in favoring the car over the pedestrian. As Bernier (2002, 192) argues, drawing from newspaper and magazine articles of the period, "Local [Los Angeles] newspapers blamed pedestrians for holding up the entire movement of automobiles.... Detroit pedestrians during the late 1920s were led step-by-step through the journeys with the 'painting of huge yellow footsteps on sidewalks ... to keep pedestrians moving in proper lines—to encourage them to turn square corners. The city also blamed street furniture for misbehaving pedestrians. It reportedly removed trashcans and abolished newsstands to stop 'confusion' and to promote a 'fluid rather than a congealed state of pedestrian behavior.'"

Municipal efforts to clear sidewalks from "obstructions" proved to be largely successful. Eventually, not only did the crates, barrels, or peddlers' carts disappear from the sidewalks, but the pedestrians themselves did. Today, visitors from other countries are often surprised to see American sidewalks devoid of social activity, especially in West Coast cities.

SIDEWALK PUBLICNESS

Sidewalks played a part in the way that urban residents understood and claimed public rights in a variety of settings. Both the proximity of sidewalks to private property and their association with adjacent property owners are at the heart of a persistent ambiguity over the sidewalks' publicness. Up to the early nineteenth century, adjacent landowners held the ownership of the land constituting the road in front of their properties (Novak 1996). Sidewalks were associated with adjacent uses, and the abutting property owners had distinct claims and responsibilities regarding their care. Property owners paid for the sidewalks, and sidewalks were constructed at their request. In some places, property owners provided sidewalks individually, resulting in breaks in the pathway along a given block. In Chicago, the sidewalks were so irregular that in certain places flights of stairs were necessary to connect the sidewalk in front of one building to the sidewalk of an adjacent building (Einhorn 1991).

As streets and sidewalks increasingly came to be perceived as public ways, indispensable for the movement of pedestrians and vehicles, municipalities quickly and aggressively extended public jurisdiction over them. In a process that was often fraught with contestation and conflict, the nineteenth-century courts "dissolved vested interests and private property rights and reinvented the roadway as a distinctly public phenomenon, an object of governance and police" (Novak 1996, 121). In this way, providing public spaces extended the municipal government's control.

Nevertheless, the status of sidewalks remained ambiguous. They continued to be associated with abutters even as pedestrians became their primary users. Although the sidewalks were dedicated to the city as part of street improvements, their maintenance fell on the adjacent property owners, who did not always willingly comply with maintenance standards.[12] Abutters maintained the sidewalks adequately for their purposes, but because this was insufficient for smooth and safe pedestrian circulation, the superintendent of streets was often granted authority to require sidewalk repair and contract for it at the abutter's expense ("Liability Concerning Sidewalks" 1918; "Municipal Liability Concerning Streets" 1918; "The City's Legal Responsibility and Powers" 1919).

Because the sidewalks were distinguished from the road, the adjacent property owners were held more responsible for sidewalks, curbs, and gutters than they were for the roadbed. New Yorkers, for example, were required to clean the area from their house to the gutter, although many failed to do so (Moehring 1981). Similarly, the city of Los Angeles in 1899 required property owners to keep the sidewalks and equivalent spaces "free from any dirt, filth, garbage or rubbish and free from any holes or other dangers to life or limbs," but it did not hold them responsible for the street.

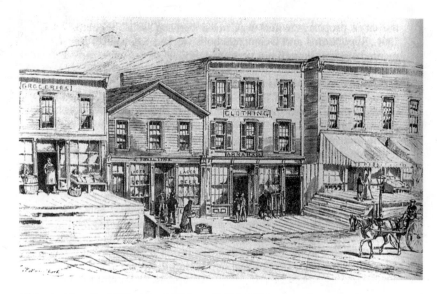

Chicago sidewalks, 1860s. *Source*: Einhorn (1991), 170.

During the same meeting, the city held the street users responsible for retrieving anything they dropped on the street; the city maintained the street paving (Los Angeles 1899).

Property owners nationwide were challenging the ordinances that required them to maintain the sidewalks. When Kansas City property owners contested the ordinances that required them "to keep the sidewalk, curbing and guttering, ... in good repair and order, and to clean the same, and remove ... all ice, snow, earth or other substance that in any way obstructs or renders the same dangerous, inconvenient or annoying to any person," the Missouri Supreme Court upheld the ordinance ("Snow Removal Ordinances" 1918). However, requiring private persons to take responsibility did not reduce municipal obligations, and cities were also becoming responsible for the safety of those using sidewalks and liable for accidents that occurred on them. This forced cities to keep sidewalks and streets—regardless if they had been formally dedicated to the city—in reasonably safe condition (in decent repair, clear of ice and snow, and free from hazards). The courts therefore established the sidewalks as public spaces, even while adjacent property owners were required to maintain them ("The City's Legal Responsibilities and Powers" 1918). The question of liability increased the importance of maintenance and emphasized that sidewalks were public facilities.

Paradoxically, expanding public powers over sidewalks meant increased control and regulation of public activities by municipalities. City after city started issuing ordinances prohibiting or regulating a number of sidewalk activities from street vending to political and commercial speech, from the display of wares on the sidewalk to loitering, panhandling, and prostitution (see tables 2.1 and 2.2 for examples of early and contemporary ordinances in Los Angeles). The invention of the public space of the sidewalks created a contested terrain among conflicting uses, users, and interests. In the process of defining and controlling sidewalk activities, municipalities articulated the pedestrian as the user for whom the sidewalks were being created. Municipal professionals facilitated the creation of a pedestrian circulation system by constructing sidewalks out of durable materials and demanding that they be maintained for the benefit of pedestrians. Although

TABLE 2.1
Examples of sidewalk ordinances in Los Angeles, 1880 to 1900

Action	1880s	1890s	1900s
Obstructions	Prohibited sidewalk use except limited displaying of wares Limited receiving and delivering of goods Required awnings at least 10 feet up	Regulated sidewalk use during construction Prohibited signs and bulletin boards	Prohibited signs, billboards, bulletin boards
Maintenance	Regulated raking and filling gravel Required • repairs to be made with durable materials in certain districts • tree trimming (and noted who must trim, either city or abutting property owner)	Regulated cleanliness Required tree trimming	Regulated the maintenance of vegetation Required sidewalks to be free of rubbish
Speech	Prohibited • defacing utility poles and lamp posts • auction bell ringing • assemblies obstructing streets, crosswalks, and entrances to public buildings	Prohibited • obscene pictures, bills, posters • defacing of poles • standing or assembly • street obstructions Required parade permits	Regulated sign boards and billboards (on private property) Prohibited • begging • street speaking • handbill distribution • soliciting patronage • advertising
Vending	Required licensing Regulated • utility posts • food wagons and carts	Required licensing Prohibited • peddlers and hucksters in certain districts • fruit peddling on certain streets Established a public market	Required licensing Prohibited • stands in certain districts • vending near private parks • exchanging goods on the street (with some exceptions)

TABLE 2.2
Examples of sidewalk ordinances in Los Angeles, 2005

Actions	Ordinance	Ordinance Overview
Loitering	41.1.41.18. Sidewalks, pedestrian subways—loitering	"No person shall stand in or upon any street, sidewalk, or other public way open for pedestrian travel or otherwise occupy any portion thereof in such a manner as to annoy or molest any pedestrian thereon or so as to obstruct or unreasonable interfere with the free passage of pedestrians."
Sidewalk cleaning	4.1.41.46. Clearing of sidewalks (added by ordinance 127,508, effective June 29, 1964)	"No person shall fail, refuse, or neglect to keep the sidewalk in front of his house, place of business, or premises in a clean and wholesome condition."
Urinating, defecating in public	4.1.41.47.2. Urinating or defecating in public	"No person shall urinate or defecate in or upon any public street, sidewalk, alley, plaza, public building, or other publicly maintained facility or place, in any place open to the public or exposed to public view, except when using a urinal, toilet, or commode located in a restroom or when using a portable or temporary toilet or other facility designed for the sanitary disposal of human waste and which is enclosed from public view."
Aggressive solicitation	4.1.41.59. Prohibition against certain forms of aggressive solicitation	No person shall solicit, ask or beg in aggressive manner in any public place

TABLE 2.2
(continued)

Actions	Ordinance	Ordinance Overview
Soliciting sales	4.2.42.00. Regulation of soliciting and sales in streets—street sale of goods prohibited (amended by ordinance 169,319, effective February 18, 1994)	"No person except as otherwise permitted by this section shall on any sidewalk or street offer for sale, solicit the sale of, announce by any means the availability of, or have in his or her possession, control, or custody, whether upon his or her person or upon some other animate or inanimate object, any goods, wares, or merchandise which the public may purchase at any time."
Street advertising and news racks	Street sidewalk—advertising	"No person shall have, bear, wear, or carry upon any street, any advertising banner, flag, board, sign, transparency, wearing apparel, or other device advertising, publicly announcing or calling attention to any goods, wares, merchandise, or commodities, or to any place of business, occupation, show, exhibition, event, or entertainment." Permits required for news racks and news stands.
Special sidewalk vending districts	4.2.42.00(m). Establishment and regulation of special sidewalk vending districts (added by ordinance 169,319, effective February 18, 1994)	"The Board of Public Works is authorized to form special sidewalk vending districts for the purpose of permitting vending goods, wares, and merchandise and announcing the availability thereof within such districts, and to promulgate rules and regulations with respect to the formation of such districts. No more than eight districts shall be approved by the Board during the first two years following the effective date of this ordinance. Each district shall have a designated police liaison appointed by the Chief of Police. Before any proposed vending districts are established, the City Council shall adopt a humane and comprehensive enforcement policy regarding sidewalk vending both inside and outside the proposed districts."

others disagreed about restrictions on their uses, a consensus developed by the early twentieth century that the pedestrian was the sidewalks' priority user and that movement was the primary purpose of streets and sidewalks.

Claiming rights to public space and imposing controls entailed a process of negotiation (Goheen 1994). Permissible activities and actions developed through both conflict and agreement among those using the spaces, and the municipal government acted as a venue through which negotiation occurred. Certain public activities have been highly conflictual and persistent, and as cities have been unable to absolutely eliminate them, they have increasingly developed techniques to segregate or contain them (Baldwin 1999; Gilfoyle 1994).

CONCLUSION

On sidewalks, the pedestrian has become equated with the public, and the formal articulation of the public has been a limiting process rather than an expansive one. This has led to municipal ordinances that favor efficient movement and prohibit other social, economic, and political uses of the sidewalk. Indeed, pedestrian circulation has justified the banning of other activities. At the same time, the city's process has provided a venue for citizens to challenge its decisions and a forum for opposing groups to present their claims to this public space. The amendments to city ordinances suggest that there was room for negotiation and reconsideration.

As urbanites adopted cars and municipal engineers envisioned public works, unobstructed mobility focused on these marvelous moving machines. Still, in the decades that followed, people continued to make claims for promenading, public speaking, expression of dissent, and street vending as well as a host of other activities on the sidewalks. In doing so, they took spaces again and again and negotiated and redefined their publicness.

II

Display, Opportunity, and Celebration

On sidewalks, people engage daily with other urbanites. They greet familiar bus drivers and baristas, observe neighbors they have never met, and cross paths with strangers. Urban residents value these fleeting and ephemeral interactions, which make cities intriguing and possibilities in public spaces endless.

People enjoy diverse public arenas—commercial streets, sidewalks and parks, open-air markets, and coffee shops. Brief encounters can be pleasurable when people display their identities, engage in playful behavior, or share smiles. Iris Marion Young's (1990) "unassimilated otherness" envisions a just city that embraces diversity. In her appealing world, savvy urbanites move through all spaces with ease, comfortably encounter others in public, enjoy differences, and return home, allowing diverse people to coexist.

People do not always go home unchanged, however. Social encounters in public spaces can create a sense of connection among strangers or simply generate interest when people see trends they may have read about and understand other people and places better. Lyn Lofland (1973, 1998) has argued that public relationships are more meaningful than urban observers and sociologists initially realized. Lofland (1998, 51–59) delineates four types of public relationships: in fleeting relationships, people interact momentarily; routinized relationships describe standardized interactions, such as those between customers and fast-food restaurant workers; quasi-primary relationships are infused with emotion, such as chats among dog owners or encounters at bars; and intimate-secondary relationships develop when people interact over long periods and become familiar.

Whether fleeting or ongoing, however, public encounters can affect people. When personal differences are observed in public spaces, others may react to, learn from, or adapt to what they see (as we discuss in chapter 3). Respectable nineteenth-century middle-class women maintained social distance in public from others, but increased freedom in public spaces allowed independent working women to develop culturally influential alternatives. Simply seeing someone may have lasting effects, even if the initial encounter is about observing and moving on. A woman who dresses in masculine clothes could give courage to other lesbian women to seek female companionship.

PART II

As urbanites see others and are seen by others, they develop and display identities, indicating similarities and differences through fashion and spatial practices, as well as claiming the right to be included in a diverse crowd. Negotiating public relationships is simultaneously pleasurable and challenging, but people also have undesirable interactions. Additionally, both changes and differences can be threatening. To prevent discomfort or unpleasantness from interfering with consumerism, cities and private developers have attempted to recreate public streets as safe, appealing, and ordered settings (as we explore in chapter 3).

Periodically, groups explicitly construct and display collective identities. In chapter 4, we discuss residents who commemorate or celebrate a communal event with a parade or public celebration and thereby both assert a group identity and insert that identity into a greater public. Parades form fleeting relationships between participants and spectators, who might enjoy the other's celebration and walk away with more information about the other. When parades make public claims or assert certain rights, they can also be challenging. The gay pride parades in the 1980s and 1990s, for example, were as political as the women's suffrage parades in the early 1900s.

Promenading and the Performance of Individual Identities

Michel de Certeau (1993) has described the city as a story that unfolds continuously as people move through space on different trajectories. Sidewalks are such spaces of movement. They facilitate social encounters among strangers and expose sidewalk users to a public gaze. As people see and are seen by other city residents, they become mindful of their differences from and similarities to others, these public interactions help construct and display individual identities.

On urban sidewalks, visitors and residents interact in countless formal and informal ways, which may allow for playfulness and openness. Observers have celebrated the sidewalks as "the breathing space of city life, offering opportunities for exploration and discovery, for the unexpected, the unregulated, the spontaneous, and the risky" (Franck and Stevens 2007, 3). Some chance encounters, however, can be unsettling. Fear of those who are unknown—those "others" against whom a group partially defines itself—has led to intolerance, violence, and regulation and has justified unequal treatment of sidewalk users.

This chapter focuses on two types of everyday interactions—(1) walking and informal strolling and (2) ritualized leisure strolling or promenading. Although sidewalks are places of opportunity, enjoyment, and playfulness, implicit and explicit rules guide public behavior. The rules have effects at different scales—from dictating clothing styles and individual mannerisms to constraining middle-class women's public activities. In some instances, rules of public presentation have explicitly enacted class differences, such as with nineteenth-century promenading or the gendered separation of public and private spheres. Public-space rules nonetheless affect all public-space users, and boundaries form around these alternatives. The rules often become obvious when they are violated, as the increasing visibility of gay men and lesbian women has made clear, but negotiating these boundaries has given expression to queer identities that were not previously articulated. Despite the rules of decorum and proper behavior, people are often relaxed and playful in public spaces, and their spontaneity and uncertainty make such spaces engaging.

This uncertainty, however, is what cities and business owners have nevertheless sought to reduce by redeveloping particular commercial streets. Destination shopping areas are contemporary promenades, and leisure shopping has become a favorite pastime for many urbanites. Diverse residents enjoy these abridged streets for shopping, observing, and socializing, but for many observers, these tightly controlled destination streets are predictable and exclusive. Whether these destination streets allow for the kinds of changes that public sidewalks have facilitated is an empirical question that deserves further study.

Urban Rambling and Promenading

The opportunity to watch urban life unfold introduces a theatrical element to sidewalks and the surrounding city. An individual strolling on city sidewalks is simultaneously the observer and the observed. In the 1920s and 1930s, Walter Benjamin (1999) romanticized getting lost in a labyrinth of city streets in nineteenth-century Paris, wandering carefree, and enjoying strangers, unexpected events, and social activities. He considered "flâneurie" (a term first coined by Parisian poet and boulevardier Charles Baudelaire in the 1850s) an escape from purposeful action. Often associated with modernity, the "rambler" or "flâneur"—an upper-class, single, heterosexual male who cruised the city sidewalks for entertainment and pleasure—personified a new, distinctly urban figure whose essential characteristics included movement, observation, and self-presentation. Other urban observers have continued in Benjamin's tradition, extolling sidewalks as sites of freedom, opportunity, playfulness, and loose behavior (Franck and Stevens 2007; Stevens 2007). For Iris Marion Young (1990, 239), enticing public interactions are erotic, bringing about "the pleasure and excitement of being drawn out of one's secure routine to encounter the novel, strange, and surprising."

In upscale neighborhoods, nineteenth-century sidewalks became an intentional urban theater as middle- and upper-class men and women displayed their social status and power through ritualized leisure walking in the form of a promenade. Unlike purposeless rambling and observing, promenading inserted a sense of order and hierarchy within the chaotic, rapidly changing streets. As Domosh (1998, 213) has found, "one of the most public and surveyed activities of the nineteenth-century city was that of the promenade, a highly scripted ritual of people both watching and being watched as they walked along the boulevards." In cities such as New York, Philadelphia, and Chicago, this ritual was not open or loose, and these wealthy residents were performing identities where "any sort of disruption, such as shouting and rude behavior, was simply not acceptable" (Domosh 1998, 213). In their best clothes and manners, residents strolled to display their social status and define their respectability by the differences they created (Rendell 1998). These wealthy urbanites claimed the streets and attempted to insert bourgeois decorum into urban bustle. Because promenading was a public act, it allowed people to insert themselves into the ritual. People from all racial groups could participate, although the participation of African Americans was only uneasily tolerated.

Appearance-based public exchanges rely by necessity on a careful "appraisal of the physical look, manner, nonverbal communication, and dress of the other. It is understood that all other things being equal, the citizen will attempt to give the best possible appearance in public.... Clearly, dependence on appearance favors those whose appearance connotes statuses that are held in high regard" (Gardner 1995, 53–55). These cues attempt to make some divisions obvious in environments where diverse people interact. This has been and continues to be oppressive because appearance alone

African Americans promenading, 1860s. *Source: New York Illustrated News*, Jan. 31, 1863, p. 196. Collection of the New York Historical Society; in Domosh (1998).

has worked to exclude certain groups from city sidewalks. City ordinances in the nineteenth and early twentieth centuries, for example, restricted people from displaying disabilities because they constituted "a disgusting sight" (Gardner 1995, 77). In the 1980s and 1990s, when a confluence of factors including deinstitutionalization of people in mental health care facilities, deindustrialization, and rising housing costs increased visible homelessness, cities nationwide attempted to remove the people who appeared homeless from the sidewalks.

The "best possible appearance in public" implies polite public behavior and the social expectation of civility, self-restraint, and culture (Valentine 1998). In the nineteenth century, these expectations pervaded women's lives. Surveying American etiquette books published between 1879 and 1922, Jessica Sewell (2000) found that women were expected to walk on urban sidewalks "wrapped in a mantle of proper reserve" (Young 1882, in Sewell 2000). City sidewalk etiquette made women in public as invisible as possible. To abide by these standards, women walking on city streets had to detach themselves from the surrounding environment by avoiding the gaze of other pedestrians (particularly men), dressing inconspicuously, talking in low voices, and not laughing in public. Unlike men—who could take their time and pace leisurely on the sidewalks, often stopping to chat—middle-class women were expected to walk with a purpose. Even when on the sidewalk, women could not be part of its social life.

When department stores developed in the nineteenth century, they offered women a limited public realm. The respectable flâneuse became possible only when shopping emerged as a socially acceptable pastime for middle-class women (Aitken and Lukinbeal 1998). This created a form of public space for commercial leisure that complied with middle-class norms and protected women from the dangers of the streets.

But neither social pressure nor an alternative environment like the department store could counter the possibilities that public spaces offered. For increasingly independent young working women in the early twentieth century, the city offered broad pleasures in public. Commercial heterosocial activities such as dance halls and movie theaters attracted young women, and despite the disapproval of middle-class reformers, these women were not solely victims but instigators of casual liaisons with the opposite sex. Sidewalk corners at night were treacherous for those intending to maintain middle-class propriety, but for adventuresome, pleasure-seeking women, they were sites of amusement (Hunt 2002; Peiss 1986).

Using sidewalks as urban theaters for promenading and flâneurie illuminates the importance of visual and ephemeral urban experiences. Urban life became a spectacle that unfolded under the flâneur's gaze, and his interactions were quick and superficial. A number of urban observers, including Georg Simmel (1950), Walter Benjamin (1999), and Richard Sennett (1977), have suggested that modernity relies on fleeting, detached, and impersonal encounters and superficial visual appearances instead of intimate social contacts and relationships (Simmel 1950; Sennett 1977; Benjamin 1999). Lyn Lofland (1998) has challenged the notion that public interactions are meaningless, however, and instead argues that within a world of strangers, urbanites may develop public relationships. Some ephemeral relationships are emotionally laden and may have meaning for urban residents, as people are affected by and affect others as they go about their daily routines.

Public Spaces and Life-Altering Encounters

Despite the existence of implicit or explicit rules of behavior in public, the diversity and anonymity of sidewalks has allowed some level of social flexibility and relative acceptance of people and activities that deviate from the norm (Sennett 1971). Indeed, "looseness of behavior" (Goffman 1980) and trangressive acts were more likely to be tolerated on public sidewalks than in private environments. This has allowed marginal groups such as queer residents to find others and socialize in ways that would be prohibited elsewhere. Sidewalk diversity helped gay men and some lesbian women meet friends and lovers and develop queer identities.

Gay and lesbian circles were not neighborhood-, family-, or work-based, and the streets' openness and diversity were critical for gay men to come into contact with each other. Men found others in public on the streets or in parks, bars, bathhouses, or picture shows (Chauncey 1994).

Meeting people in public and cruising (visiting known streets or parks to find sex partners) have been common for gay men since the late nineteenth century, and the word *cruising* was in use by the 1920s (Chauncey 1994).

Publicly presenting gender-nonconforming traits helped gay men meet and also presented alternative male identities. The most visible queer citizens in the late nineteenth century were effeminate "fairies," who could be seen on public streets (Chauncey 1994). Both flâneurs and fairies bounded a range of masculinities, and both exposed themselves to others. Fairies were visible enough that an 1870 guide book for Latin American businessmen included an image of them among other street people, including a prostitute, a shoeshine boy, a beggar, a policeman, and a flâneur (image depicted in Chauncey 1994, 32). Not all queer men were as effeminate as fairies, and many had no feminine characteristics. Subtle fashion differences (such as wearing a red tie) and mannerisms (including a slightly feminine stance of hands on hips and fingers facing forward) could alert gay men to another's presence. Maintaining eye contact could also suggest interest. The binary understanding of gay and straight had not yet taken hold, and there were many names for variations of homosexual practices and gendered identities (Chauncey 1994).

Whether seeking sex or friendship, gay men who wanted to avoid notice sought sites for meeting others that allowed them to linger. Window displays that offered middle-class women a way to stroll on city streets without violating social norms also gave gay men a justified reason to be on the sidewalks. A man who expressed interest in another could stop in front of a window display, and the other, if interested, could begin a conversation without attracting attention. Indeed, in 1913, a Macy's saleswoman in New York identified an area on Third Avenue in the East Fifties as a common gay strolling place (Chauncey 1994, 190).

Sidewalks amenable to gay cruising could also be found in areas where local bars accepted gay patronage. In the 1920s, Times Square was a center of female and male prostitution and offered an area where men could meet without monetary exchange. Men leaving the theaters could further their evening activities through sidewalk encounters (Chauncey 1994). From at least the 1920s, San Francisco's Embarcadero was a cruising area for gay men and offered bars that only men frequented (Rubin 1998). Sidewalks were attractive because they were less regulated than parks or bars. Although street sweeps did occur, the complete elimination of street activity was difficult.

Gay social circles depended on the identification of other gay men, but public streets and sidewalks had also another important dimension for the gay community. When gay men participated in gay street life, they did so as one group among many public socializers. Within a larger public realm, visibility was an informal claim to being part of a diverse, visible public.

Lesbians and women who passed as men sometimes could partake in masculine privilege and move more freely in the streets than other women. Sally Munt (1995) has argued that lesbians could be flâneurs, taking a masculine role of a watchful dandy as their masculine dress gave opportunities that conventional women—particularly those concerned with propriety—would not have had. By the 1950s, a butch identity—with masculine characteristics including clothing—for women had been clearly established. On the street, butch women with short hair wore slacks and men's shirts, challenging heterosexual norms and raising the possibility of alternative identities for other women who saw them (Kennedy and Davis 1993). Public visibility has been important for lesbians, and it helped define a public identity and mark an area as "lesbian" (Munt 1995; Rothenberg 1995; Podmore 2001).

Sex was one relationship that gay men found in public, but they were not alone. During the late nineteenth and early twentieth centuries, some people found more privacy and freedom for sex outside the confines of family and community. Men sought prostitutes or other casual sexual encounters, and young working women traded sexual favors on public sidewalks. Because working-class young men and women lived in cramped quarters with their parents or in supervised rooming houses, relationships were pursued in the anonymity and relative privacy of dark sidewalk nooks and other public spaces (Chauncey 1994; Peiss 1986; Hunt 2002). Even though gay men were not unique in this use of public space, cruising and public sex became an acknowledged aspect of gay community life.

Cruising is perhaps the most controversial ongoing use of sidewalks and other public spaces that is associated with gay men. Casual and anonymous sexual encounters fall outside the heteronormative view of sex associated with romantic love and problematize public-private distinctions (Bell 1995). As David Bell explains (1995, 306), "In terms of the location of the sex act, then, nominally it is taking place in *public space*: the park, the public toilet, the alley, the beach, the parking lot, the woods, the docks, the street. But in terms of the identities of the participants, their knowledge of each other, and the wider 'public' knowledge of the activities that go on in a particular setting, public (homo)sex can be very private."

Although visibility had positive aspects, it could also be dangerous. Fairies often became targets of violence from youth gangs and others (Chauncey 1994). By not conforming to gender norms, butch women were the most visible lesbians and, like fairies, were subject to harassment and at times violence. Displays of affection (such as holding hands or kissing in public) that go unnoticed in heterosexuals can appear indecent or even perverted when done by gay or lesbian couples because they confront the unwritten rules of the heterosexual street.

CONSTRAINED PARTICIPANTS IN CONSUMERIST SPACES

A sometimes uncomfortable tension between consumerism and social differences has been at the crux of the debate around the privatization of public space. After World War II, flâneurie in many cities became inextricably related to commercial activities as new downtowns, shopping malls, and commercial streets were designed to promote shopping as entertainment (Loukaitou-Sideris and Banerjee 1998). Many observers have argued that Americans have retreated from public life and moved from public to private spaces (Sennett 1977; Lofland 1973, 1998). The idea of a city as an unfolding play where anything can happen has been replaced by the provision of safe and controlled places for strolling where consumption is an assumed payment for participation.

In the last fifty years, shopping plazas, shopping centers, and shopping malls have proliferated. These public spaces are under private ownership and strict private control, and they increasingly replace traditional town squares and main streets (Kowinski 2002). Suburban shopping centers have become the de facto downtowns of the suburbs and the functional equivalent of a sidewalk in a public business district (Cohen 1996, 1069). According to a national survey, 94 percent of the adult population visits a shopping center at least once a month (Kowinski 2002), and studies have documented how teenagers, seniors, and families view shopping centers not simply as places to shop but also as places where they can stroll, hang out, socialize, and be entertained (Kowinski 2002).

In the 1990s, complaints grew louder that malls and shopping plazas feel sterile when contrasted with dynamic city streets. To encourage people to return to city centers to shop, cities have attempted to "reinvent" the publicness of sidewalks and to encourage promenading in environments that carefully screen the dark and unpredictable elements of street life—homelessness, prostitution, cruising, and strip clubs. These newly developed or redeveloped streets and sidewalks emulate the ambience of traditional streetscapes (with sidewalk cafés, open-front shops, and public seating) but exclude all their messy elements. They have become leisure shopping destinations that are more like a department store or mall than a chaotic street.

Cities invest in these commercial streets and open them to many groups, but actual participants are those who can afford and wish to consume the services offered. The desire to keep these destination spaces orderly and comfortable has justified formally and informally excluding others, and the intended user has been limited to the pedestrian shopper rather than the traveling public.

Nonetheless, destination streets have become very popular, and people promenade, shop, and hang out along designated street segments that extend only a few blocks. In the following section, we discuss the socio-physical characteristics of three categories of Los Angeles streets—gentrified streets, themed or "invented" streets, and "ethno-streets."

THIRD STREET PROMENADE: A GENTRIFIED STREET

If you are near Westside's upscale neighborhoods in Los Angeles and wish to promenade with Angelenos, be entertained by street performers, shop in trendy establishments, and dine in gourmet eateries, you will most likely visit the Third Street Promenade (TSP) in Santa Monica. TSP was completed in 1990 by the Third Street Development Corporation, a nonprofit, public-benefit corporation formed by the city of Santa Monica to revitalize and reclaim a decaying open-air pedestrian mall. The promenade occupies three city blocks that are lined with specialty stores, galleries, cafés, restaurants, and movie theaters. Rigid guidelines regulate streetscape and façade design, and a public-private company (the Bayside District Corporation) oversees its management.

On a Saturday night, people of different ethnicities and walks of life fill the promenade. They observe the unfolding scene with the sound of a pulsing guitar of a Latin folklore group, the stroke of a bamboo flute, and the melancholic beat of a piano. The music animates the crowd, their faces backlit by the neon signs of Banana Republic, Abercrombie and Fitch, and other upscale retailers. Many carry shopping bags, and the strollers provide entertainment for those seated at the cafés and restaurants.

This public promenade is heavily regulated. A Santa Monica ordinance bans roller-skating, skateboarding, and cycling on TSP (Santa Monica Municipal Code 6.112.050). Street performers have to purchase a performance license and pay a $37 annual fee to the city so they can perform from 9 a.m. to 11 p.m. on weekdays or 9 a.m. to 1:30 a.m. on weekends. Business owners generally like the performers because they attract crowds that will then enter the stores (Barna 2002). Even so, the performers have to move at least 120 feet every two hours and also maintain a distance of at least 40 feet from each other (SMMC 6.112.050).

TSP was one of the first gentrified streets in the Los Angeles region. Others include Melrose Avenue in West Los Angeles, Colorado Boulevard in Pasadena, and Pike Avenue in Long Beach. Indeed, cities throughout the nation—Times Square in New York, Harborplace in Baltimore, Fremont Street in Las Vegas, Quincy Market in Boston—have turned to the redevelopment of selected street segments to transform them into urban theaters for strolling and shopping as entertainment. Banerjee, Giuliano, Hise, and Sloane (1996, 20) call them "re-invented streets"—copies of the original Main Street whose planners are "searching for ways to resuscitate the diminished public realm."

Third Street Promenade, Santa Monica, California, 2007. Photograph by Anne McAuley.

Sign on Third Street Promenade, Santa Monica, California, 2007. Photograph by Anne McAuley.

These street segments reflect the municipal desire to revitalize the physical environment of decaying commercial streets to attract pedestrians and shoppers. To accomplish this goal, cities are designating pedestrian-oriented districts where only specific retail uses (those deemed as pedestrian-friendly) are welcome. They typically include cafés and bakeries, upscale restaurants, flower shops, boutiques, bookstores, and galleries. Architectural design, landscape embellishments, and street furniture are used to orchestrate an environment for promenading and leisurely shopping. Design guidelines often instill a theme on the street that may be inspired from the existing architecture or may be independent of it. Themes include art deco, country western, Mediterranean, and modern.

Beautifying the physical environment and emphasizing certain retail uses frequently lead to the effects of gentrification—expensive land, high rents, and the replacement of small independent shops by chain stores and upscale retailers. Gentrified streets strive to create an upscale atmosphere to attract the "right kind" of pedestrians and shoppers. The identity of the stroller is intertwined with the identity of the shopper.

CityWalk: An Invented Street

Even in the most constrained public spaces, visitors come to enjoy themselves. Competing with the Third Street Promenade for pedestrians and customers is CityWalk in Universal City, a multibillion-dollar development whose theme is scenes from Los Angeles's streetscape. Located in L.A.'s Westside along a previously existing road on a hilly location that now is on land owned by Universal Studios, CityWalk connects the Cineplex Odeon Theaters with the main gate of Universal Studios' theme park. Designed by architect and urban designer Jon Jerde (the designer of San Diego's Horton Plaza), CityWalk opened its doors to ever-increasing crowds in 1993 and was expanded by an additional 93,000 square feet in 2000.

CityWalk is an idealized street that uses eclectic architecture, neon lighting, and the blending of building and sign. This idealized street borrows liberally from quintessential L.A. to emulate and blend the excitement of Sunset Boulevard, the hyperbole of the Venice Boardwalk, and the fantasy of Disneyland's Main Street to recreate the sense of city walking. Banerjee et al. (1996, 26) call it an "invented street" that intends to "create a programmed experience similar to much older processional architecture. It is designed with a clear sense of arrival and departure and careful parameters guiding the experience."

Sidewalks are aligned with stores, offices, restaurants, theaters, piano bars, and dance clubs. LA's iconic images—the freeway, the beach, and Hollywood—are all represented here. The architecture is extravagant and outrageous, using "every outlandish, visual trick in the book to wow the passing crowds" ("Seeing Stars: The Ultimate Guide to Celebrities and Hollywood" n.d.). It blends the ideal with the real to the extent that visitors do not know where fantasy ends and reality begins. Does the "UCLA Extension" sign on a building façade signify a real community classroom that is operated by the city's major public university, or is it simply one more sign in a superficial pastiche of signifiers? Are students entering the building to attend an evening class, or are those people tourists who appear to be students?

CityWalk aspires to be perceived as a city street, but it eliminates the elements that make sidewalks unpredictable. The panhandlers, prostitutes, and bag ladies are absent. Even skateboarders are banned, and walking becomes the safest of activities. As the developers of CityWalk have argued, "A new and improved Los Angeles was needed" because "reality has become too much of a hassle" (Wallace 1992, A1).

The crowds seem to appreciate this abridged street. Over 8 million people visit CityWalk each year, and it is an economic success. On a Saturday night, a mostly young crowd of many different races and ethnicities swarms the sidewalks. As with those who visit TSP, people have come here to walk, shop, eat, be entertained, and watch others do the same. In this environment of "make believe" streets and sidewalks, people can pretend for a night that they are the stars featured in the movies of Universal Studios. Walking becomes a theatrical act: it is framed by a built environment that acts as a stage set, is carefully monitored and regulated by the private management and security officers, and costs a $10 parking fee.

CityWalk, Universal City, California, 2002. Photograph by Anastasia Loukaitou-Sideris.

PACIFIC BOULEVARD: AN ETHNIC STREET

Los Angeles's Eastside is a blue-collar neighborhood that also has pedestrian magnets. Ethnic commercial strips have appeared in the urban fabric of many North American cities, transforming formerly decaying street segments into thriving commercial districts. One such segment is Pacific Boulevard, a one-mile stretch of a commercial strip in Huntington Park, a heavily Latino municipality. The boulevard and the city experienced a "white flight" in the 1960s and 1970s after extensive riots in the Watts neighborhood (Rodino 1998). The strip's buildings became run down, and the street was crime-ridden and desolate. Today Pacific Boulevard is booming again with new businesses that attract Latino shoppers from the metropolitan area. Behind the street's comeback was a city council strategy to reposition Huntington Park as the center for Latino economic activity through a multi-million-dollar redevelopment targeting Pacific Boulevard (Rodino 1998).

The physical environment of Pacific Boulevard is a collection of new and old buildings with an eclectic mixture of Mexican, mission revival, and Aztec architectural elements. Most façades have received facelifts in a festive mix of sign and color to become "decorated sheds" (Venturi, Brown, and Izenour 1977). Unlike the stores in the Third Street Promenade or City-Walk, those on Pacific Boulevard are mostly discount stores "para toda familia," bridal shops, jewelry and music stores, fast-food eateries, and some sit-down restaurants. Most are small independent stores, but some Mexican chain stores have also entered the scene. Formal and informal economies coexist here as vendors occupy parts of the sidewalk and are often joined by store merchants who open their storefronts to display their goods on the sidewalk. The boundaries between the sidewalks and the abutting shops disappear as the store interiors extend to the street.

People stroll and hang out on the sidewalks, and they are the most dynamic elements of the streetscape. They are predominantly Latino—Mexican and Central American. Promenading up and down the one-mile stretch, they come mostly in families, with babies and young children, and spend hours on the sidewalk socializing, window-shopping, and entering a shop when a window display catches their attention. All ages visit

Pacific Boulevard. Children play or bike on the sidewalk and care for their younger siblings when their parents enter stores. Teenagers come to the boulevard to see and to be seen. Adult men and women come to shop in the numerous discount stores, and sidewalk benches provide retreats for older men, who spend long hours watching the life of the sidewalk (Loukaitou-Sideris 2002). The social activities and performing identities on the sidewalk create an "enacted environment" (Rojas 1993)—sounds, voices, and music that provide a Latin identity for this street segment. Although consumerism is a dominant activity here, it blends with the cultural and social ritual of promenading, a common activity in many Latin American public spaces.

CONCLUSION

These new shopping streets function differently than historic sidewalks because they are destinations rather than daily spaces of travel. Historically, overlapping activities allowed urbanites to watch a diverse city unfold, and sidewalks served as urban theaters where people observed others and developed and displayed social identities.

In the nineteenth and early twentieth centuries, rambling, promenading, and shopping took place on city sidewalks that were integrated into the urban fabric. There was plenty to see—other strollers, street vendors, and merchandise in store windows. Sidewalks' overlapping functions allowed people to bend expected norms and develop and articulate relationships and identities. Participating itself was a public claim. In public, gay men and women challenged limited visions of social roles, and dangerous tensions developed between those who upheld gender norms and those who did not conform. Nevertheless, public sidewalks have allowed individual and collective identities to develop and have provided physical settings for contesting or deviating from rules, stereotypes, and norms of appropriateness. This idiom of public sidewalks is absent from today's malls, destination streets and plazas, which seem to homogenize their users under the identity of consumer.

Teenagers on Pacific Boulevard, Huntington Park, California, 2002.
Photograph by Florian Urban.

Families on Pacific Boulevard, Huntington Park, California, 2002. Photograph by Florian Urban.

Making urban spaces resemble privatized public spaces could limit the changes that are brought about by defining and violating rules, which raises empirical questions that require further study. Although some urban observers criticize the sterility of "reinvented" and privatized streets, most users appreciate them. Nonetheless, a just city requires the flexibility that allows diversity to stimulate greater diversity and that creates opportunities for people to find their niches by constructing parochial spaces in public cities.

PERFORMING COLLECTIVE IDENTITIES: PARADES, FESTIVALS,
AND CELEBRATIONS

talk about how they march through the streets for the public language day

Sidewalks transcend their ordinary functions when people "take to the streets" to celebrate, protest, and mourn—either formally or in an impromptu fashion. In these instances, groups come together as a community. A sport team's victory can instigate joyful celebration. A senseless death caused by a hit-and-run driver or a drive-by shooter brings neighbors together to mourn an incomprehensible loss. A neighborhood block party, a marriage or funeral procession, or even street picketing may momentarily unite individuals, engendering a sense of commonality as people share roles as fans, neighbors, friends, or coworkers.

Some formal events occur at regular (often annual) intervals. Processions to celebrate civic, national, religious, or secular holidays (such as the Cinco de Mayo, Chinese New Year, Fourth of July, Labor Day, Thanksgiving, Christmas, or Carnival) temporarily redefine the purpose of streets and sidewalks. They override the functionality of streets and sidewalks, blocking the smooth flow of traffic, and forcing people to stop, observe, or participate.

Parades are planned rituals that allow people to display collective identities publicly. Spontaneous and planned festivities and rituals break the rhythm of everyday life and give collective expression to people's joy, sorrow, hope, claims, or aspirations (Kazin and Ross 1992). Erving Goffman

(1980, 21) has noted that "the decorum of serious everyday life is typically subverted momentarily by parades, convention antics, marriage, and funeral processions." By breaking ordinary rhythms, a group also inserts its concerns into the public realm where they can be acknowledged by others.

Considering parades historically reveals some changing trends in urban society. In the early republic, parades helped forge a native national identity. By the second half of the nineteenth century, Roman Catholic Irish immigrants paraded on the streets, making public claims to a public realm that had been dominated by white Protestants of English heritage. A century later, public celebrations nationwide expressed the growing diversity of an increasingly heterogeneous public, and a unified, national identity was superseded by multiple claims to the public realm. In this way, various groups staked a claim to a greater public and defined spaces for themselves within the city.

Because public commemorations insert cultural practices, issues, and interests into public consciousness, they are not neutral events. Quentin Stevens (2007, 52) has argued that such "ruptures" are publicly tolerated because they are seen as temporary and nonthreatening to the normal urban order. Nevertheless, they have the power to bring people together, focus attention, and intensify interactions and playful engagement. Whether counterhegemonic parades have the potential to subvert the dominant order is debatable. At times, they have been instruments of social movements for change. Although an individual parade may do little to subvert social order, labor union, suffrage, and gay pride parades have demonstrated that they can demand public attention. Their communicative power may make some parades controversial, but because public streets and sidewalks are presumed to be open to allow urbanites to engage in expressive activity, parades are— if at times uneasily—tolerated.

COLLECTIVE IDENTITIES ON PARADE

Parades are linear processions of an orderly crowd moving with a sense of direction, purpose, and ceremonial significance, providing the means for social identities to be crafted and displayed in public (Brown-May 1998).

Historically, groups have used the parade to claim the streets and sidewalks and make themselves visible to a greater audience (Stevens 2007). Marchers use their bodies, banners, and other visual and auditory props to convey a particular group identity and make a public statement. On some occasions, parades spawn other statements or counterparades (Santino 1999). Bystanders observe the spectacle, interact with participants, react by cheering or jeering, and at times join them, as with the case of "second lines" in New Orleans.

Parades can be seen as territorial acts. Their participants temporarily claim the public space of streets and sidewalks and stir local and sometimes even global audiences. Participants appropriate the pavement and "enact the streets" for their own performances of ethnic, sexual, political, or religious identities. As O'Reilly and Crutcher (2006, 248) have argued, "Parade territorialities involve simultaneous and complex spatial and social claims. Territoriality and identity are fused." Different parades use the physical space of public streets and sidewalks to communicate a variety of scaled power relations (Marston 2002). Some parades display elite identity and power, while those at the margins display alternative identities (Goheen 1993).

Parades are a spectacle of a group imaginary (Stychin 1998). By choosing to participate in the procession with others, the individual becomes a de facto member of a "community." Through a linear procession along the street, the community presents itself to society as a whole (Davis 1995). Parades bring "a performative, spatial component to cultural identities—particularly those of ethnic and racial minorities—by way of their routes through the urban landscape" (O'Reilly and Crutcher 2006, 249).

A parade's meaning depends on confluent factors. Parade participants define a community as they envision and organize the parade. This identity is shared with others through the parade itself. The meaning of the parade changes by neighborhood, and adjacent properties contribute to the way that parades are interpreted. This means that the public claims differ by neighborhood, and outsiders perceive the parade differently depending on where it is inserted. Parades are events that deviate from the ordinary life of the street and make almost everyone pause and watch.

From National to Class Identity

During the colonial era in the United States, public displays, feasts, festivals, and parades filled town streets, sidewalks, and public squares. Local militia interrupted everyday life by marching to drums in a procession that culminated in the town common. These public festivities were mostly organized by and for the local elite to celebrate the power of the throne and their own affiliation with the ruling society (Newman 1997).

In the young American republic, parades became a significant site for national identity formation, serving as both narrative and performative spaces for the new nation (Stychin 1998). The first notable parade of the new nation celebrated the ratification of the Constitution in Philadelphia in 1788. More parades followed. Grand processions on public streets paid honor to the nation's fathers—celebrating the birthdays of George Washington, Thomas Jefferson, and John Adams and commemorating the nation's independence every Fourth of July. Fourth of July celebrations helped display national unity and fostered a national festive culture (Newman 1997).

These parades forged a composite national image and identity out of diverse but assimilated social groups (Stychin 1998). The distinct marching units were composed of individuals associated by occupation. According to Ryan (1989), in the Erie Canal Procession that took place in New York on November 5, 1825, all parading men were grouped in specific contingents, with the more prestigious occupations (civic officials, judges, lawyers, physicians) at the front and the less prestigious ones (tradesmen, laborers) following.

Despite this hierarchical parade structure and group arrangement, scholars have argued that early parades served as an inclusive ritual for participants. Civic pride tied individuals through a sense of citizenship. National identity was expressed through shared symbols of flags, banners, and other regalia and through shared collective ideals and values (Lawrence 1982). According to Mary Ryan (1989, 134), early American parades had several essential features. They were composed of distinct marching units, each representing a preestablished social identity; they involved a large portion of the local population but excluded many others based on race and gender; and they lacked a particular "plot" but rather were "a march for the sake of marching" along major streets of the town.

During the nineteenth century, parades became common events in American cities. As Ryan (1989, 132) has argued:

> The parade stands out in the chronicles of American public life as the characteristic genre of nineteenth-century civic ceremony. A grand procession of citizens was "of course" the central event in the cyclical patriotic rite, the Fourth of July celebration, and to a lesser extent of Washington's Birthday. It was also the focal point of local holidays: Evacuation Day in New York, Admission Day in San Francisco, and the anniversary of the Battle of New Orleans. When it came to celebrate civic improvements—the Erie Canal, the Atlantic cable, the transcontinental railroad—or the erection of any number of new monuments in public squares, a parade was again in order. The parade was called into ceremonial service on somber occasions as well. The procession that accompanied Lincoln's casket through the streets of New York was, in structure and organization, if not in mood, like a classic American parade.

Seeking to construct a typology of nineteenth-century parades in Melbourne, Brown-May (1998, 178) identified eleven purposes. Civic parades celebrated the opening of institutions and the consecration of new civic buildings and infrastructure; royalty and loyalty parades celebrated events relating to local authorities or state rulers; public execution processions conveyed the condemned prisoner to the executioners; mutual-aid and charitable societies paraded to make their missions visible; funeral processions mourned the deceased; proselytizing parades (employed, for example, by the Salvation Army or the temperance and prohibition movements) had a moral or missionary objective; military parades displayed the might of local militia; political parades were protests and demonstrations; calendrical parades displayed patriotic, religious, political, or ethnic groups; benefit parades were associated with charitable causes; and celebratory parades welcomed political leaders or celebrated particular noncalendrical events.

In the second half of the nineteenth century, streets and sidewalks were increasingly used to express specific group identities rather than an integrated national one. Almost three-quarters of a century had passed from the time that the nation had gained its independence, and the collective anxiety to display national unity had subsided. After the 1850s, the higher social ranks stopped marching. Professional and mercantile classes soon exited, and parades became almost exclusively populated by the labor classes, which started forming labor associations and unions (Ryan 1989). After the 1850s, Irish Americans increasingly participated in parades, so much so that in 1858 the *New York Herald* commented that "parading had become almost synonymous with the ethnic label Irish-American" (in Ryan 1989, 146). In doing so, Irish residents also symbolically displayed their claim to citizenship.

By the end of the century, growing class identification was proudly displayed annually on city streets and sidewalks each Labor Day. The first Labor Day celebration took place in New York on September 5, 1882, when the Central Labor Union staged a spectacular parade on city streets. Estimates of participants varied, but there were at least 10,000 men and very few women marching from lower Broadway to Union Square, holding banners and flags under the cheers of an audience of about 250,000 New Yorkers (Kazin and Ross 1992).

The unprecedented success prompted the union to repeat the festivities in the following two years, and by 1886 similar parades appeared in other cities across the nation, often enhanced with a variety of props such as floats, banners, music, and speeches. The hours spent marching on the streets created a bond among parade participants. This street display of unified labor was so important that in 1884 the Federation of Organized Trades and Labor Unions called on "all wage workers, irrespective of sex, calling, or nationality [to] observe the day in an organized fashion" (in Kazin and Ross 1992, 1302). In a nation composed of different interest groups, mobilizing diverse labor groups in a mass parade helped develop class identity.

Labor Day parades continued into the twentieth century, but their attendance fluctuated from a high of 50,000 union members during times of labor crises and massive strikes to a low of 5,000 participants when few problems existed for labor. Union membership and Labor Day parades saw an upsurge in popularity during the Depression, when thousands of workers marched. Labor Day parades continued into the 1940s, but their class identity and militancy weakened. Despite the efforts of labor leaders to attract participants by offering entertainment and even Hollywood stars in Los Angeles parades, the crowds dwindled, and the parades eventually stopped.

A Spectrum of Identities in a Multifaceted Society

Parades have never been inclusive. Women rarely marched in public processions. They were confined to the role of the spectator: middle-class women applauded from balconies and windows, and working women crowded the street (Hickey 1995; Ryan 1989). Only during the first decade of the twentieth century did women suffragists take to the streets demanding the rights of equal citizenship and gaining a representative place in the public ceremony (Ryan 1989). Similarly, African Americans were excluded from participation in nineteenth-century parades of the white population. In the nineteenth and twentieth centuries, African Americans established their own parades and public traditions. By the late twentieth century, various queer groups inserted themselves into the public by claiming the streets and sidewalks.

Suffrage Parades

Parading on public streets and sidewalks has been used by some groups as a tactic to make a cause known by appealing to a broader audience and demanding equal citizenship. The tactic proved to be effective for suffragists in the early twentieth century who took to the streets. Women actively participated in nineteenth-century political and reform efforts including city improvement work, and the abolition, temperance, and women's rights movements, but women's activity was couched in language that reflected their role as homemakers and moral guardians. In this context, the appropriation of streets and sidewalks by suffragists to demand political equality was a risky move.

Realizing that parades would invoke stronger reactions than quieter strategies such as education and advertising, suffragists took to the streets. The first suffrage parade took place in Oakland, California, in August 1908, when 200 to 300 women marched in front of surprised city residents (McCammon 2003). After tentative beginnings, the Women's Political Union and other suffragist organizations around the country staged much larger processions, and parades became common after 1913 (McGerr 1990).

The parades brought thousands of women as participants onto the streets and many more spectators on the sidewalks. Frequently, women activists would choose the time and location of their parade strategically to draw more attention, such as with the parade that took place in Washington, D.C., in March 1913, the day before the inauguration of President Woodrow Wilson (McGerr 1990). Two years later, in 1915, a parade in New York City drew 20,000 to 25,000 women participants, who marched with bands, horses, and decorated automobiles (Bzowski 1995). Mostly, however, suffrage parades were focused, and women marched solemnly in formation and carried signs and banners stating the reasons that they wanted the right to vote (McCammon 2003). Suffragists needed to be taken seriously and project a dignified but courageous image to bystanders (Lumsden 1997).

Parades helped activist women "redefine the sexual hierarchy of the streets" (Finnegan 1999, 46). Rather than onlookers, women became active agents and protagonists of the "street ballet" (cf. Jacobs 1961). Marching down the streets and demanding a legitimate political role "not only allowed women to claim the streets as women's terrain, but the parades permitted women to lay a symbolic claim to the polity as they demanded the right to vote. The use of this tactic helped them redefine themselves as men's equals in the public sphere" (McCammon 2003, 789). In 1919, Congress passed the Nineteenth Amendment, establishing women's right to vote.

THE HIDDEN CARNIVAL AND SECOND-LINE PARADES IN NEW ORLEANS

In New Orleans, an alternative Carnival and second-line parades played out in the backstreets of the city's poorest Creole and African American

Suffragettes on Parade, Los Angeles, California, before 1920. Courtesy of the Los Angeles Public Library.

neighborhoods in the days before Ash Wednesday. They provided an alternative to the splashy Mardi Gras (Fat Tuesday) carnival parades and implicitly challenged the hegemony of the elite groups that put it together.

The Mardi Gras celebration originated in France in 1700 and was introduced to New Orleans in the 1700s (Gotham 2002). Since early in the town's history, participation in the carnival—who was included or excluded—was an issue of contestation between the white elite and the poor Creole segments of New Orleans society (Roach 1993). As early as 1781, the attorney general warned the city commission of the trouble generated by "a great number of free negroes and slaves who, with the pretext of the Carnival season, mask and mix in bands passing through the streets, looking for the dance halls" (Brasseaux 1980, 144, quoted in Smith 1994, 47).

Mardi Gras parades began in New Orleans in 1827 (Lipsitz 1988), and after the Civil War, white elites began dressing like royalty to recapture, if ephemerally, their social dominance. Throughout the nineteenth century, black people were excluded from the secret carnival societies (called *krewes*) that held themed balls and parades with floats and masked revelers. Legislation even forbade blacks from participating in Carnival (Lohman 1999), although separate black carnival societies began to flourish in the early twentieth century. Not until December 1991 did the New Orleans city council require carnival societies to integrate if they paraded on city streets or took part in public festivities that required public funds (Roach 1993).

The Zulu Social Aid and Pleasure Club was established in 1909, and in 1915 this African American krewe began parading on city streets. Although the Zulu parade once took place on the city's back streets, it now rolls on Fat Tuesday along a designated route with a parade permit. Zulu parodies the Mardi Gras tradition of white royalty-inspired elite. Riders wear black face and grass skirts, and the parade's most coveted thrown favors are decorated coconuts.

With different social objectives and in response to historic discrimination, black New Orleanians developed social clubs and organized street festivities and parades on the streets of black neighborhoods. Despite police efforts to prevent, outlaw, or at least control what they perceived to be renegade activities, these parades continue (Smith 1994). The Mardi Gras Indians parade on Fat Tuesday and St. Joseph's Day, a tradition that began in the late nineteenth century (Lipsitz 1988). These black Indian "gangs" remain defiantly outside the regulatory imperative of the official establishment. They circumvented laws that used to prohibit African Americans from masking by wearing face paint and headdresses. They do not apply for permits but rather march on the streets as they please under the tunes of their own music drawing on Native American references and African cultural rituals and celebrations (Smith 1994; Lipsitz 1988). The Indians sew and bead their own suits, and their tradition is based on both commonality and difference, as tribes may have common or different themes, may choose their own colors, and at times compete over verbal and suit-making skills (Lipsitz 1988).

In addition to offering opportunities for joyful and playful expressions of community in some of the city's most blighted neighborhoods, the appropriation of streets and sidewalks by the revelers has a symbolic meaning. As Lipsitz (1988, 115) argues:

> Much of the power of this Mardi Gras ritual stems from its force as a counter-narrative challenging the hegemony of New Orleans's social elite.... The elite mask themselves in expensive costumes and ride motorized floats along the city's main thoroughfares, throwing beaded necklaces and souvenir doubloons to the crowds. The Indians subvert the spectacle by declaring a powerful lineage of their own, one which challenges the legitimacy of Anglo-European domination. They make not buy their costumes, avoid the main thoroughfares, and walk through black neighborhoods. They define the crowds along their route as participants, not just as spectators.

While most parades have a clear bifurcated role between performers and marchers and between spectators and bystanders, New Orleans' African American parades merge the two roles. The observers form an active "second line" that follows the rhythm of the marching dancers by beating on bottles with sticks and dancing to their music and chants (Kinser 1990). Thus, the organizing social club and its band form the "first line" of the

St. Joseph's Day, New Orleans, Louisiana, 2007. Photograph by Renia Ehrenfeucht.

Masked riders throwing beads, Mardi Gras, New Orleans, Louisiana, 2006. Photograph by Renia Ehrenfeucht.

parade, while their families, friends, and neighbors also actively participate in the festivities as a "second line" (Regis 1999). Such parades may well attract 5,000 to 10,000 second-liners stretching over ten to twenty city blocks (Smith 1994).

Second-line parades do not take place only during the Mardi Gras season. They are employed by the social clubs of the city's black community to celebrate many festivities, holidays, and birthdays. On almost every Sunday afternoon from mid-August to late March, New Orleans social aid and pleasure clubs parade through their central city neighborhoods. "Jazz funerals" also wind their way through the neighborhoods to honor the life of a deceased community member.

These parades, which historians and cultural anthropologists link to early African American freedom celebrations (Smith 1994; Regis 1999), create a counterstatement, an alternative social order that momentarily transforms the marginalized neighborhoods into spaces of emancipation.[1] As Regis (1999) argues:

> The majority of participants in this tradition are not "owners" of homes, real estate or large public businesses. Yet, through the transformative experience of the parade, they become owners of the streets.... This collective ownership of the streets that is experienced by participants in the second line has important political implications (478).... The parades empower participants to walk through terrain that they might otherwise perceive as hostile, dangerous ground (479).... Second liners can partake in this order, this joyous space of power, dignity, self-reliance, and freedom, transcending the quotidian struggles of the ghetto (480).... In the U.S. only in New Orleans has the black community created and sustained such a year-round cycle of massive commemorative celebrations of dignity, freedom, solidarity, and blackness (494).

By creating a space of conviviality, solidarity, and freedom, this exuberant and defiant taking of public streets and sidewalks allows members of the black community to celebrate black culture and history despite the chronic unemployment or underemployment, racism, segregation, and crime that many communities still endure.

Second-line parades continue to confront the city's expectations of order. In fall 2007, New Orleans police interrupted a jazz funeral, charging musicians with playing without a license and disturbing the peace, when they did not stop playing "I'll Fly Away," when the police demanded them to do so. The police subsequently dropped the charges (Reckdahl 2008).

GAY PRIDE PARADES

Other social groups have also used parades to capture the public's attention and, by their presence in the public realm, to claim respectful recognition and equal citizenship. Like the suffragists, gay and lesbian activists have inserted themselves into the public realm through pride parades, temporarily subverting the heterosexuality that pervades public space. Gay parades both demand acceptance of differences and assert the "everyday sameness" in a larger community (Stychin 1998, 288). They affirm a positive queer identity that is nevertheless distinct from the mainstream (O'Reilly and Crutcher 2006).

A fairly recent tradition, pride parades commemorate a 1969 event when transgender and other queer patrons of New York's Stonewall Inn resisted a police raid. Although a nascent gay movement had been developing since World War II, the Stonewall rebellion gave voice to feelings that many shared in the gay community—no more police harassment, no more prohibitions on gender identities or relational and sexual desire, no more shame that allowed such injustices to continue. In contrast to the organizing before Stonewall, visibility and pride thus became critical political acts for many queer groups.

Visibility and pride have taken symbolic form in annual parades in U.S. cities and other countries worldwide (Polchin 1997; Kates and Belk 2001). The first national parade for gay and lesbian pride took place in Washington, D.C., in 1979. Today such parades have become annual events in some cities (hundreds of thousands celebrate gay pride in San Francisco each year). Gay pride parades are playful, satirical, and frivolous. They combine "in your face" politics with fun, and in their most visible manifestations (such as in New York and San Francisco), they offer the chance to throw a gay street party that infiltrates the entire city for a weekend. Men and women come to the streets and sidewalks in leather and heels, gowns or work boots, masks of mock political figures or homophobic spokespeople, or simply silly wigs and colorful clothes. Many gay neighborhoods and cities—San Francisco, New York's Greenwich Village, and West Hollywood, California—also host Halloween street parties in the same spirit. Costuming and silliness offer an opportunity to be irreverent for at least one evening.

Public celebrations—gay pride parades, Halloween celebrations, New Orleans's Southern Decadence, San Francisco leather community's Folsom Street Fair—have been critical to queer visibility and an influential way that queer communities have inserted themselves into the public realm. Queer parades and street parties also accomplish critical political work. Gay pride offers an opportunity for various segments of queer communities to come as distinct but connected groups. Members of gay political and service organizations and transgender groups build floats, don costumes, throw condoms, and by their presence on the street assert their public rights and claims. Such ephemeral events also transform a street, a neighborhood, or even a city temporarily into gay space. The humor and parody challenge and reclaim the heterosexual street: "Fifty thousand homosexuals parading through the city streets, of every type, presenting the Other of heterosexuality, from Gay Bankers to the Gay Men's Chorus singing 'It's Raining Men,' a carnival image of space being permeated by its antithesis" (Munt 1995, 123).

Gay events have become increasingly citywide and public rather than strictly local and parochial. The route often takes the parade outside of gay neighborhoods (Kates and Belk 2001). In San Francisco, for example, the parade rolls down Market Street, and an afternoon celebration unfolds at the Civic Center. This has both positive and negative aspects. Increasingly, pride parades have become more open to outsiders, but to some, such events have become more mainstream, and scripted and result in a sanctioned city festival rather than the earlier grassroots celebrations (Kugelmass 1993).

Who gets represented in public events remains controversial. Although people of color participate in pride and gay community events,

Gay Fathers of Los Angeles, Gay Pride, West Hollywood, California, 1987. Courtesy of the Los Angeles Public Library.

many nonetheless find these parades exclusive, unwelcoming, and politically narrow (Bulwa 2005). The significance of inclusion and representation in other citywide events has not diminished. Not all parades are open to gay and lesbian contingents. For example, gay men and lesbian women had to fight for inclusion in Boston's and New York's St. Patrick's Day parades (Davis 1995).

To some heterosexual residents, queer pride forces "deviant" sexuality on unwilling parties (Brickell 2000). Media coverage of lesbian and gay pride parades often depicts the participants as inserting gayness into the public realm. This emphasizes that in public spaces, "heterosexuality is invisibly visible" (Brickell 2000, 166). For some but not all participants, the parades are an opportunity to engage in playful sexual teasing and some public sex. The very fact that gay events are seen as uniquely sexual, however, demonstrates that elements of the broader society continue to equate queer communities with sex. Carnival traditions that are also sexualized, public playful events do not receive comparable criticism about promiscuity or deviant heterosexuality (Brickell 2000).

In recent years, pride parades have also raised internal controversy in the gay community. For some, public nudity and sexuality do little to further gay rights but convey the sense that sex dominates queer communities. For others, the commercialism and emphasis on youthful beauty reflect neither the community's diversity nor its values. Both debates highlight the importance of public representation, which is not *only* fun. Some simply think that the time has passed when gay pride is needed because the community is visible. Gay men and lesbians have gained greater acceptance, and the politics of daily life—marriage, housing, employment, children— are the pertinent battles. Although this might indicate progress, we still look forward to a day when queer publicity poses no controversy or challenge and the public celebrations are simply play.

CONCLUSION

Urban critics have observed the demise of a spontaneous street culture and impromptu street festivities in early twenty-first century U.S. cities. Parade processions now have to be preplanned and licensed and are thoroughly monitored and controlled by municipal police forces. The dominance of motor transport and the emphasis on uninterrupted movement has stripped streets and sidewalks of many of their social meanings (Brown-May 1998). Although parades continue, some critics have argued that their recent commercialization has led to opportunities to display corporate logos and have corporate sponsors. Similarly, parades such as the Mardi Gras in New Orleans, the Rose Parade in Pasadena, and the Macy's Parade in New York seem to sacrifice the collective or local interests to become tourist attractions. Today, the tourist industry aggressively markets such street festivals and parades as part of a larger tourism-oriented strategy to encourage visitors to come and spend money in particular cities.

Nevertheless, at specific moments, street parades, festivals, and celebrations still provide opportunities to forge and assert a collective identity, claim rights to equal citizenship, and display pride. Public celebrations, processions, and festivals offer opportunities to display counternarratives. By participating in the rites and symbols of peaceful street parades and festivals, groups insert new ideas into street politics and use public spaces to make their claims (Newman 1997, 186). Because the focus is often celebration, commemoration, or public expression of emotion (whether it is rage, sorrow, or happiness), these ephemeral events are tolerated, and although they interfere with daily life, they do not appear as disruptive as intentional political acts.

III

Disruption and Confrontation

As sites of daily routines, sidewalks facilitate both expected and unexpected interactions. Neighbors greet each other from doorways or meet on sidewalks as they walk with their children or dogs. On busy downtown streets, pedestrians negotiate sidewalk space with others, sometimes purchasing a hot dog from a sidewalk vendor or dropping a coin into the cup of a street person. At sidewalk cafés, people watch passersby, enjoying fleeting encounters like smiles or brief comments. These street encounters are unscripted although some may be anticipated, and the breadth of possibilities—even when only few are realized—enhances the urban experience.

Some interactions, however, may be undesirable, uncomfortable, or even disruptive. At times, disruption can also be confrontational. In part III, we discuss disruptions. In chapter 5, we focus on everyday politics—micropolitical acts and violations of social norms. Engaging with different people invariably results in encounters (sometimes intentional) that confront established norms. Protests like sit-ins and micropolitical acts such as refusing to step aside on the sidewalks challenge social hierarchies. But not all disruptions are political. Talking loudly in public or lingering for a long time on sidewalks run counter to expected behavior but may not be intentional political acts. Through repetition, such acts can also change a space, altering expectations and making it public for people who previously did not feel comfortable there.

In chapter 6, we discuss large political events—large-scale, intentionally confrontational disruptions. Public protests and picketing are political acts and necessary dimensions of a just society, even though they interrupt ordinary street life. Unimpeded transportation has been the assumed primary purpose of sidewalks, and on this basis cities have in the past banned disruptive sidewalk activities. Public protests are now widely accepted to be constitutionally protected free speech. Even if a group's position is abhorrent to the larger community, protecting the group against an a priori decision by municipalities about what is acceptable takes precedent over the community's standards. Although some actions (such as hanging nooses) are forbidden as hate speech that is intended to threaten, and other actions (such as falsely crying "Fire!" in a crowded theater) are banned as threats to public safety, free-speech rights must be protected. Even these rights have become debatable, however, in the current antiterror era.

Many who support the principle of free speech may not support actions that disrupt their daily routines or disturb city events and conventions. Protest acts have less effect, however, when they are not disruptive. Because the interruption is part of the message, public confrontations and expressions of dissent are integral functions of public space.

People who gather in the streets can challenge injustices, demand inclusion, or simply offer information. Because they are visible, sidewalks have been favored political and communicative spaces, and those engaged in expressive and disruptive activities can reach others. Sidewalks are spaces for travel, and so everyone has a purpose for being there. They are also traditional public forums where cities must exercise restraint when regulating expressive activities.

Despite a legacy of positive social and political changes—activities that challenged segregation have become unremarkable a generation later—sidewalk users have an ambivalent relationship to disruptive events and people. There are three reasons for this. First, events that interfere with mobility and block or delay passage violate the notion of the pedestrian as the primary sidewalk user (Ehrenfeucht and Loukaitou-Sideris 2007). Second, protesters also violate the principle of civil inattention (Lofland 1998) by specifically demanding others' attention (instead of simply capturing it as a street performer might do). Finally, the issues being publicized might be troubling. Although disruptive interactions are usually fleeting, since sidewalk skirmishes pass quickly and passersby redirect their attention away from protesters, they are emotionally and morally laden, and their impact lingers. This power makes them confrontational and necessary.

Everyday Politics and the Right to the Sidewalk

Daily interpersonal interactions offer opportunities for sidewalk users to disrupt and counter social expectations. Sometimes this is simply playful, as when rambunctious teenagers take over a sidewalk, but at other times, people intentionally act in unexpected ways to challenge unjust social norms. Sidewalks are sites of both domination and resistance (Fyfe 1998). To emphasize and maintain their status, some social groups have in the past demanded deference from members of other groups that they encountered on public sidewalks, and these norms were backed by city ordinances. For example, African Americans were historically expected to act deferentially in shared public spaces. Stigmatization and exclusion were additional mechanisms for maintaining status differences among urban groups in public interactions, which were open and difficult to control. Women used to be stigmatized for appearing in public, and since the nineteenth century, children have been mostly excluded from streets and sidewalks. Some of these exclusions produced reactions, and when they have been discriminatory or oppressive, people have asserted their equality and right to the city (Fyfe 1998).

As shared spaces that people traverse by necessity, sidewalks have provided arenas for negotiating exclusion and inequality. As Dailey (1997, 585) has argued, sidewalk altercations have served as "a metaphor for broader questions of racial domination and subordination." Because public encounters both reflect and reproduce social hierarchies, transgressions were and continue to be disruptive. Transgressions were dangerous and could result in social approbation or violence—from either the state or other people—but they were nebulous enough to disrupt without always eliciting immediate retribution.

Acts of deference or domination were negotiated as people passed each other. Deferring to someone meant stepping off the sidewalk and into the roadway or gutter. Deference by low-status individuals was expected and even demanded, while an uninterrupted walk reflected high status. This was even true in the case of middle-class women, who moved uninterruptedly but privately, wrapped in a mantle of reserve. When men acknowledged women's privacy by allowing women to pass without comment, they conferred respect, even if acting privately was a woman's attempt to avoid being stigmatized. In this way, movement on the sidewalks reinforced various conflicting hierarchies and social norms. Norms are repetitive micro actions, however, and when sidewalk users failed to step aside or interacted in unanticipated ways, social relationships were unsettled.

Through public encounters, hierarchies are both upheld and challenged. Disruptive encounters represent interactions among groups. The open hate stares that white southerners directed toward African Americans in the mid-twentieth century were not intended for the individual but meant to reiterate status differences between white and black residents. Hate stares violated an expectation of behavior in public—"civil inattention" (Lofland 1998, 29; Goffman 1969)—and by doing so, they reaffirmed that those who received the stares did not deserve respect. Likewise, African Americans challenged daily subjugation by "accidentally" tripping white residents.

Perceived misbehavior poses a significant threat because it is an interaction among individuals who are representative of groups. Otherwise, it would simply be an annoyance. Daily acts on public sidewalks legitimize those who warrant basic respect and, more fundamentally, those who comprise the public body and have a right to the city.

In this chapter, we first discuss two cases where sidewalk norms changed for the better—African Americans who negotiated public rights in everyday life, and women who claimed the sidewalks and weakened the dichotomy between public and private spheres. We then turn to children and youth, who have been increasingly missing from public streets and sidewalks since the late nineteenth century, and whose presence on the sidewalks still elicits handwringing. The street continues to be construed as threatening to children, and the presence and safety of children in public (like women in the past) has become a mechanism to discuss multiple concerns about city life.

MICROPOLITICS ON PUBLIC SIDEWALKS

Historians have long drawn attention to the political importance of everyday acts and manners as mechanisms of resistance and subjugation (Kelley 1993; Dailey 1997). When state actions and dominant public opinion supported inequality (such as institutional and pervasive racism in the United States), oppressed people developed micropolitical acts of resistance that challenged social inequality and helped maintain their integrity. Many of these acts took place on public sidewalks.

In the nineteenth century, African Americans had more freedoms on public streets and sidewalks than they did in other spaces of the city, but sidewalks were still controlled. Ceding sidewalk space was one mechanism for retaining inequities. White urban residents used the distinctions between the sidewalk and the gutter or the roadway to enforce social status. This was formally established at times. According to Richard Wade (1964), before the Civil War, the relative freedom that black urban residents, both enslaved and free, exercised led Southern cities to institute ordinances that required African Americans to defer to white residents. The 1857 Richmond (Virginia) code, for example, specified that "Negroes shall not at any time stand on a sidewalk to the inconvenience of [white] persons passing by. A negro meeting or overtaking, or being overtaken by a white person ... shall pass on the outside; and if it be necessary to enable such white person to pass, shall immediately get off the sidewalk" (Wade 1964, 108).

The distinction between the sidewalk and street was not lost on urban dwellers. In 1863, white Confederate soldiers outside Jackson, Mississippi, feared that they would be prohibited from using city sidewalks and instead would be forced to walk in the middle of the street. Although it is unclear if the Jackson city council meant to take such action, this illustrates that being denied equal status with the rest of the white Jackson society meant being denied access to walk with them on an equal basis (Dailey 1997).

Denying access to sidewalks as a means of denying status led to opposing actions—the refusal to cede the sidewalks. In the late nineteenth century, as African Americans asserted their citizenship through various mechanisms, white southerners repeatedly noted that African American men and women would not yield the sidewalk and even sometimes forced them into the gutter. Through these acts, which were not inconsequential, the relationships among groups were being negotiated. They were perceived as important enough that, in 1883, a conflict between a black man and a white man over a sidewalk encounter in Danville, Virginia, led to a riot in which white residents massacred African Americans (Dailey 1997).

During the Jim Crow era, white supremacy was enforced by laws that kept African American and white residents physically separated. Throughout this period, claiming public space continued to be an important way for people to participate publicly and form public identities. Robin Kelley (1993) has argued that in the repressive 1930s and 1940s, urban public sites in the South—streets, public buildings, and especially public transportation systems—were places where African Americans resisted racial oppression and where repressions occurred daily. Morning and evening commutes on buses and streetcars were places where African Americans resisted laws that forced them to board at the center door or prohibited them from sitting in the front seats. Although the color line could not be drawn with the same precision on streets and sidewalks as it was in restaurants, theaters, buses, and trains, by the 1930s the inner side of the sidewalk in a number of southern cities was customarily reserved for white people (Doyle 1937).

In addition to asserting their public rights on sidewalks and in other public-space encounters, African Americans sought voting rights and the right to enter into contracts. But the right to participate equally in public space was an important claim to full citizenship. People negotiated their social status by claiming access to all spaces in physically differentiated environments. Although the interactions were a way to negotiate power, the practices by which this occurred used the distinction between the sidewalk and gutter to enact these relationships.

Reconciling Distinctions between the Public and the Private

Sidewalks posed many challenges for those attempting to maintain hierarchies or promote order. In the nineteenth century, the public and private spheres were rigidly separated in American cities, and they distinguished male and female domains, work and home, and private and public spaces. Men moved from private realms into public spaces and were expected to easily navigate both spheres, but women who wished to maintain middle-class propriety were relegated to private realms.

In practice, however, women had to walk on sidewalks, take streetcars, and move through public spaces regularly between their homes and their destinations. Although it affected all women, the private sphere was a middle-class construct, and working-class women could not and did not want to always follow its dictates. Most low-income women had to work, although some worked more publicly than others. For female peddlers on sidewalks and in public markets, being in public was necessary and unremarkable. Working women had to travel regularly in public, and women servants often had to escort middle-class women to social visits and return alone.

Although middle- and upper-class women actively created and maintained the private/public distinctions, they also challenged them. Middle-class women who did not work for pay also chose to engage publicly, by taking care of daily business and volunteering in philanthropic organizations and city beautification efforts. This contradiction was reconciled in many ways. Middle-class women couched their public work in the language of the private sphere (such as municipal housekeeping for city beautification) and moved within a private bubble of reserve when on the sidewalks.

Public and private boundaries were maintained by stigmatizing women who acted improperly and by using public behavior as a lens for interpreting social status. No respectable nineteenth-century middle- or upper-class woman would be seen in public unescorted. In the daytime, only working-class women walked alone, and at night, a woman alone was considered a prostitute or "night-walker" (Baldwin 2002). Women exposed to the public environment of the street, especially at night, were inviting danger, and those present presumably lacked dignity (Ryan 1990). Women were not only corruptible but also corrupting, and they invited temptation as well as danger on themselves (Hickey 1995).

Harassment and at times violence also helped maintain boundaries. Men considered women on the street as a spectacle. They intimidated them with "lecherous gazes" and followed, insulted, and abused them with sexual comments (Ryan 1990, 69). By the middle of the nineteenth century, cities such as New York, San Francisco, and New Orleans started passing ordinances against the harassment and insulting of women on public streets (Ryan 1990), which also suggested that class and gender relationships were negotiated around women's public appearance. If allowing people to walk unimpeded suggested status, working-class men who violated middle-class women's veil of privacy used gender privilege to challenge class norms.

The multiple concerns that surrounded women in public reflected both male anxieties about women and worries about cities. Women embodied the erotic potential and freedom (and associated dangers, both to individuals and to shifting family, community, and class structures) that cities offered. Women on city streets were the source of public anxiety, as Rendell (1998, 88) eloquently explains in the following passage:

> In streets, the threat to social order posed by a mixing of classes and genders was cause for middle- and upper-class angst. So too was the worry that female forms of male property (mothers, wives, daughters) would be visually and sexually available for other men. In such public spaces, the masking of social identity through deliberate disguise or class emulation led to fear of working- and middle-class contamination of the public realm; such fears were represented by concerns with female sexuality in these spaces. The body of the urban female was the site of conflicting concerns—those of

public patriarchs seeking to control female occupation of the city and of consumer capitalists aiming to extend the roles of women as cheap workers and consumers of household and personal commodities. The representation of women as sexual commodities in the rambling class narratives as Cyprians in upper-class venues and prostitutes in working-class taverns articulated male concerns with female sexuality.

The politics of public space distinguished women by class and categorized them as dangerous or endangered, respectable or undignified (Ryan 1990). Proper women visited public spaces but were not supposed to linger or venture on public streets and sidewalks. Therefore, the sight of working-class women—who enjoyed public sociability and sought opportunities to meet men, display fashion, and have fun—was troubling. Living in the congested residential quarters of tenements, these women had few spaces in which they could socialize. Public sidewalks provided a venue for sociability and for escaping the protective control of the family. Sidewalk leisure also generated more opportunities for heterosocial contact (Hunt 2002, 15) because young women could meet men in public and even spend time with male gangs (Peiss 1986). Public activities (appearing in public, shopping, and amusing themselves) were liberating for working girls, who used their wages to buy clothes, jewelry, and entertainment (Hickey 1995). Although women had fewer freedoms than young men did, they enjoyed street life (Peiss 1986).

Nevertheless, working-class styles and public habits conferred working-class status, and middle-class residents considered those habits to be vulgar, inappropriate, and "low-class" (Sewell 2000). Those who defied sidewalk etiquette were considered "available," "loose," and of "low morality" (Stansell 1986). Working women waiting on sidewalks were harassed by the police, who assumed that they were prostitutes or had stolen the clothes or jewelry that they wore (Hickey 1995). The behavior of working girls appalled middle-class reformers, who were concerned about the eroticization of public space (Stansell 1986, 184) and feared that respectable women could become endangered or tempted by nonrespectable people or activities.

By the late nineteenth century, when paid labor and paid leisure were contributing to an increasingly heterosocial public life, women's use of public space had expanded greatly. Businessmen saw women as consumers of goods and of leisure opportunities. Women went on excursions to dance halls and movies and could increasingly afford inexpensive fashions (Peiss 1986). Merchants and advertisers also began perceiving women as the primary consumers in a capitalist economy, and women increasingly viewed posters, billboards, advertisements, and store windows that courted their gaze (Ryan 1990). Downtown department stores created a domestic public realm for upper- and middle-class white women. Store interiors and merchandise associated this public realm with the domestic sphere, but department stores also blurred the line between their interiors and the sidewalks. Plate-glass windows of the storefronts, originally designed to increase natural light, were soon used for window displays. The displays and the downtown shopping districts extended women's realm to the sidewalks, which were under the purview of the stores and therefore clean and controlled.

Sidewalks linked the department store's public realm with the rest of the downtown. In 1911, women suffrage activists in San Francisco used sidewalks for political ends. Because sidewalks were not segregated by gender and department stores and accompanying shopping districts were associated with women, women used this space to access the men that they needed to support their efforts. Sidewalks in the shopping district provided platforms for street speeches and other political activities, and the windows displayed political exhibits (Sewell 2003). Thus, middle-class women moved from the department stores to the sidewalks, where they were able to access the political realm of multiple constituencies and public actions.

In the twentieth century, women's increasing presence in the paid labor force increased their presence on the streets and sidewalks. Today women move freely on U.S. sidewalks, but some argue that at times they are still the wrong gender in the wrong place (Beazley 2002). Women are underrepresented in public spaces, and parental admonitions, highly publicized media stories, crime-prevention advice, and warnings by the police encourage women to consider streets and other public spaces as dangerous (Loukaitou-Sideris 1995, 2005, 2006). As a result, many women avoid some areas or routes or stay home at night, fearing harassment or violence (Gardner 1995).

Sidewalks as a Dangerous Adult World

Although the access of women and African Americans to sidewalks eventually increased, that of children and youth has been progressively curtailed over the past two centuries. In the nineteenth century, children were common participants in sidewalk activities, but their presence became an indicator of disorder and neglect, which allowed the state to intervene in their care. The common opinion was that streets were no place for children, and today few children travel independently on the streets. Similarly, the presence of teenagers on streets and sidewalks may appear disruptive and even threatening.

By the late nineteenth century, working-class youngsters filled urban sidewalks as they peddled, ran errands, and distributed newspapers. Sidewalks were places for employment and leisure. Having no private territories for play and living in cramped apartments, thousands of immigrant children used the sidewalks as immense playgrounds. As Baldwin (2002, 600) argues, "the street remained at least as powerful an influence on the working class child in the early 1900s as the home and the school.... Even though hundreds of supervised playgrounds, gymnasia, and vacation schools opened in the early twentieth century, the street was the favorite play space."

In the eyes of middle-class residents, the image of "delinquent," "rowdy," and "unruly" children embodied the pathologies of tenement districts and the tenement classes. In 1849, New York City's chief of police, George Matsell, warned against the "deplorable and growing evil of poor children overwhelming the streets and causing crime and disorder" (Stansell 1986, 194). New York's vagrancy and truancy laws soon forbade "delinquent" children from wandering unchaperoned on city streets under the threat of arrest and institutionalization (Jackson 1998).

In the eyes of middle-class reformers, the presence of children in the streets implied inadequate parental supervision and moral dangers. Reformers feared that "innocent" children would be corrupted. After the cholera epidemic of 1849, reformers were also alarmed by the epidemiological dangers of allowing children to live in unsanitary conditions and spread diseases (Stansell 1986).

Restrictions on children's street jobs, such as newspaper vending and errand running, became widespread. These restrictions were part of a movement to reduce vending and other street activities but also to instill a sense of order in the expanding industrial city (Baldwin 2002; Boyer 1983).

Between the 1880s and 1920, juvenile curfew ordinances were enacted in more than 3,000 cities and banned the presence of unaccompanied children from the sidewalks after 8:00 or 9:00 p.m. During this period, 80 percent of cities with a population over 30,000 adopted such ordinances. President Harrison considered them as "the most important municipal regulation for the protection of the children in American homes from the vices of the street" (Hemmens and Bennett 1998–1999, 280). Many are still in place.

Sidewalks and streets became perceived as an adult and dangerous world, and children on the streets increasingly symbolized disorder. As the years passed, the rhetoric of protecting the young from the evils and dangers of the street intensified. In the 1960s, activist Abbie Hoffman (1968, 187) highlighted how danger and kids encapsulate a middle-class moral order: "The street has always been an interesting symbol in middle-class American life. It was the place to avoid. There is 'violence on the streets,' 'bad people in the streets,' and 'danger in the streets.' It was always 'let's keep the kids off the streets' as a honkie America moved from outside to inside." And indeed, in the early twenty-first century, few middle-class children walk alone on city sidewalks, wait at bus stops and train stops, or bike to school unaccompanied by adults.

Today, the perceived dangers of the street permeate children's lives and mobility. Researchers have observed that children became less independent and less mobile in the late twentieth century because adult anxieties about their safety on sidewalks and public transportation led middle-class parents to drive them everywhere (Cunningham and Jones 1999). These fears lead parents to impose more restrictions on their children's use of the street than they experienced in their own childhood (Valentine and

McKendrick 1997; Jones 2000). An early 1980s survey found that only 16 percent of a total of 323 seven-year-olds in the United States were allowed to go farther than their block without adult supervision (Boocock 1981), while a California survey revealed that nearly 30 percent of the eleven- and twelve year-olds asked had not visited any public space on their own (Medrich, Roisen, Rubin, and Buckley 1982).

Children in both "safe" suburbs and "dangerous" inner cities are constrained. Grim media reports about street gangs that loiter on street corners and sidewalks affect both urbanites' and suburbanites' views of the street. In the cities, fear of violence and drive-by shootings force many parents to keep their children indoors. But, children are also restricted in the automobile-dependent suburbs, where they are unable to walk from their homes to schools, parks, malls, and friends' houses. Suburban children often stay "prisoners of a thoroughly safe and unchallenging environment" (Duany, Plater-Zyberk, and Speck 2000, 116).

Perceived problems with teenagers in public spaces exemplify the tensions that disruptions may pose. Unlike children, teenagers are mobile and likely to use public spaces for many purposes. As Crouch (1998, 164) has argued, "The youth culture finds the street valuable for its own practices. These include display, and gauging and swapping representations visually and in conversation. For youth the street is not only an actual material place, but embodied with all sorts of meanings and metaphors; of escape, discovery, and home too. The street offers an opportunity, a place to be (as well as to be seen). It becomes a place of sharing; of conflict, confrontation between different members; of ownership."

Teenagers test boundaries and insert themselves in adult worlds, and in doing so may appear disruptive. In the late twentieth century, municipal ordinances against lingering, roller-skating, and skateboarding were enacted to restrict teenager activities in public spaces (Owens 1999; Wooley and Johns 2001). Teenagers who linger or skateboard on city sidewalks trouble businesses and residents, and their complaints lead police to move teenagers along (Valentine 1996).

Skateboarding teenagers use sidewalks and street furniture in unintended ways, and their speed, noise, and unpredictable movements can make an area less usable for others. Skateboarding is not purposeful movement (such as walking) or a consumer activity (like outdoor dining) and often is perceived as a "nuisance," "urban pathology" or "civil disorder" by municipal authorities and other sidewalk users (Howell 2001; Oc and Tiesdell 1997). These reactions suggest that the playful adaptation of sidewalks, benches, stairs, and ledges by skateboarders is wrong. Moreover, skateboarders are sometimes intentionally countercultural in their appearance and mannerisms, which deviate from accepted social norms. By consciously defying the ordinances that ban their sport, skateboarders challenge and test established norms of behavior and movement on the sidewalks.

CONCLUSION

When disruptions occur on public sidewalks, one group's interests may appear appropriate or normal, while another group may appear to violate those interests. As some urban observers have noted, however, definitions of "normality" are often "privileging the lifestyles of white, middle-class, heterosexual adults over 'others'" (Valentine 1996, 206; also Mitchell 1996, 1998). Those whose presence or activities were banned or excluded from sidewalks have at times defied social expectations or municipal ordinances by challenging discriminatory practices. Such reactions may lead to disruptions, discomforts, and even conflicts, and some argue that these are negative aspects of urban life that should be eliminated or contained (Ellickson 1996). The history of civil rights, however, has shown that challenges, contestations, and disruptions may indeed be necessary when the goal is a just society and an inclusive public realm.

Sidewalk as Space of Dissent

Wherever the title of the streets and parks may rest, they have immemorially been held in trust for the use of the public and, time out of mind, have been used for purposes of assembly, communicating thought between citizens, and discussing public questions. Such use of the streets and public places has, from ancient times, been part of the privileges, immunities, rights, and liberties of citizens.
—*Hague v. Congress for Industrial Organizations (CIO)*, 307 U.S., 496, 515 (1939)

Although the protesters outside the 2000 Democratic National Convention chanted "These are our streets," the heavy police presence indicated otherwise. A federal order had guaranteed protesters access to Los Angeles's Staples Center, but city officials, mindful of the protests during the 1999 World Trade Organization meetings in Seattle, were determined to contain the activities as much as possible. They created a protest zone that was defined by concrete blocks and a twelve-foot chain-link fence. Despite the city's efforts, protesters slowed downtown business and disrupted traffic. To many, public speaking and protest—central aspects of public spaces—had become an impediment to the streets and sidewalks' primary purposes.[1]

More than sixty years and a sea change in the perception of streets and sidewalks separate the above two incidents. They illustrate two opposing views of sidewalks as political spaces. The first perceives sidewalks as the political realm par excellence—an inclusive public forum that enables debate, dissent, and political action. This view celebrates sidewalks as spatial settings where "subversive forces, forces of rapture, ludic forces act and meet" (Barthes 1986, 96) and where "marginalized groups make themselves visible enough to be counted as legitimate members of the polity" (Lees 1998, 115). The right to "take to the streets" thus underlies freedom of expression and democracy (Mitchell 1996).

The second view perceives dissent as street obstructions that are fraught with possible violence and disorder. Demonstrations and protests threaten the safe rhythms of everyday life by hindering the free flow of pedestrian and vehicular traffic and creating chaos. Sidewalk protests interfere with others' movement or passage, and this disruption is uncomfortable and undesirable. This view privileges public safety and order over the rights of dissenters.

Public sidewalks are necessary sites for protest. Public acts of dissent counter more powerful interests, and to be effective they must be both visible and disruptive. Although walking is no longer the primary mode of transportation in U.S. cities, sidewalks are still important and visible as a circulation system that winds through the city and abuts roadways and private properties. Even people who do not walk all the way to their destination may walk a portion of the way and will use the sidewalk space to enter or leave their destination. Sidewalks are also visible to motorists. Because of this, sidewalks provide demonstrators critical access to the rest of the city, precisely because they are sites of movement that can be disrupted and because they are visible.

In the United States and other countries, public sidewalks have been used by groups to express opposition to governmental or corporate actions and to demand the privileges of representation in public life. Various groups have fought for racial, social, economic, or political justice and social change. By taking to the streets, staking a claim and interrupting normal traffic flows, these groups forced society to notice them (Mitchell 1996; Mitchell and Staeheli 2005).

Demonstrators picketing in support of fair housing, Torrance, California, 1963.
Courtesy of Los Angeles Public Library.

Local disruptions are no longer solely local, however, and effective events now receive global attention. The 1989 student and citizen protests in Tiananmen Square were instantly carried to the living rooms of American and European households by international television networks. Aware of this opportunity, many protesters carried banners in English designed for international audiences (Hershkovitz 1993). Meetings for global institutions attract people from around the globe, and coverage of the events—including the protests against them—is broadcasted internationally as well. This visibility raises the stakes for cities. Fearing bad publicity, municipalities try to manage protest events.

More than almost any other sidewalk use, intentional speech and expressive activities are constitutionally protected in the United States. Cities therefore cannot prohibit protests, but they have leeway to control how and when protests occur to decrease the disruption and thereby to render protests ineffective. This often leads protesters and their allies to turn to the courts to arbitrate the constitutionality of municipal ordinances and determine the scope of municipal authority. In the post 9/11 security era, however, cities have increasingly attempted to stop protests and to prevent the disruption of secured events.

In this chapter, we use two early conflicts around free speech—between the Socialist Party and the city of Los Angeles from 1902 to 1908 and between the Industrial Workers of the World and the city of San Diego from 1906 to 1917—to discuss how cities created "no-protest" zones to ban sidewalk speaking. We also discuss the laws surrounding expressive sidewalk activities and the ways that freedom of speech and freedom of assembly in public space have been defined by the courts. To examine contemporary conflicts over the use of sidewalks for the expression of dissent, we discuss protests and reactions during three large events—the 1999 World Trade Organization (WTO) meeting in Seattle, the 2000 Democratic National Convention in Los Angeles, and the 2003 Free Trade Area of the Americas (FTAA) meeting in Miami. In an era when many cities want to attract large conventions and international investors and tourists, municipal governments are eager to quell controversies and render protesters invisible so that large events remain uninterrupted.

EARLY SIDEWALK CONFLICTS OVER FIRST AMENDMENT RIGHTS TO FREEDOM OF SPEECH AND FREEDOM OF ASSEMBLY

Because people take space and make it public when the need arises, public political actions have been recurrent. In the early years of the American republic, the streets and sidewalks were sites of local draft riots and political marches. As American cities industrialized in the late nineteenth and early twentieth centuries, as the economy was transformed from a mercantile to a corporatist and Fordist economy, and as the modern capitalist state emerged, new forms of collective action developed. Picketing and protesting by industrial workers, labor unions, and women's suffrage workers in the early 1900s targeted small and local stakeholders, centralized corporations, and state institutions (Tilly 1986). Those who marched for civil rights for African Americans in the 1950s and 1960s and against U.S. military involvement in Vietnam in the 1960s and 1970s presented demands to the national government, and since the late 1990s, protesters have focused on global governance institutions such as the WTO.

In the early twentieth century, public-speaking controversies began to debate First Amendment rights. The Salvation Army and other religious groups frequently proselytized on sidewalks, and street meetings attracted hundreds and at times thousands of people. Democrats, Republicans, and members of other political parties spoke on street corners, and to a large extent municipalities tolerated these assemblies. When political speech challenged the state and labor organizers threatened corporate interests, however, cities became less tolerant and enacted ordinances to curb speaking on sidewalks. These efforts were backed by downtown merchants who felt that street speaking was a nuisance and detrimental to their businesses. In the following sections, we detail the actions of two western cities, Los Angeles and San Diego, that enacted numerous techniques to curtail sidewalk speaking by two political organizations challenging business interests—the Socialist Party and the Industrial Workers of the World (IWW). The importance of these conflicts was not simply parochial, as the ensuing debate around free speech and free assembly on public sidewalks eventually extended across the country.

THE SOCIALIST PARTY'S FREE SPEECH FIGHTS IN LOS ANGELES[2]

In the 1890s and 1900s, trade unions proliferated nationwide, and by the early 1900s the labor movement in Los Angeles was gaining strength. Although union organizing occurred through direct communication with workers in different trades, political parties like the Greenback Labor Party, the Union Labor Party, and the Socialist Party focused on labor relations. In the 1900s, reflecting the national trends, the Socialist Party became more visible in Los Angeles and more involved in local politics. In the 1911 municipal election, a socialist mayoral candidate almost unseated the incumbent mayor. The Socialist Party also made its ideas visible by holding weekly meetings on sidewalks and open spaces ("The Week" 1901, 3).

Because the Los Angeles city fathers felt threatened by the activities of labor unions and radical political parties, in 1901 they issued the city's first ordinance that required permits for any "public speaking, meetings, debates, or discussions" in parks (Los Angeles City Council 1901, ord. 6503 N.S.). The ordinance targeted the Socialist Party, whose members were speaking to crowds of hobos and tramps, the migratory men who came through the city by the hundreds and passed their days in public spaces. H. Gaylord Wilshire, a socialist millionaire developer, challenged the ordinance, but the city appealed to the Superior Court and prevailed, and the challenge died.

Permitting was the city's first attempt to control street speaking, and soon the city began to extend its permitting requirements. In 1903, it amended an 1887 sidewalk obstruction ordinance to forbid "meetings and public speaking debates or discussion in public streets" without a permit (Los Angeles City Council 1903, ord. 8539 N.S.). The city exercised considerable discretion when it issued permits for street speaking, and it routinely denied them to Socialist Party members. In response, the Socialist Party organized a "Free Speech League." In a petition to the city council, the League argued that the ordinance was unconstitutional because it discriminated among groups and was "contrary to the genius of democratic institutions, because it deprives the people of their rights of free speech and free assemblage." The League vehemently objected "any discrimination by our city officials in favor of one Creed, or Party, or Cult" (Los Angeles City Council 1903, pet. 1202).

The ordinance was enforced inconsistently, but in a few years the Socialist Party directly challenged it. In early 1908, party members spoke without permits, were cited and jailed, and demanded jury trials because, as they argued, the ordinance violated the U.S. and California state constitutions. Few posted bail, and they crowded the city jail.

The city's response acknowledged the problem entailed in the discretionary use of permits and instead sought to utilize a tool that cities uniquely can draw on—land-based controls. In July 1908, the city unexpectedly repealed the speaking ordinance and released the prisoners. A week later, it enacted another ordinance that prohibited all speaking in the downtown central district because it interfered with traffic (Los Angeles City Council 1908, ord. 16857). The new ordinance no longer focused on individuals but instead designated a district where free-flowing traffic was protected. The new ordinance placed everyone on the same terms, and for the Socialists a nondiscriminatory restrictive policy was preferable to a policy that allowed city council discretion. But the Salvation Army and other religious groups that accepted the first ordinance that required permits contested the new ordinance and challenged its legality. Nevertheless, the courts upheld the new ordinance.

The city's main newspaper, the *Los Angeles Times*, reflecting the opinion of the Merchants and Manufacturers Association, sided with the city council, and argued a position that would increasingly dominate. In the paper's September 18, 1903, edition, transportation was the priority, and political uses such as street speaking were not the sidewalk's "legitimate purpose" (Ehrenfeucht and Loukaitou-Sideris 2007). Many organizations countered this position—including the Los Angeles Fellowship League, the Democratic League, and the Los Angeles Liberal Club—and submitted petitions in support of free speech.

Despite these free-speech arguments, the city's no-speaking zone was established, and its boundaries were expanded many times based on requests by residents and business owners, who felt entitled to the same protection from public-meeting nuisances that the residents of streets within the no-speaking zone enjoyed. Ultimately, the no-speaking zone was negotiated within a growing consensus that sidewalks and streets were for travel and that the interests of abutting property owners weighed more than those using the sidewalks to communicate.

THE FREE-SPEECH FIGHT OF THE WOBBLIES IN SAN DIEGO

The free-speech fights of the Socialists in Los Angeles were only the beginning of a series of battles over the right to political dissent and protest on the sidewalks. Members of the Industrial Workers of the World (IWW) began to use sidewalk speaking as a political tactic throughout western U.S. cities during the turbulent era of 1906 to 1917. The Wobblies (as IWW members were called) were a revolutionary group of about 25,000 registered members dedicated to the cause of radical unionism (Miller 1972). On soapboxes at street corners, the Wobblies shouted slogans and distributed leaflets to gathering crowds and passersby against the "extortionist practices of labor agents" (Genini 1974, 102).

Municipalities felt threatened by this wave of "irrational" behavior and arrested street speakers for violating ordinances against obstructing the sidewalk, blocking traffic, vagrancy, unlawful assembly, or violating public-speaking restrictions. With more people than money, the Wobblies intended to overwhelm city jails. As Rabban (1994, 1062) writes, "They [the Wobblies] openly violated laws that restricted speech, successfully provoked arrests, overcrowded the prisons, and clogged the courts. With these tactics of direct action, the Wobblies tried to force communities to allow street speaking."

There were twenty-six documented IWW free-speech fights during this era in Missoula, Spokane, Seattle, Kansas City, and Fresno, among other cities, but none was more dramatic than the conflict in San Diego (Miller 1972). Following its northern neighbor's example, in January 1912 the city of San Diego enacted an ordinance patterned after Los Angeles's no-speaking zone and established a no-speaking zone in forty-nine square blocks of its downtown. Merchants in the area had petitioned the city, complaining that "street speaking was a nuisance and a detriment to the public welfare of the city" (in Miller 1972, 216). Although the city used traffic flow to justify the ordinance, it exempted religious groups such as the Salvation Army. This exemption revealed an underlying concern that the municipal government was aligning itself with business interests that were antagonistic to the ideas and principles espoused by the Wobblies.

The Wobblies' main audience was transient workers who spent most of their time on city sidewalks. Therefore, no other space would have been equally effective to reach them. Although the Wobblies' strategy was to overwhelm the city facilities and court system, they also framed the fight around First Amendment rights, speaking to those who might have not supported their mission or politics but would support their right to act on them. As Margaret Kohn (2004, 29) describes:

> The Wobblies believed that free speech would never be won by appealing to the conscience or principles of the ruling class. The only viable tactic would be to exert power and the only power that the IWW possessed was manpower. Their strategy was to crowd the jails and overwhelm the resources of localities until they were forced into at least a tacit acceptance of soap box oratory. The strategy was victorious in Spokane and became a model for dozens of free speech fights. Whenever the police arrested someone for getting up on a soapbox, another supporter from the crowd stood up to replace him.

More than 5,000 Wobblies and sympathizers from other cities came to San Diego for the fight, and the conflict became violent. An underground vigilante movement developed, which the police tolerated and possibly supported. Vigilantes stormed the San Diego jail at midnight, abducted imprisoned Wobblies, transported them to the county line, and assaulted them (Miller 1972). Turning a blind eye to this brutality, the council enacted another ordinance that gave San Diego police authority to disband any meeting on public streets and sidewalks within the city limits (Mitchell 1996). The conflict reached its zenith when on May 7, 1912, a Los Angeles Wobbly, Joseph Mikolash, was killed during a dispute with the police, and on May 15 vigilantes kidnapped and tortured Ben Reitman, the partner of famous anarchist Emma Goldman, who was visiting the city (Miller 1972).

The national attention to the police actions and vigilante brutality prompted the governor of California to threaten military action against the vigilantes. The threat seemed to have an effect. The vigilantes backed down, the city repealed the street-speaking ordinance, and by 1914 the Wobblies were free to resume their sidewalk activity without police interruptions (Mitchell 1996). Fights involving the Wobblies also erupted in other western cities (Genini 1974), but the IWW became less visible and less influential in the subsequent decades. Nevertheless, the free-speech debates that the organization instigated highlighted issues that would be negotiated in public discussion, municipal councils, and the courts for the years to come—the reasonableness of sidewalk restrictions, the need for access to public space, and the discriminatory application of municipal ordinances.

Legal Construction of Sidewalks

Before World War I, the U.S. Supreme Court did not confront any public-speech or public-assembly cases. Lower courts responded to such issues by upholding municipal ordinances that restricted the uses of sidewalks. In doing so, the lower courts were following what Margaret Kohn (2004, 6) calls a "property rights approach," essentially treating sidewalks as a private space that was owned by a government that had the right to forbid citizens from accessing and using it. The interest of early courts was not to protect the citizens' right to express dissent but rather to control disruptive behavior. This did not stop people from taking to the streets. As Don Mitchell (1996, 167) has argued, "Even as the court continued to restrict the politics of the street, the issue continued to be contested on the streets themselves. Workers continued to picket and organize in public spaces. And localities continued doing what they had always done when speech and expressive activity seemed to threaten existing political and economic interests—they banned speech and arrested dissenters."

It took a landmark 1939 U.S. Supreme Court decision, *Hague v. Congress for Industrial Organizations (CIO)*,[3] to reverse the legal precedent that denied dissenters access to the streets and sidewalks. The city had established a permitting system for protests and demonstrations and denied a permit for public assembly to the Congress for Industrial Organizations (CIO) under the pretense of possible violence. The CIO sued Jersey City and its mayor,

Frank Hague, for refusing to grant it a permit. A lower district court ruled in favor of the CIO, finding no evidence that the proposed assembly would inevitably lead to violence. The case reached the U.S. Supreme Court, which ruled that the city was violating the group's constitutional right to assembly. In a formulation that later became known as the *public-forum doctrine*, the Court established the political role of streets, sidewalks, and parks and emphasized the government's responsibility for protecting the right of speech and assembly in traditional public spaces.

Hague v. CIO did not, however, prevent the government from enacting restrictions that guided political uses of public spaces, stating that public speech and assembly have to be "exercised in subordination to the general comfort and convenience ... peace and good order" (*Hague v. CIO*, 515). Although cities could not prohibit protest, the decision confirmed their authority to control how spaces were used.

Subsequent U.S. Supreme Court decisions established guidelines for municipalities. Three classes of public forums were designated: (1) "traditional" or "quintessential" public spaces that have always been open to the public (such as streets, sidewalks, and parks); (2) "dedicated public spaces" that are dedicated to the purpose of speech and assembly (such as college campuses or plazas in front of federal buildings); and (3) other publicly owned spaces that have primary purposes that precludes open access (such as jails or military bases) (Mitchell 1996). Even in the traditional public forums, the most open of the three, the Court has allowed time, place, and manner restrictions as long as they meet three criteria: they ensure content neutrality by not discriminating against any particular view; they are narrowly tailored to serve a significant governmental interest; and they leave open ample alternatives for communication (Janiszewski 2002).

Cities have exercised control by requiring permits (Janiszewski 2002), and the public-forum doctrine has led municipalities to develop intricate local rules governing the settings for protest—forbidding the use of certain sites, allowing the use of others, and specifying the duration and noise levels of protests (Mitchell and Staeheli 2005). Orderliness and public safety are significant governmental interests that justify regulation, and most if not all

U.S. municipalities have established permit systems for any public assembly (Mitchell 2004). As Mitchell and Staeheli (2005, 801) have argued, "free speech" became in reality "permitted speech."

Court decisions have emphasized that city officials should have little discretion when granting permits. In 1969, in *Shuttesworth v. Birmingham*,[4] the U.S. Supreme Court held that "we have consistently condemned licensing systems which vest in an administrative official discretion to grant or withhold a permit upon broad criteria unrelated to proper regulation of public places" (*Shuttesworth*, 153). Similarly, in *Forsyth County, Georgia v. Nationalist Movement*,[5] the U.S. upheld the government's right to impose a permit requirement for regulating uses of public forums but warned that government officials should not have overly broad licensing discretion (*Forsyth*, 123).

These decisions have shifted municipal control from the regulation of expressive activities to the regulation of spaces of expression and the practices through which the rights are exercised. This assumes that safe and orderly settings are necessary to the free "trade of ideas" (Cole 1986, 891), but as Mitchell (1996, 170) argues, "This quintessentially liberal formulation writes power out of the equation by assuming that all actors have equal access to the market." These guidelines also downplay the role that disruption has in expressing alternative views. Disruption is part of a demand to pay attention to an issue that might be overlooked. It is precisely those benefiting from situations who have an interest in ignoring—intentionally or not—opposing opinions.

Court decisions have increasingly used the notion of a space's primary purpose to justify restrictions of ordinary political communicating, petitioning, or information sharing. The logic of designating primary uses has developed by differentiating among public, quasi-public, and nonpublic forums. Initially, these differences served to distinguish between a jail and a sidewalk. However, this logic has been extended at times to traditional public forums. In *United States v. Kokinda*,[6] the U.S. Supreme Court held that a sidewalk on postal service property between the parking lot and the post office is not a traditional public forum because the post office is run as a business. The post office could prohibit political activists from setting up information tables on its sidewalk (Kohn 2004). This differs from the Ninth Circuit Court of Appeals decision that sidewalks outside casino hotels, regardless of who holds title to the land, function as public sidewalks and are traditional public forums (Blumenberg and Ehrenfeucht 2008). The sidewalks in these cases differ because in one case the sidewalks abut a roadway, while in the other a parking lot. In *Kokinda*, the U.S. Supreme Court argues that the resemblance of a sidewalk between a parking lot and post office building to a sidewalk along a street was irrelevant to a public forum. Sidewalks, in other words, differ from one another.

The increasing economic dependence of U.S. cities on visitors and on large events such as conventions means that municipal governments need to ensure that controversial events (such as meetings of international organizations, political conventions, and corporate gatherings) are not disrupted. They do so by designating areas where protests can or cannot occur, either by delineating a highly controlled space for protests or by designating a "no-protest" district around a controversial event. The city's ability to control activities and land use rests on the notion that sidewalks and streets are intended to be used for transportation.

By eliminating dissent from places where it could be visible and effective, municipal governments have traveled a full circle to the days of the Wobblies' free-speech fights in the early twentieth century (Kohn 2004). Municipal attempts to reduce disruption and disorder make the message of dissenters difficult to hear and their voices ineffective. Mitchell and Staeheli (1995, 810) have argued that these tactics are insidious and destructive to democracy:

> If constitutional jurisprudence after the 1939 *Hague* decision led to a politics of location aimed at moving protests to where they are bound to be least effective, then this politics of location was now supplemented by police practices that led protesters to locations where they could most easily be arrested. An interesting dialectic is at work. The legal incorporation of dissent has been accomplished by constructing spatial strategies that have had the effect of routinizing protest. This leads to what many see as protest's ineffectiveness.

FREE SPEECH OR SPEECH-FREE? THE CONSTITUTIONALITY VERSUS SECURITY DEBATE

In a globalizing world, sidewalks and streets have become venues for accessing global governance institutions. Mass demonstrations have been an important stage for protesters to voice human-rights and antiwar concerns, demand responses to impending environmental disasters, and act against the practices of national governments and transnational organizations (such as the World Trade Organization, the Free Trade Area of the Americas, or the World Bank).

The protesters' interactions with conventioneers and their disruption of the scheduled events direct the world's attention to dissenting perspectives. But the attention and disruptions run counter to municipalities' interest in being perceived as safe and attractive places for hosting large venues. Large conventions and visitors infuse cash into local economies, and image-conscious cities want the positive publicity that they receive from the ensuing media coverage. This attention becomes a liability if something goes wrong, so cities have incentives to help event organizers prevent disruptions. Organizers of global governance meetings have also increasingly attempted to minimize large protests by choosing cities or meeting locations that are hard to access (Boski 2002). Thus, cities have even greater reasons to ensure that events take place unimpeded.

To be influential, however, protesters must have access to both the conventioneers and the press and must be disruptive enough to attract the attention of the national and international media. For national conventions, activities outside the conventions raise awareness of issues and priorities that may not be addressed inside, and protesters demand that elected officials be accountable. For transnational organizations, protesters build alliances and make moral demands so that global institutions and the participating nations become obligated to respond. Sidewalks become critical protest spaces because these are areas where people access decision makers and the media. Unlike a park, which a controversial event can avoid, sidewalks go virtually everywhere.

Municipalities have used their authority to determine where and how protests occur by designating protest areas, and by doing so, they keep protesters from occupying salient spaces. Cities have attempted to fence in or zone out dissenting groups to control sidewalks. Cities have designated "no-protest zones," or they have delineated "protest pens" with fences and barricades away from an area where protesters could disrupt scheduled events. These techniques are reminiscent of the "no-speaking zones" in cities a century ago.

To legitimize their controls, cities and supportive organizations such as newspapers present the protesters as threatening and highlight the need for policing to guard against potentially dangerous people and to ensure security (Brand 2006). This framework justifies significant police presence and controls and can also block the participation of protesters from permitted events, as happened outside the Free Trade Area of the Americas conference in Miami, where in separate incidences, police refused to allow Amnesty International to its permitted event and turned away participants from an AFL-CIO rally (Schneider 2003).

When the U.S. Supreme Court's decisions limited the authority of municipalities to regulate activities and conflicting uses on sidewalks and other public spaces, cities redefined free speech as an activity like any other. In such a framework, public speaking or protest events must then be balanced with other activities, including conventions during which conventioneers must be able to enter and exit buildings and move through the city. As protest events become defined as activities, cities increasingly control how the events unfold and deemphasize what is necessary to ensure effective communication. In the following sections, we discuss three conflicts that all involved the freedom to express dissent on public streets and sidewalks—in Seattle, Los Angeles, and Miami.

SLEEPLESS IN SEATTLE: THE WORLD TRADE ORGANIZATION CONFLICT, NOVEMBER 29 TO DECEMBER 3, 1999

In late November 1999, 40,000 protesters from the United States and the world gathered at the Washington State Convention and Trade Center in

Seattle, Washington, prepared to spend days and nights on city sidewalks outside the World Trade Organization (WTO) meetings to demand that the WTO address issues of global importance. About 6,000 officials from 135 countries had come to Seattle to participate in the WTO's ministerial conference. The high visibility and high attendance of the conference and its coverage by international media provided a unique opportunity for protesters. They could capture global attention for their dissatisfaction with the effects of globalization and the practices of transnational corporations—worsening of labor conditions, increased inequity between wealthy and poor nations, and widespread damage to the environment (Comfort 2001).

Most protesters were peaceful. Some, however, came prepared to nonviolently disrupt and, if possible, shut down the WTO meeting. While protesters were getting ready to spend some sleepless nights on the pavement, the Seattle Police Department was caught unprepared for the extent and intensity of the impromptu protests. Police officers used pepper spray and tear gas on protesters, hit them with batons, and shot them with rubber bullets at short distances ("WTO" 2000, B5). As the conflict escalated, some demonstrators broke windows, tagged buildings, and damaged property in other ways, and the police made multiple arrests. Seattle Mayor Paul Schell declared a state of civil emergency and imposed a limited curfew in downtown (Perrine 2001).

The curfew covered two dozen downtown blocks where WTO conference attendees, business owners, and their employees and residents were allowed entry. Police officers heavily patrolled the borders of this "no-protest zone." The American Civil Liberties Union (ACLU) sought a temporary restraining order to eliminate the no-protest zone, but Judge Robert Bryan of the District of Tacoma denied the motion on December 1, 1999, stating that "free speech must sometimes bend to public safety" (Ith 2001, A1).

On March 7, 2000, the ACLU filed a second lawsuit in the U.S. District Court in Seattle on behalf of citizens who were kept or forced out of the "no-protest zone" by police because they were carrying anti-WTO signs. The lawsuit also challenged the zone's legitimacy and enforcement. Kathleen Taylor, executive director of the ACLU of Washington, argued

Police in front of boarded buildings at the World Trade Organization meetings, Seattle, Washington, 1999. Photograph by Renia Ehrenfeucht.

that the city was violating the protesters' First Amendment rights and that "An American city must not get away with such flagrant violations of citizens' freedoms" (ACLU 2000). When the case reached the Ninth Circuit Court of Appeals in 2005, the court ruled that the government could not arrest demonstrators because of the content of their messages. The court did not find that that the "no-protest zone" itself violated the constitutional rights of protesters. It remanded the case to the lower court to determine whether, in practice, the city's policy was to create such a zone where people could not enter solely on the basis of the content of their speech. In doing so, the lower court would have to determine if the rights of two ACLU clients, Victor Mennoti and Doug Skove, were violated when they were arrested (ACLU 2005). The lower court did not have the opportunity to decide on the case because the city settled in September 2006.

Eight years later, Seattle still feels the fallout. The city has settled dozens of lawsuits for illegal arrests and excessive use of force by the police during the WTO incidents. A class-action suit on behalf of about 200 arrestees was filed against the city, and in January 2007 a federal jury found that the city was liable for violating the rights of 175 protesters who had been seized and searched. The court did not find that the city had violated the protesters' First Amendment rights ("Seattle Is Found Liable for WTO Protest Arrests" 2007).

SEALED OFF IN LOS ANGELES: THE DEMOCRATIC NATIONAL CONVENTION CONFLICT, AUGUST 14 TO 17, 2000

On August 14, 2000, delegates who had come to the Staples Center in Los Angeles, California, for the Democratic National Convention (DNC) felt sealed off in its cool interior. They could see on television the commotion that was taking place in the sweltering heat outside, where thousands of protesters who were fenced inside a parking lot a block north of the Staples Center were demonstrating for a variety of causes—including the failed war on drugs, workers' rights, environmental protection, corporate greed, and homelessness (Gorov 2000). "During these hot, heady days of marches and street battles," described a *Los Angeles Times* editorial, "delegates and demonstrators have inhabited separate realities, kept apart by the security measures that have sealed off Staples Center. The delegates sit in air-conditioned buses and are waved past check-points by police—they hear the voices of the protesters as faint, muffled sounds in the distance or see them on TV" (Tobar 2000, A1).

Mindful of the WTO events in Seattle just eight months earlier, the Los Angeles Police Department (LAPD) and Los Angeles mayor Richard Riordan were expecting 30,000 people to come into town and hold mass demonstrations. The mayor had attempted to preempt similar events and wrote an op-ed in the *Los Angeles Times* that warned potential protesters that "Los Angeles cannot tolerate nonviolent civil disobedience" (Schneider and Stuteville 2000). He admonished the police to take action. Unlike the Seattle Police Department, the LAPD put together a six-inch-thick security plan that outlined causes of action under different scenarios (Shuster and Newton 2000). People who wished to demonstrate had to obtain a permit indicating their purpose, the estimated number of participants, and their proposed location or route. The LAPD had the authority to grant or deny a permit, choose the date, time, and location of a demonstration, and monitor the group's behavior.

The city also decided to restrict the areas where protests could take place. It erected barbed-wire fences of concrete and steel around the Staples Center and cordoned off and declared as off-limits for demonstrators many of the blocks that surrounded the Staples Center. An official protest area was designated. It was a surface parking lot that was enclosed by a chain-link fence and was a considerable distance from the convention venue. Activists observed that their efforts would be ineffective if they were caged far away from the convention and lambasted "the protest pit."

In a lawsuit filed before the convention in July 2000, the ACLU challenged as unconstitutional the city's efforts to contain and control the demonstrations, arguing that the designated zone was too far away from the convention delegates and that the city's parade and permit policies gave officials too much discretion over the exercise of First Amendment rights of speech and peaceful assembly. As the ACLU's Ramona Ripston argued in a

Protest pen outside the Democratic National Convention, Staples Center, Los Angeles, California, 2000. Photograph by Tom LaBonge, SPNB Collection. Courtesy of the Los Angeles Public Library.

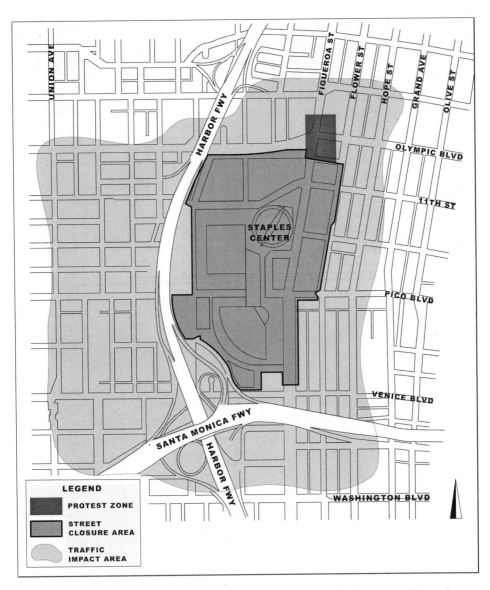

Map of the Staples Center area, Los Angeles, California, 2000. The Democratic National Convention's protest zone is the solid area in the top right, outside the black line.
Credit: Map redrawn by Konstantina Soureli.

letter to the editor of the *Los Angeles Times*, "Protests challenge accepted opinion and are therefore essential to the health of our democracy and our growth toward greater freedom and equality as a society. But they also challenge our society in a more immediate way: They force us to implement our democratic values, and in doing so, put those values to the test. They force us to create a real, not hypothetical, space for public dissent" (Ripston 2000, 6).

U.S. District Court judge Gary A. Feess granted an injunction striking down the security zone around the Staples Center. "You can't shut down the First Amendment about what might happen," the judge was quoted as saying. He also found that the city "made no attempt to accommodate or balance free speech interests of the protesters against the need for security at the convention site" (Rabin and Shuster 2000, 1). Unlike Judge Bryan, who upheld the constitutionality of the "no-protest zone" in Seattle, Judge Feess in Los Angeles argued that the city was "setting a dangerous and constitutionally dubious precedent by enacting 'prior restraints' on speech based on the mere speculation that violence might occur" (Kohn 2004, 39).

Although the Seattle "no-protest zone" was not in the plans prior to the events but was a reaction to the demonstrations and to perceived dangers, Los Angeles sought to preempt disruptive demonstrations by making a broad area around the convention inaccessible to protesters. By placing time, place, and manner restrictions on political speech in the name of safety and order, Los Angeles attempted to provide an alternative for communication—an official "protest zone." But the zone's location, blocks away from the center of action, gave protesters the ability to speak without being heard—effectively, if not literally, silencing their voices.

CLAMPED DOWN IN MIAMI: FREE TRADE AREA OF THE AMERICAS, NOVEMBER 17 TO 21, 2003

In November 2003, when the Free Trade Area of the Americas (FTAA) meeting came to the Inter-Continental Hotel in Miami, Florida, protesters faced post-9/11 security measures. Businesses were closed. The city's elevated rail was quiet. At staffed checkpoints, police asked pedestrians for pieces of identification and checked their bags. The estimated 20,000 people who had come to the sidewalks outside the hotel to register their concerns about environmental responsibility, work conditions, and growing inequity were treated like criminals.

Seattle's WTO fiasco led all parties to understand what Miami was not going to allow, and the police were out in force. As one reporter described, "Miami has been transformed into an armed camp of police.... They have a SWAT team on every corner" (Pacenti 2003b). Even the city's independent review panel agreed that "For a brief period in time, it appeared as if Miami was a 'police state'" (Reynardus 2004, 2).

As the delegates met in the Inter-Continental Hotel, a security fence surrounded the protest perimeter. It allowed protesters to speak within reasonable distance but also ensured the FTAA meetings would not be disrupted. Those wanting to enter the security fence needed an FTAA badge and two other forms of identification (Pacenti 2003a).

To the chagrin of some businesses, the city planned to detour traffic away from a fifty-block area, more than twice the area covered by Seattle's curfew, and the city's Metro-mover did not operate over downtown (Pacenti 2003b). Some businesses decided to close for the week or moved employees to other branches (La Corte 2003). The transportation system and traffic circulation were modified, and city employees were employed to ensure the FTAA's security.

The Miami-Dade Police Department prepared well in advance, spending 40,000 work hours on training for the forty security and law enforcements agencies that participated in the event. The city removed trash bins and enacted a new negotiated ordinance that prevented people from carrying bottles and lumber on city sidewalks. Its original ordinance also prohibited people from wearing bullet-proof vests and carrying gas masks, sticks, poles, baseball bats, and assorted other items and encountered strong resistance from the ACLU. The city left nothing to chance, and on the Saturday prior to the meeting, five protesters were arrested for blocking the sidewalk (Pain 2003). Security costs were estimated between $8 and 12 million, but

Congress allocated $8.5 million for the FTAA conference as an appendage to an Iraq war bill that had passed one month prior to the meeting (Clifton 2003).

Mitchell and Staeheli (2005) have observed that the politics of location leads to protests where protesters can most easily be arrested. This sounded true in Miami, where the streets of the district surrounding the FTAA meeting became a contained space where police felt comfortable indiscriminately asking for names and information, requiring people to empty their pockets, and generally intimidating passersby. Checkpoints staffed with officers blocked pedestrians who were not carrying proper credentials. In one case, police blocked Amnesty International members from accessing the Torch of Friendship for their permitted demonstration (Reynardus 2004, 7).

On Thursday, November 20, 2003, the clashes between protesters circling the protest perimeter and police became violent, and at Southeast First Street and Southeast Third Avenue, the police started clubbing protesters (Nielson 2003). Amid allegations of police violence and brutality, the City of Miami's independent review panel investigated the police response. It found that (Reynardus 2004, 13)

> The police response was successful in protecting the FTAA ministerial from disruption but was not successful in protecting the anti-FTAA peaceful demonstrations from being disrupted. Police did not give the same consideration to the protection of demonstrators' civil rights as it did to the protection of the FTAA ministerial.... Actions to show police preparedness to protect the ministerial from attack were more evident than actions to protect committed peaceful protesters from police actions that would limit the constitutionally protected peaceful protest.

The independent review panel further concluded that although the police were trained to contain protest, they were not educated about the protesters' rights (Reynardus 2004, 5–6). In the following year, the Democratic National Convention in Boston disrupted the entire city—the streets were empty—but no protesters interrupted the convention itself.

CONCLUSION

Disruption has its purposes, but municipal interests favor order over demands for freedom of speech or justice. Because municipalities cannot prohibit speech activities outright, they control the time, place, and manner that they occur. They issue permits, designate areas where protesters cannot go, and deploy police to contain protest actions.

Increasingly, image-conscious cities want to avoid being perceived negatively, and safeguarding free speech has been a lower priority than the national preoccupation with public safety, which has intensified since the 9/11 attacks. Effective communication matters less than ensuring security and lack of disruption of planned events. Municipal strategies let protesters talk but ensure that they are not heard, seen, or able to disturb their intended audience.

Sidewalks have been defined and transformed by the concepts of power and resistance (Law 2002) and have been characterized as being "simultaneously a space of political struggle and of repression and control" (Lees 1998, 238). The discretionary powers of municipalities in the early twentieth century to issue public-speech permits to some groups and deny them to others defined "insiders" and "outsiders" in the public realm. Similar to the early "no-speaking zones," the recent "protest pens" and "no-protest zones" are artifacts of the powerful who have the ability to control and regulate—municipal governments, police authorities, and global capital.

Still, resistance to power occurs at multiple levels and with more or less intention. Protesters engage in civil disobedience, defy ordinances and regulations, and appropriate public spaces for oppositional purposes. As Hershkovitz has argued, the "tension between the domination of public space and its appropriation as a platform from which to communicate alternative or oppositional political messages is part of the social process that continually produces and transforms social space" (Hershkovitz 1993, 416, quoted in Law 2002, 1643). Because streets and sidewalks provide space to stage acts of dissent, they are "reviled as the front of low culture or feared as a signifier of dangerous territorialisation" (Keith 1995, 297), and it is the streets' potential to transform society that makes them dangerous.

IV

COMPETING USES AND MEANINGS

Accommodating diversity in public is a critical and necessary ideal of democracy. Sidewalks can be spaces that facilitate "unassimilated otherness" and where people of varying affiliations and identities coexist (Young 1990). Because civility in the face of diversity is expected in such public spaces (Lofland 1998), most sidewalk encounters are trouble-free and often pleasant or useful.

Notwithstanding the need for urban residents to live together and an expectation of civility, competition and conflict over specific spaces are at times unavoidable. Activities that are not intentionally disruptive can still be incompatible in small public spaces. Sidewalks present a paradox. Many sidewalk uses have overlapping purposes, and this variety creates diversity and draws people to the street. At the same time, coexisting activities can conflict with one another. Sidewalks are functional parts of the roadway but also useful to abutting spaces. In many cases, abutters' interests differ from the interests of other sidewalk users. Broad agreements about what should be permitted on sidewalks may be irrelevant when the debate is about a particular strip of sidewalk for specific, competing desires.

The interests of street vendors and shopkeepers, which we discuss in chapter 7, are a case in point. Although shopkeepers can and do benefit from a vibrant street life, they usually object to having street vendors outside their establishments. Street vendors compete directly with merchants by selling similar goods for less. Their business may also interrupt pedestrian flow, and the scents of street food may damage clothes and fabric. Nonetheless, both vendors and shopkeepers want busy—if different—sidewalks.

Legitimate objectives can compete, and those promoting exclusion might be furthering a desirable outcome such as a small business district. When cities intervene, economic interests are given priority, and municipal authorities ally themselves with property or business owners. Cities privilege activities that contribute to economic vitality, defined as increasing property values or tax revenues. In these struggles, those with fixed property win. While this may make economic sense for a city, not all groups have equal resources and alternatives.

People who are dependent on street activities become the problem. Regulations must further a public purpose, but because the public is composed of groups with varying needs and interests, this concept is ambiguous. We follow Young (1990, 158) and argue that a politics of difference allows for and requires treating people differently: "The assimilationist ideal assumes that equal social status for all persons requires treating everyone according to the same principles, rules, and standards. A politics of difference argues, on the other hand, that equality as the participation and inclusion of all groups sometimes requires different treatment." In some circumstances, activities that appear to be counter to a city's economic objectives and that interfere with others' use of space should be tolerated.

This issue is further complicated because sidewalks differ from one another and may have different meanings and uses for different people. Neighborhoods are also unique. People who are homeless need to be somewhere, for instance, but sometimes cities offer them space that is not where they want to be or that does not suit their purposes, as we discuss in chapter 8. A person who intends to ask for money might want to be near many other sidewalk users.

Although soliciting money on sidewalks is characterized as using public spaces for private activities, public and private activities are integrated. People do many personal activities in public: they have private cell-phone conversations, act intimately with lovers, have business meetings, and maintain friendships. The use of public spaces for private activity increases the complexity of what the "public" aspect of public space is meant to convey (Lofland 1998; Valentine 1996). Sidewalks support public activities and public relationships, but they also allow people to fulfill personal needs through economic exchanges, social encounters, and at times basic survival.

Sidewalks also serve large public interests that may conflict with individual priorities. Street trees, for example, can cool a city, reduce pavement stress, and improve air quality. Individual trees can also block a garden's sunlight or hide business signs. Recognizing this complexity does not lead to immediate solutions, as street-tree provision shows in chapter 9. Activities, priorities, and people overlap and compete along sidewalks. The interests of sidewalk users include personal gain, social encounters, and regional environmental improvements, leading to negotiations over each linear stretch.

Sidewalk as Space of Economic Survival

The geographer Edward Soja has noted that "relations of power and discipline are inscribed into the apparently innocent spatiality of social life" (Soja 1989, 6). When ordinary activities such as mobile or stationary vending, displaying wares outside stores, and day laboring become conflictual, they reflect larger struggles over social change and attempts to manage it. Established merchants and middle- and upper-class citizens have tried to deny mobile vendors the opportunity to use sidewalks for economic activity (Bromley 2000). Street vendors and day laborers, driven by economic need, have negotiated their presence, evading or challenging regulations and asserting claims to the city in the process.

Street vending wars have been characterized as a struggle over the meaning and uses of public space between a public with a specific ideal for order and a counterpublic (composed of immigrants, poor residents, and ethnic minorities) who need a venue for various economic and social activities (Coombe 1995; Fraser 1992). Street vending, day laboring, and other informal economic activities are driven by large national and supranational forces, but they are also sites where transnational migrations become visible to established residents and merchants. Cultural differences, a discomfort with these differences, and the changing circumstances that bring them about underlie the local tensions.

The vending wars also reflect a conflict among sidewalk users who compete over the narrow concrete strips. Businesses that compete directly with vendors oppose sidewalk peddling. Established businesses also fight for an image that they want their neighborhood to convey. Municipalities typically align themselves with property and business owners, by collaborating with them through business improvement districts (BIDs) and by enacting and enforcing vending regulations.

This chapter provides a historic perspective for the conflicts over street vending and display of wares. Using primary and secondary sources and moving from the late nineteenth century to contemporary times, we detail the nature of street-vending conflicts and the municipal responses to street vending on sidewalks in New York and Los Angeles. Recent immigrants traditionally have used street vending as an economic entry point. When they do so, they compete with long-standing businesses and invoke the wrath of the established classes who are troubled by such appropriation of public spaces.

THE "PUSHCART EVIL" IN NEW YORK

Street vending (or street peddling, as it used to be called) once had a ubiquitous presence on American sidewalks. Nineteenth-century sidewalks were crowded with vendors, sidewalk displays, day laborers, and solicitors. Most early peddlers were men, but some women worked alongside their husbands, and widows supported their families through vending. Peddlers worked long hours, often well into the night under acetylene torches. Pushcart peddlers, itinerant hawkers, and street-stall operators sold fruit, vegetables, and sundry household goods. Peddlers pushed carts through the streets with produce, fish, and meat. Carts sold popcorn, sandwiches, candy, and drinks to lunch crowds and evening bar goers. Lunch wagons and news, cigar, and bootblack stands were established sites for social interaction, and at newsstands citizens exchanged the news as well as bought it. On foot, boys sold newspapers, and girls sold flowers. Although the peripatetic peddler was an important figure in urban neighborhoods, stationary carts eventually became more common (Burnstein 1996). Attracted by the profit at specific sites, formerly mobile peddlers started congregating during the last quarter of the nineteenth century. That was when they were first described as the "pushcart evil."

Because street peddling required minimal capital outlay, it was pursued by less wealthy residents. It was not a high-status occupation, but it offered an alternative to sweatshops or piece work. Street peddling, however, pitted some citizens against others and led to vending wars between the well-established, native-born merchants and their poorer, immigrant counterparts. Reformers and city officials nationwide opposed street vending in the name of "public health," "aesthetics," or the public's right to "unobstructed movement" on the sidewalks. Street vendors were frequently painted in the public imagination as "loud," "undignified," and "undesirable" (Isenberg 2004). Ordinances regulating street commerce were adopted to eliminate noise, congestion, and filth (Bluestone 1991). By the late nineteenth century, the uninterrupted pedestrian traffic became the explicit reason that municipalities gave for controlling street vending in a way that would have been unimaginable in earlier decades.

Street peddling was common in New York, and from the seventeenth century, the city curtailed, controlled, and regulated it. As early as 1691, the city prohibited selling on the streets until two hours after the markets opened, and in 1707, street hawking was forbidden outright. By the late nineteenth century, vending became ubiquitous. Daniel Bluestone (1991) has delineated four distinct but overlapping phases in New York's pushcart commerce. Between 1880 and 1913, peddlers established illegal street markets at specific locations, defying city ordinances that forbade peddling at one spot for extended times. From 1913 to World War I, the city sought to contain peddling by allowing it in designated areas, primarily under major city bridges. In response to the food shortages during the war, the city decided to tolerate, legalize, and even expand pushcart markets, which were now seen as providing inexpensive food. When the war hardships ended and again during the later La Guardia administration (1933 to 1945), the city abolished the open-air street markets and tried to confine peddling in enclosed locations.

Essex and Hester Streets, New York, c. 1900. Picture Collection, The Branch Libraries, The New York Public Library, Astor, Lenox and Tilden Foundations.

During the late nineteenth century, particular ethnic groups—Jews, Italians, and Greeks—dominated street vending in the lower East Side, Harlem, Brooklyn, and Greenwich Village. They faced strong opposition from merchants with similar products and from upper-class citizens who saw them as dirty and disorderly (Burnstein 1996). The city, favoring merchants' concerns, responded in two ways. Traffic cops moved peddlers, and a hastily issued city ordinance prescribed a maximum standing time of thirty minutes on city sidewalks. As Burnstein (1996, 57–58) explains, "Peddlers were arrested for obstructing traffic; violating sanitary regulations; breaking Sunday blue laws; standing too close to a corner; standing on a restricted street; failing to obtain a peddler's license; and breaking the thirty-minute rule. Ordinances were often enforced in a capricious manner; local custom, corruption, and political favoritism precluded neutral enforcement."

Local public-health officials scrutinized peddlers and their goods because they believed that foul air spread disease. Middle- and upper-class New Yorkers were terrified that epidemics would begin in tenement districts and spread throughout the city. They sent letters to the press and to elected officials when they felt that their neighborhoods were being invaded by unhygienic pushcarts. These concerns about sanitary conditions were sincere, but they were compounded by hostility toward immigrant ethnic groups, whose presence was associated with social disorder (Burnstein 1996).

New York City reformers called for street regulations that would impose order on the street vendors. In many other American cities, reformers worked to move vendors from the sidewalks to public markets. The reformers' concerns were many, including an evolving desire for an orderly circulation system that would clean up dirty and crowded streets. In poor and working-class neighborhoods, women and children walked freely on the sidewalks, which challenged the dominant middle-class philosophy that public and private spheres should be separate. The ubiquitous hodge-podge of carts that were owned by immigrant vendors lined the tenement districts and threatened both public health and good morals. The image of rough peddlers arraying their wares on sidewalks was also antithetical to the reformers' calls for "Americanization" and attempts to instill middle-class manners and respectability standards (Bluestone 1991).

To analyze urban problems before acting on them, New York reformers convened a conference on pushcart reform in 1904 and established a Push-Cart Commission in 1906. The commissioners were appointed by the mayor and included well-known housing reformer Lawrence Veiller and settlement house advocate Lillian Wald. The commission found that peddlers were responsible for an array of sidewalk problems. They created congestion, odor, and litter, delayed merchant deliveries, increased fire danger, offered improper and dirty food, prevented children's play on sidewalks, and presented unfair competition for shopkeepers. At the end of this litany of complaints stood the most serious concern: by giving immigrants a means for their livelihood, committee members found, peddling attracted them to New York City (Burnstein 1996).

The commission recommended that pushcart vendors be restricted to four locations on any block, limited to twenty-five feet away from each corner, and be required to purchase licenses for peddling. These licenses would be limited to a restricted area bounded by Fourteenth Street, the Brooklyn Bridge, Broadway, and the East River (Bluestone 1991). Additionally, reformers wanted to establish designated public markets that would be under bridges or enclosed and would concentrate all street peddling activity in one public space.

These reform proposals were doomed, however, by inadequate space, the cost associated with establishing markets, and peddlers' concerns that they would be too far from their customers. New York street peddlers fought back by organizing protests and demonstrations. Peddler associations brought their complaints to city commissioners and found allies in Tammany Hall representatives and ward politicians. They also found support in the established merchants who collected rents from the peddlers who stood in front of their stores. Caught in this contested terrain were mayors and city politicians, and their ambiguity frequently led to policies of "least resistance" and inconsistent enforcement. As Burnstein (1996, 79–80) explains:

> By 1912 the system of extortion, favoritism, and insecure legal standing created discontent, not only among reformers but among peddlers themselves. Corrupt public officials and store owners had a stake in the status quo; the

city lacked funds to build adequate markets; competing retailers, Department of Street Cleaning officials, and conservative New Yorkers opposed reasonable compromise.... at the most basic level there was conflict between two public goods—between the desire to provide inexpensive food for the poor and to achieve greater public health and well being through more sanitary, orderly surroundings.

Concerns about social order and public health dominated the rhetoric against street vending on sidewalks during the Progressive Era, but a vision of the street as a modern thoroughfare that accommodated vehicular and pedestrian traffic dominated discussions in the 1920s and 1930s. This view coincided with the search by city planners for rationality and order, exemplified by the fragmentation of the American city by zoning into segregated monofunctional cells (Boyer 1983; Baldwin 1999). In subsequent years, proposals to move pushcarts from sidewalks to city markets were guided by this vision of the street as the modern traffic artery. Alternative uses of the sidewalks and streets that involved social gatherings, entertainment and play, demonstrations and celebrations, or commercial activity were considered "obstructions." During the La Guardia administration, the number of pushcarts on New York streets decreased significantly, and nine enclosed markets were built.

EARLY VENDING WARS IN LOS ANGELES[1]

As in New York, many immigrants in Los Angeles became vendors, and their presence threatened native-born residents. Public-health rhetoric justified the opposition to street vending, and native-born merchants and other residents attempted to exclude new immigrant groups from the streets (Ehrenfeucht and Loukaitou-Sideris 2007). In the late nineteenth century, Chinese vegetable vendors frequently sold their wares on the streets of Los Angeles. During the Chinese exclusionist movement in the 1870s and early 1880s, city businessmen promoted regulation of street vending, laundries, and day labor (table 7.1). In 1876, the city licensed the vendors, but three years later, in response to rising anti-Chinese sentiments, the city council increased the monthly license fee for vegetable vendors from $3 to $20.

TABLE 7.1

The origins of sidewalk vending regulations, Los Angeles and New York

Year	New York	Los Angeles
1691	Vending prohibited until two hours after markets open	
1707	Street vending	
1876		Vendors required to purchase a license
1878		Chinese vegetable peddlers strike
1879		Fruit vending license fees increase from $3 to $20
1885		California Supreme Court rules any sidewalk obstruction is a street obstruction and a nuisance
1890		Peddler and huckster wagons prohibited from standing on streets
1893		Fruit vending prohibited on major downtown arteries
1896		First public market opens downtown
1897		Meat vending license fees increase to $50
1901		Public market moves and quickly fails when no vendors rent stalls
1904	Push-cart reform conference	
1906	Push-cart commission created	
1910		Selling fruit, vegetables, produce, eggs, or fowl on the streets prohibited
1913	Vending allowed only in designated areas	
1933–1945	Nine enclosed vending markets built	

This was an overt attempt to force the Chinese residents from the area (Lou 1990).

Most opposition arose from merchants who sold produce and bread and who felt threatened by competition from the vendors. In January 1890, shopkeepers who sold fruit complained to the city council about the fruit peddlers in downtown. The council enacted an ordinance that prohibited peddler and huckster wagons from standing on streets within a defined downtown district. Vendors had three minutes to make a sale when approached by a purchaser. In 1893, peddling fruit was forbidden outright along seven blocks of Main Street, Spring Street, and Broadway in downtown Los Angeles. In 1897, at the meat sellers' request, the city enacted a $50 monthly licensing fee for street vendors who sold meat from wagons. This fee greatly exceeded other street peddling licenses, which ranged from $1 to $5. When flower vendors refused to sign exclusive contracts with established stores with guaranteed minimum purchases and instead began purchasing directly from independent growers, Signal Hill Florist and other established florists asked the council to eliminate flower vending on sidewalks ("All Along the Line" 1897; "Obnoxious Class Legislation" 1897; "Florists Are Again Making War on Flower Vendors" 1908; "Won't Disturb the Flower Vendors" 1908).

At times, vendors became defiant and acted against municipal pressures. In 1878, the Chinese vegetable peddlers went on strike. Because 80 percent of the vegetables for Los Angeles came from these vendors and no sellers came forward to fill this void, the city reduced the license fee to $3. It again climbed to $5. The Chinese exclusionists again raised the license fee to $20, tacked on an additional $5 tax, but again lowered it to $3 (soon to be raised again to $5) in response to popular sentiment against the license. The vendors also successfully challenged the ordinance in court (Locklear 1972). A disparity remained between fruit vendors, who were charged $1 monthly, and vegetable peddlers, who were charged $5 monthly. Many peddlers, not exclusively those who were Chinese, were cited for license violations in the 1890s. Given the relative frequency that the same Chinese peddlers were cited, it appears that they resisted the license fee. At any rate, the low fines, from $1 to $3, and overall low enforcement rate (a total of 37 license violations in 1893 and 68 in 1897) made it worth the risk (Los Angeles Police Judge Reports 1893, 1897).

Public protests, notably from middle-class consumers, rose against the excessive taxes on vegetables and meats because consumers benefited from the peddlers. Thousands demanded their repeal. The probusiness *Los Angeles Times* opposed shopkeepers' sidewalk use in the name of unobstructed circulation, but it found the restrictions on meat peddling "obnoxious class-legislation." Ultimately, the council reduced the fee for meat and vegetable peddlers ("Obnoxious Class Legislation" 1897).

Vending wars continued well into the 1890s resulting in a fruit-peddling prohibition ordinance, and the city fined merchants for obstructing the sidewalks. But police commissioners disagreed over to what extend they should enforce ordinances that caused hardship (Los Angeles Police Commission Minutes 1890; "The Merry War" 1890; "Police Matters" 1890). The conflicts among vendors occasionally became violent such as when Loui Palma, an Italian fruit vendor, shot and dangerously wounded Cyrus Donato. According to the *Times*, the basis for the conflict was that Joseph Donato, the wounded man's father, sold fruit in his shop ("Murderous Assault" 1890).

Like New York, Los Angeles tried to solve the street-vending conflict by confining and enclosing street vendors and in 1890 offered a public market as a solution. For its advocates, a public market had numerous benefits. It could procure rents from the vendors, remove competition from the streets, ensure access to good-quality produce, and build a local market for food and products that could be produced regionally. As the *Los Angeles Times* editorialized, "The thing of great need in this city at present is a public market place.... The farmer, the gardener, the fruitier and the dairyman would realize a fair profit for their products, and the consumer in the city would obtain his supplies at a much less cost" ("A Market Place" 1890; "A Public Market and Its Benefits" 1890). In 1896, Los Angeles established a public market at Ninth Street and Los Angeles Street in downtown.

Although many residents supported the meat and produce vendors when they faced high licensing fees or strict prohibitions, their goal was inexpensive food, not enforcement of the peddlers' rights. When public markets that offered food sold by producers were proposed, middle-class citizens favored them over the street peddlers. In fact, the "horde of peddlers" became the "lowest rung of the [middle men] ladder" and were one group they hoped to eliminate. By the 1910s, when the city was actively establishing public markets, it was illegal to sell "fruit, vegetables, eggs, chickens, or other fowls, or any farm or country produce" on the streets (Ordinance 19,867).

Small merchants had a mixed response to markets because they moved rather than eliminated the competition. In Los Angeles, shopkeepers complained about the market's hours, and in 1899 the city attempted, ultimately without success, to limit the market's operation to between 4 and 9 a.m. The vendors immediately protested the restriction because it was instituted after they rented the stalls and because it would decrease business, and the city backed down, partly because withdrawal of the vendors would decrease municipal revenue. In 1901, with much protest, the city moved the market into an enclosed warehouse at Third and Central Streets, but the new market immediately failed when produce vendors did not rent the stalls. Nevertheless, in the years that followed public markets including curb markets became common.

Lunch wagons and snack vendors received less support than produce vendors did from middle-class consumers. Storefront businesses objected to lunch wagons for several reasons, including competition, messiness, and general disorder. Shop owners often petitioned the city council to remove food vendors, complaining that the latter were obstructing pedestrian movement on sidewalks and "degrading" their establishments with their "mess and odor" (Petition 3018 1917). The LAPD's 1901 and 1902 annual reports recommended closing the food stands an hour earlier to eliminate the attraction for "drunk and dissolute characters" after the bars closed (Los Angeles Police Department 1901, 1902).

Without middle-class support, many popcorn, candy, peanut, lemonade, and root beer vendors appealed to the city to support their economic self-sufficiency. They were old men, some were disabled, and their stands were their only source of income. "We are all old men," six root beer and lemonade vendors petitioned, "and some of us crippled with rupture, so we are not able to do any kind of hard work.... To go to the Poorhouse would be our fate.... Our root beer and lemonade wagons are small and do not take up much space" (Petition 3018 1917). Thirty-eight "poor peddlers"—many of whom claimed to be "old, sick and crippled up men who are not able to do any hard work, who should not be able to earn a living for themselves and their families, but who now can do so"— requested that they be allowed to vend (Petition 1136 1910; Petition 658 1909).

Although street vending was allowed, vendors had to comply with many regulations, and their position was precarious. Even so, few peddling citations were given. For example, from July 1912 to July 1913, only three of 11,575 infractions were peddling complaints. Two years later, twelve citations were issued (Los Angeles Police Department 1913, 1915). Nevertheless, vendors could be cited for various offenses, such as calling out their wares, standing for too long on the sidewalk, peddling in a prohibited zone, and violating standards for food quality, preparation, and storage. Although ordinances were not issued frequently, the recurring public discussions suggest that they were enforced occasionally and thereby weakened the street vendors' claim to the sidewalks.

CONTEMPORARY CONFLICT ZONES: THE TALE OF TWO CITIES

A hundred years later, street vending has again become a contentious issue on U.S. sidewalks. Global economic forces have accelerated the pace of immigration to the developed world. Not all unskilled immigrants find work in the formal economies of receiving countries, leaving many unemployed, underemployed, and underpaid. In this context, the informal economy offers needed economic opportunities.

Since the 1970s, street vending has resurged in large U.S. cities (Bromley 2000). Business improvement districts (BIDs), the entities that represent established businesses, have contested the vendors' presence on the sidewalks. BIDs are often established in areas that Bromley characterizes as "conflict zones." As Bromley (2000, 15) explains, "In every city there are a few 'conflict zones' where many interest groups are concerned about the high density of street vendors.... There are a few exclusive and elite areas where street vendors are aggressively excluded. The conflict zones make up less than 5 percent but it is in these areas that most of the tension and conflict is acted out. Conflict zones are typically the CBDs, various suburban commercial centers, the transportation terminals, the major sports and entertainment centers, and all major tourist attractions."

On one side of the conflict are the mostly immigrant vendors and their advocates (such as immigrant-rights groups and vending associations). On the other side are established merchants and some middle- and upper-class residents. The power differential between the two sides and the interest of cities in tax generation lead authorities to be more attentive to the demands of established residents and merchants than to those of street vendors. Municipalities typically enact regulations to limit the locations and types of products that can be legally sold by street vendors. Vendors in the poor immigrant neighborhoods meet with less opposition.

Beginning in the 1990s, U.S. cities began to adopt sidewalk ordinances to control "sidewalk disorder" and regulate public space (table 7.2). Sidewalk regulation and enforcement have limited the number of vending licenses, raised their fees, designated more sites as off-limits, and restricted the terms of operation. Some cities have tried to contain street vendors by designating specific vending districts, requiring permits for restricted areas, and confining vendors within them. Other cities prescribe maximum times for staying in one location, minimum distances between vendors and other vending establishments, sidewalk clearance areas, and cart appearance and size (Ball 2002). As in earlier years, the matter has reached the courts, which have typically upheld local vending ordinances (Austin 1994). Enforcement of these ordinances is often inequitably applied, however. It is often determined by the BID's power, the political climate, and the municipal police force's workload. Although vendors frequently evade the rules, thus avoiding the licensing costs and taxes and the hassle of compliance, they risk fines and prosecution.

The vending wars reflect dramatically different notions about appropriate public-space uses and perceived conflicts between activities (Cross 2000). To explore this further and understand the conflicts over sidewalk use, we again turn to New York and Los Angeles.

TABLE 7.2

Contemporary sidewalk vending regulations, Los Angeles and New York

Year	Los Angeles	New York
1982		Local Law 2 passed authorizing creation of business improvement districts in the city
1985		Mayor Koch creates a New York Police Department Street Vendor Task Force
1986	Street Vending Association formed to advocate for vendors	
1988		Vending licenses capped at 853 for general merchandise and 3,000 for food
1989	Street Vending Task Force created by the city	
1993		Community court established to handle quality-of-life infractions
1994	Ordinance 171913 passed to allow creation of vending districts on commercial corridors in eight areas	Mayor Giuliani prohibits vending on 125th Street
		Ordinance passed allowing creation of vending districts in eight areas
		125th Street vendors relocated to open-air market on 116th Street
1995		Street vendor review panel created to establish vending districts
1997		U.S. Supreme Court denies Giuliani's appeal that visual art should not be protected by the First Amendment
1999	First vending district inaugurated in MacArthur Park under 1994 ordinance	
2001		Street Vendor Project created as a grassroots vendor advocate
2005		Executive Order 41 prohibits New York Consumer Affairs from questioning vending applicants about immigration status
2007	MacArthur Park vending district suspended	

New York: BIDs and Mayors against Vendors

"New York," says Sean Basinski, director of the Street Vendor Project, is the "historical capital of street vending in the country—a city where a hundred years ago Jewish and Italian immigrants were vending on the Lower East Side" (Basinski interview).[2] The resurgent street-vending conflicts have been accentuated by two events—the passage of Local Law 2 in 1982, which authorized the creation of BIDs throughout the city of New York, and the arrival of Senegalese vendors on Fifth Avenue in Midtown Manhattan during that time. The BIDs and vendors found themselves on a crashing trajectory because the established merchants' cultural and economic expectations differed significantly from those of their African counterparts. As Stoller (1996, 785), argues "In NYC, many 3rd world spatial, social, and religious practices, which are themselves inextricably interconnected, have taken place in spaces zoned as 'first world'—all of which create spatial arenas of multiple contestation and struggle."

Complaining that "Africans" constitute a blight that diminishes their businesses as well as the good image of Fifth Avenue, in 1985, the Fifth Avenue Merchant Association, headed by Donald Trump, asked Mayor Koch to remove street vendors from that street (Coombe 1995). Koch responded by creating a new arm of the NYPD, the Street Vendor Task Force, consisting of thirty-four officers who would enforce vending ordinances. The Task Force had the full support of the BID, which according to its current president, Tom Cusick, "is known throughout the city as the most effective supplemental enforcement agent on the topic of street vendors" (Cusick interview).[3]

Vendors were prosecuted, fined, and often arrested, and in 1988 Mayor Ed Koch capped vending licenses. He limited the number of legal vendors in New York City to 853 general merchandise vendors and 3,000 mobile food vendors. But the cap, which remains in effect today, has not resolved the "vendor problem." With thousands on a waiting list, "it becomes impossible for people to get a license; they have to vend without it and this is what they do," says Basinski (Basinski interview). About 10,000 vendors do business on New York sidewalks, and only a few are licensed (Ricci 1994).[4] Incentives to obtain a license are few because the sites where

Street vending, Manhattan, New York, January 2006. Photograph by Renia Ehrenfeucht.

vendors can sell legally are limited (Basinski interview). Although in theory street vending is allowed everywhere in New York City, it is excluded from the city's most important commercial thoroughfares, where vending can be most profitable. As Basinski explains the situation, "If you get a license, there is no place to vend because so many streets have been closed off to vending. It is very difficult to find a place to vend where you can make any money whatsoever.... There are so many rules, and it's so impossible to follow them, and they are enforced in such an arbitrary way that it makes it very difficult for vendors" (Basinski interview).

The New York City Administrative Code and the New York Penal Law Code regulate street vending. These codes define four categories of street vendors: (1) general merchandise vendors, (2) food vendors, (3) vendors of print material, and (4) disabled veterans. Each category is subject to different regulations (Ricci 1994).[5] The codes restrict the vendors' behavior, including the placement of carts and the maximum size of their vending tables; prohibit vending in certain locations; and impose other street, day, and hour restrictions. Fines can be as steep as $1,000 per citation or imprisonment of up to three months, although the courts rarely exercise the latter option.

In the early 1990s, immigrants from Mali and Niger appeared on Harlem sidewalks selling African items, leather goods, and fabrics (Coombe 1995). By 1992, Harlem's 125th Street Market was booming with activity and had become a popular New York attraction (Ball 2002). But the success of street vendors brought them into conflict with the area's businesses. The Harlem Business Alliance appealed to Mayor David Dinkins's administration to disperse the vendors. The street vendors resisted the administration's attempts to enforce the vending ordinances. In one instance, they shut down the 125th Street Market for a day in protest. Fearing violent conflicts between the police and BID members on one side and the street vendors on the other, the mayor cancelled his enforcement plans. In 1993, the mayor established a community court to arraign quality-of-life infractions, including unlicensed street vending.

In January 1994, a new mayor, Rudy Giuliani, assumed the city's leadership. Giuliani was elected on a law-and-order platform. He promised

New Yorkers to clean their streets from panhandlers, beggars, and vendors and to reduce crime. One campaign promise was to disperse the African market in Harlem. Making good on this promise, Giuliani issued an order prohibiting any street vending on 125th Street as of October 17, 1994. On that date, the street was filled with policemen who arrested twenty-two vendors (Stoller 1996). The vendors were moved to an open-air market on 116th Street, nine blocks south of Harlem's retail hub, and many claim they have been hurt economically or forced out of business because the area was less profitable than 125th Street (Ball 2002).

The Giuliani administration's regulating of street vendors was not limited to the African market. In 1994, ARTIST (Artists' Response to Illegal State Tactics), an organization that represented street artists, brought a federal lawsuit against the city. It claimed that street artists' right to freedom of expression was being violated by the city's prosecution of street artists and the confiscation of their work. In response, some of New York's most powerful BIDs (the Fifth Avenue Association, the Grand Central Partnership, the Alliance for Downtown New York, the 34th Street Partnership, and the Madison Avenue BID in association with the SoHo Alliance) filed a brief in federal court that declared visual art to be unworthy of First Amendment protection (Lederman 1998). A lower court ruled in favor of the city's artist arrest policy, but in 1996, the Second Circuit Federal Appeals Court overturned the lower-court ruling and issued a ruling in favor of ARTIST (*Bery et al. v. City of New York* 1996). The case reached the U.S. Supreme Court, which in 1997 rejected Mayor Giuliani's appeal. According to the federal court (*Bery et al. v. City of New York* 1996, 698):

> Displaying art on the street has a different expressive purpose than gallery or museum shows; it reaches people who might not choose to go into a gallery or museum or who might feel excluded or alienated from these forums. The public display and sale of artwork is a form of communication between the artist and the public not possible in the enclosed, separated spaces of galleries and museums.

In 1995, Mayor Giuliani also created the Street Vendor Review Panel and charged it with determining which streets should be closed to vending.

Over the next decade, the panel blocked vendors from more than 130 streets. By 1998, the city, with the full support of the BIDs, sought to prohibit vending from most sections of Manhattan. In response to protests and lawsuit threats, the city compromised and allowed limited vending on only some Manhattan streets but restricted the times it could occur. More protests took place in 1999, when vendors rallied outside City Hall to protest a public hearing on a proposal to ban street vending from 165 additional street blocks.

In 2001, in response to increasing restrictions, the Street Vendor Project (SVP) was established. The SVP is a grassroots advocacy group for New York street vendors. Its mission is "to correct the social and economic injustice faced by these hardworking entrepreneurs" (Street Vendor Project n.d.). In 2005, after much advocacy from the SVP and other groups, New York City council member Philip Reed introduced a proposal to restructure the city's vending laws in ways that would be favorable to vendors. The bill suggested increasing the number of vending licenses, reducing fines, and allowing six vendors per block on all streets. The proposed bill faced strong opposition by business interests and has not been enacted into law. Mayor Bloomberg, however, signed another important bill into law in the same year. Executive Order 41 (or as it is commonly called, "Don't ask, don't tell") prohibits the Department of Consumer Affairs from questioning applicants for street-vending licenses about their immigration status.

Why have the BIDs adamantly opposed the street vendors? The root of the problem is competition. "If you are selling scarves in your shop for $20 a scarf and the guy selling from a table right outside on the sidewalk doesn't have to pay the rent or the overhead or the gas and electricity that you have to pay, he sells it for $10. That is unfair competition," argued Tom Cusick, director of the Fifth Avenue Association, the BID that has led a successful battle since the mid-1980s to remove the predominantly African street vendors from downtown (Cusick interview). "Some of the complaints that we receive come from store owners paying rent on those streets and selling in some cases the same things the street vendors want to sell," added Jen Hensley, assistant vice president of the Alliance for Downtown New York, another New York BID (Hensley interview).[6]

According to the BID executives that we interviewed, street vendors and other street people create a bad image for potential customers and interfere with the financial success of established businesses. According to Hensley, "The idea of the vendors with their rickety looking tables, or the illegal vendors who just put blankets on the ground with their purses and things laid out detracts from the historic value of our neighborhood and does create that image problem" (Hensley interview).

The smells and sounds that vendors generate bother customers who frequent established businesses and also damage those businesses' merchandise. As Cusick argued, "Sometimes with a vendor who sells very spicy type food from a grill, the smoke will go up into the air and filter into a store that is selling sweaters, for instance. The smell penetrates into the clothing. So it's an incompatibility issue" (Cusick interview).

The BID representatives identified trash as a major problem because BIDs pay for extra sanitation services. "Trash and litter are also problems. We have a sanitation crew that goes around and cleans up, and every night they bag the trash that's left and sweep up the street. But it's an extra burden on our resources," Hensley explained (Hensley interview). Cusick made a similar point: "We have our own sanitation crew. And we know from experience that some of the vendors do not abide by the rules that they must take care of their own trash, and often times we wind up having to clean it up" (Cusick interview).

For BIDs, there are only two appropriate sidewalk uses: it is a corridor for unobstructed pedestrian circulation and a container for hardscape improvements that enhance the street's image. As Mark Wurzel, general counsel for the Grand Central Partnership, explains, "What we are striving for is to provide these clear paths for people to walk and to shop and to travel to and from home and work. Our other issue is aesthetics. We want an inviting environment for people to live and work in. . . . Our streets are lighted better, you see things you never saw before like lush baskets of flowers, trees, and plants, clearer signage, and eliminating some of the clutter has also helped. What has helped is the enforcement of the vendor regulations" (Wurzel interview).[7]

Municipalities and BIDs agree that the pedestrian is the only legitimate sidewalk user. In other words, the pedestrian is defined as the public for which sidewalks should be provided, and the goal of unobstructed pedestrian circulation justifies prohibiting other "disruptive" activities. As Tom Cusick explains (Cusick interview),

> As a retailer, I have a better chance of selling more merchandise if I have a large number of people walking by my store everyday. We want to have as much of a flow as possible of that traffic and not interfere with it and not bottle it up in any way.... Let's assume for a moment that it's lunchtime and you have a food vendor twelve feet from a store entrance. People start standing on line waiting for the food vendor to serve them. Then they stop traffic completely. Traffic then starts to back up, and as it backs up, all the pedestrians who were walking in that direction stop.

In the eyes of established merchants, the vendors and their wares represent unwanted and "unnecessary clutter." In the tradition of the improvement societies that sprang up in cities during the City Beautiful era, contemporary BIDs prefer to view sidewalks as a landscaped strip—beautiful, tree-lined, well-lit, and orderly. The Grand Central Partnership, for example, has initiated a program of street furniture that adds 800 planters, 100 to 150 hanging baskets, and 600 street lights on New York City sidewalks (Wurzel interview). Vendor advocates, however, deem the BIDs' priorities as "hypocritical," pointing out that the planters also impede pedestrian circulation. As Basinski argues (Basinki interview),

> This gets to the hypocrisy of the BIDs and big businesses that say they are concerned about sidewalk congestion and then they put these gigantic things [planters] out on the sidewalk that have very minimal public utility.... So we get back to this sense of controlling how the street looks, and they think they own the streets, so they put these things out there ostensibly to beautify the sidewalks.... When you have a vendor blocking the sidewalk, the police come running immediately. When you have a planter that is generally bigger and more difficult to move, you try to get something done, just try to get the city to take action.

Vendors and their advocates contest the view that the sidewalk is a beautiful space for unobstructed and orderly pedestrian circulation that is to be protected by the NYPD and private security officers. They articulate a multipurpose vision for the sidewalks and view economic survival as a legitimate use. As Basinski explains (Basinki interview),

> We think that sidewalks are for living. In New York, this is more important than anywhere else because we don't have cars and our apartments are all so tiny that we live our lives on the sidewalks. Sidewalks are for meeting your neighbors or walking with a friend of yours or walking your dog in the morning. Or they are for buying coffee from your local coffee guy or a hot dog and talking and eating while you stand there and observe life or sitting there reading the paper or selling merchandise. Most people I think would recognize that especially in New York that is why we take pride that we have such a vital street life—for stopping and watching a street preacher or walking around engrossed in your own thoughts as you observe the city. So that is why we need to make space for different uses, even if there might be conflict.

LOS ANGELES: A VENDING DISTRICT OF ONE AND LATER NONE

Street vendors are a familiar sight in Los Angeles. They populate Broadway Street, downtown's major Latino thoroughfare, and La Placita, the city's historic plaza. They set up tables on sidewalks at the edges of downtown in the neighborhoods of East Los Angeles, Pico-Union, and Hollywood. They display their wares on chain-link fences in the first-ring suburbs of Huntington Park, San Gabriel, South Gate, and Pacoima. In a city that is almost exclusively geared toward the automobile, street vendors have found ways to appeal to passing motorists by selling fruit under freeways and near freeway ramps or offering cold water bottles along street medians in high-traffic intersections. Scholars like Margaret Crawford describe them as components of "everyday urbanism." She romanticizes the small, temporary, and nondescript spaces that are frequented by vendors, arguing that they help humanize the otherwise harsh urban landscape (Crawford 1999). Others do not have such a benevolent view.

Ice cream vendor, Los Angeles, California, 2003. Photograph by
Anastasia Loukaitou-Sideris.

Street vending on a fence, Los Angeles, California, 2006. Photograph by Anastasia Loukaitou-Sideris.

In Los Angeles, street vending subsided after World War II, when the manufacturing sector offered working-class Angelenos robust employment opportunities (Kettles 2004). But in the 1980s, a series of events resulted in a resurgence of the informal economy and street vending in the city. The manufacturing sector declined, and local plants closed (Soja, Morales, and Wolfe 1983). At the same time, waves of mostly unskilled Latino immigrants were making the city their new home. Having limited access to jobs and capital, many of them found the means for economic survival on the sidewalks. By 1991, city officials estimated that about 3,000 unlicensed street vendors were on the streets, and vendor advocates thought that the number was about 6,000 (Martinez 1991). Los Angeles had once again acquired a "vendor problem."

In response to pressure from local merchants, the city dusted off its old street-vending ordinances. These were among the strictest in the country (Berestein 1995). They stipulated that: "No person . . . shall on any sidewalk or street offer for sale, solicit sale of, announce by any means the availability of, or have in his or her possession, control or custody, whether upon his or her person or upon some other animate or inanimate object, any goods, wares, or merchandise which the public may purchase at any time" (Los Angeles Ordinance 4.2.42.00, Regulation of Soliciting and Sales in Streets). Street vending is considered a misdemeanor in Los Angeles (as in New York), and violators can be fined up to $1,000 and serve up to six months in jail. Street vending becomes a felony if street vendors are selling contraband items (Harris interview).[8] The city periodically enforces vending prohibition by conducting raids in commercial areas, issuing citations, and confiscating merchandise. The *Los Angeles Times* estimated that there were about 2,700 arrests in 1990, nearly double that of the year before (Abrams 1992).

Street vendors have fought back against the rigid controls. As early as 1986, they established the Street Vending Association, and by 1988 the association had over 500 members (Casillas 2005). In collaboration with the Central American Resource Center (CARECEN), the association lobbied the city council for a change of vending laws and for the legalization of street vending in public spaces. It also sought the support of unions, churches, and other nonprofit organizations. In response to these efforts, the Los Angeles City Council created the Task Force on Street Vending in 1989 to assess the extent and nature of street vending in the city and recommend regulatory actions.

In response to the pressures of vendors and their advocates, the city council did not legalize vending but instead designated specific permitted zones or vending districts. In 1994, the city council adopted an ordinance that allowed the creation of vending districts along commercial corridors in eight areas. Succumbing to business interests, the council legislated an arduous process for creating a vending district. It involved getting a petition signed, forming a community advisory board, and demonstrating support from residents, local businesses, and city agencies.[9] Additionally, vendors could use only carts that were approved by the city's Community Development Department, and they had to be placed at least eighteen inches from the curb. They could vend only in a designated location, sell only specific goods, and had to display their permit at all times.

Throughout the next twelve years, only one vending district was established, and it was not on a sidewalk but along the outer rim of a park. The MacArthur Park vending district had only limited success (between twenty and thirty-three vendors participated) and was hampered by the many constraints imposed on the vendors. According to Joe Colletti, the executive director of the Institute of Urban Research and Development (IURD), a nonprofit organization that subsidized vendors that participated in MacArthur Park's vending district, "As long as the ordinance calls for the carts to remain stationary, their sales would be restricted" (Colletti interview).[10]

The carts were also expensive. "Without subsidies, the people in the neighborhood cannot afford to operate the official vending carts," argued Sandi Romero, the owner of Mama's Hot Tamales, a café that sold wholesale tamales to vendors in MacArthur Park (Romero interview).[11] Vendors were also constrained by being required to sell only very specific merchandise (small items of general merchandise and hot food) and having to compete with the many other unlicensed vendors who flooded the surrounding streets and sidewalks. "The vending district was very limited in its growth and potential because of all of the other illegal vending that surrounded it," explained Joe Colletti, who hopes to be able to revamp a stalled program (Colletti interview). Indeed, the city suspended the sole vending district in 2007 in response to safety concerns. Vendors were being hassled, and one was shot.

The Los Angeles street-vending ordinance has not eased the conflict between street vendors and long-standing stores. Not surprisingly, the roots of the conflict in Los Angeles are similar to those in New York. The most overt claim against street vendors is that they provide unfair competition for shop owners who have to pay taxes and cover the cost for the rent and maintenance of their establishment (Harris interview). Other complaints include concerns about overuse of the sidewalks, increased garbage, and public-safety risks for consumers who purchase merchandise from unlicensed street vendors (Kettles 2004; Harris interview).

The primary use of the sidewalk is considered to be a pedestrian thoroughfare that is threatened by the "illegal encroachment" by street vendors. Chief investigator Gary Harris made this explicit: "If you come down to Los Angeles Street on a Saturday, there are so many vendors on the sidewalk in competition with the illegal encroachment from the businesses on the sidewalk and the pedestrians on the street. It is very, very dangerous. You don't want pedestrians walking out on the street in downtown Los Angeles because they can't get by on the sidewalk" (Harris interview).

As in New York City, a less explicit but omnipresent complaint against street vendors is rooted in a cultural clash between the vendors' "third-world imagery" and the first-world expectations as articulated by merchants and BIDs (Kettles 2004; Schwada 1990). Their feelings are expressed by Chief Investigator Harris, who works closely with the downtown BIDs (Harris interview):

> We think it adds to the business when the sidewalks are clear and clean. If you go to some of the surrounding cities where they don't have the vending problem: you go to Glendale, you go to Burbank, or even one of the better parts of our city where you can walk down Melrose and enjoy the atmosphere with the buildings, the walking district, and the street life. It

just adds to character of the area and is going to be good for business. We think that downtown can maintain its flavor with the illegal vendors removed.

To make street vendors less visible and threatening, the city wants them constantly mobile, uniform, and color-coded like taxi cabs. As Chief Inspector Harris explains (Harris interview):

> We are looking at creating a program for mobile vendors so there would be no stationary vendors on city sidewalks.... The scheme would have uniform appearance for the operators, including a color scheme for the operators who work under a particular fleet or vendor group so the public can readily identify a legal vendor from an illegal vendor.... That supported group of allowed mobile vendors has to stay mobile except for the time that they are actually engaged in a sale. So you wouldn't have a vendor setting up shop in front of a business that sells the same item and is competing with it. You wouldn't have vendors constantly pushing all the pedestrians out into the streets.

The arguments and counterarguments presented in the above quotes point to two conflicting images for sidewalks. One image is held by a public that wants to keep sidewalks safe, clean, predictable, orderly, and aesthetically pleasant urban landscapes that connect points of origin and destination and serve as forecourts to commercial, retail, and residential establishments. This image is threatened by another image that is held by a mostly immigrant counterpublic that actively appropriates (through their bodies and wares) the sidewalk for trade and economic exchanges. Using historical and contemporary examples, the clash of these two images has generated disputes time and again.

CONCLUSION

Street vending has spawned heated debates and conflicts in U.S. cities. Common at the end of the nineteenth century, such conflicts have resurfaced as global economic forces have led to new waves of immigration, outsourcing, and a general decline of the manufacturing sector and formal employment opportunities for unskilled workers. In this economic climate, the informal economy provides work for many residents. Incorporating people from developing countries into the socioeconomic context of the first world has been an uneasy process that has created clashes between cultural worlds and economic interests.

Street vending takes advantage of public space, but here is where the problem lies. The murky arena of what is permissible and legal on the sidewalks has been debated on the streets, in city halls, and in the courts by vendors and their supporters, long-standing commercial interests, and municipal and enforcement authorities. On the one side, the vendors defend their right to the city and its public spaces for economic activities. On the other side, established merchants and middle- and upper-class residents claim to be hurt by the messiness, congestion, disorder, and unfair competition imposed by street vendors. Between the two sides but favoring established residents and merchants are municipal authorities that issue ordinances and regulations that impose a technical rationality on a conflict between values and cultural norms. But political struggles over the use of public spaces are rarely fully resolved by city ordinances, zoning, and nuisance regulations. The century-long conflicts around street vending in New York and Los Angeles attest to this reality.

Sidewalk as Shelter

In 2005, *Los Angeles Times* columnist Steve Lopez dismayed Los Angeles residents when he investigated the city's skid row[1] streets. He described streets and sidewalks that were filthy, gutters that teemed with garbage and feces, and alleys that reeked of stale urine. Thousands spent the night outside in the streets. Some had sex in outhouses. Others used drugs or alcohol or had mental health problems. The articles revealed to Angelenos the perils facing people who survived on the city's inhospitable downtown sidewalks.

For *Los Angeles Times* readers, homelessness was unacceptable, and therefore sidewalks could never legitimately be used for shelter. The condition of homelessness was equated with sidewalk use by people who are homeless, and within this framework, both were problematic.

In public spaces, activities can directly interfere with one another, or one group's use may disrupt another group's vision for a space. Sleeping on a sidewalk, for example, should not be someone's only or best option for shelter, and someone who sleeps on a sidewalk forces others to confront this use of the space and also makes the space less accessible for other activities. But sidewalks are spaces for both housed and unhoused residents and should be accessible for necessary activities. Indeed, some public spaces should be available to people who do not have access to private space to sustain themselves.

Most activities that are associated with homelessness are common—including sitting, talking, asking questions, and sleeping—but they are perceived differently when people appear to be homeless. Grooming, possessions, time spent on the sidewalk, and asking for money all mark people as homeless (whether they are or not). Few would argue that anyone should be completely banned from public space. Nonetheless, many cities have assumed that causing other people discomfort is sufficient harm to prohibit ordinary activities by those who are homeless.

In the early twenty-first century, homelessness has generated active public discussion. The *Los Angeles Times* has published 162 articles about the L.A. skid row since January 2004 (Wolch, Dear, Blasi, Flamig, Tepper, and Koegel 2007). In this chapter, we discuss how homelessness has become a public-space issue and explain why it conflicts with other uses. We argue that when planners prioritize public-space activities, they should create a just public-space policy that allows groups to be treated differently at certain times and that acknowledges that homeless people's survival should take precedence over other people's comfort. Using public sleeping as an example, we highlight the complexities that are nonetheless involved in granting such rights to one group.

CONCEIVING OF HOMELESSNESS

Homelessness was rare in eighteenth-century American cities. When people were prevented from working through illness or disability, their families generally supported them. For people who did not have families that would support them, colonial town governments provided almshouses, workhouses, hospitals, and asylums. In colonial society, people in need were seen as community members who needed help (Chudacoff and Smith 2005).

During the late nineteenth century, migratory workers came through cities by the thousands, creating a street population and eroding the sense that poor residents came from within the community. Railroads enabled men to travel rapidly to find work, and the mines, forests, and fields of the United States and Canada demanded labor. Migratory men roamed from city to city, worked intermittently, and owned few possessions. Using late nineteenth-century police records, Eric Monkkonen estimated that 10 to 20 percent of the population had a family member who tramped to find work (Monkkonen 1984, 8). The *Los Angeles Times* ("For the Homeless" 1896) reported that 60,000 urban homeless people lived in New York in 1896. In 1908, 60 percent of an estimated 30,000 homeless men in New York were nonresidents ("Thirty Thousand Homeless" 1908). In 1923, Nels Anderson estimated that 30,000 men in good times and up to 75,000 in bad times lived in Chicago; a third were permanent city residents. From 300,000 to 500,000 migratory men passed through Chicago during a given year (Anderson 1923, 3).

Between jobs, workers relaxed in cities and spent the days on the streets, especially in the districts bordering downtown where commercial services and inexpensive residential hotels concentrated. These districts were known as skid row. Migratory men and casual workers stayed in skid row homes and cheap lodging houses (Groth 1994). Young women who independently migrated to cities did not develop a significant street presence (Meyerowitz 1988).

Migratory men were also known as tramps (because they tramped along roads) and hobos.[2] Their identification as such came about from the stories that they told, the humorous stories that circulated about them, and the social scientific inquiry that explored marginal people in the city, (Cresswell 1991). In the early twentieth century, religious groups established shelters and soup kitchens in skid row neighborhoods. Service providers began using the word *homeless* to describe the people they served and to invoke compassion and uplift in response. Although transitory men used shelters and other services, the word *homeless* had a different connotation: the words *tramp* and *hobo* implied independence and mobility, whereas the word *homelessness* suggested helplessness.

Migratory men posed a problem for industrialists and other established businessmen. As much as these workers were needed, business and industry leaders worried that these men were too picky about the conditions under which they toiled. Vagrancy ordinances had been used since colonial times to eliminate uprootedness, and they addressed this problem by prohibiting

many of the activities that were associated with migrant workers—
including loitering, begging, refusing work when offered, and spending
extended periods without work. In 1916, the California vagrancy ordinance
addressed the concerns of businessmen. The statute's first three provisions
defined a *vagrant* as any healthy beggar, any person who roamed from place
to place without a lawful business, and any person who was physically able
but did not seek work or did not work when offered. Vagrancy regulations
focused on repetitive behaviors, and a person was classified as a vagrant if he
or she begged or loitered repeatedly. A person convicted of vagrancy could
be expelled from the city.

Vagrancy ordinances gave cities considerable discretion because they
could arrest someone based on past actions even when the person was acting
lawfully. They took on new importance when tramps appeared on city sidewalks, and municipalities nationwide enacted similar regulations. Both men
and women (usually women who worked in prostitution) were cited for
vagrancy. In addition to vagrancy ordinances, late nineteenth-century city
councils, backed by business leaders, enacted activity-specific ordinances
against begging and loitering (Ehrenfeucht 2006).

As cities grew in the early twentieth century, tramping decreased, and
by midcentury, vagrancy citations increasingly were used against perceived
criminality rather than migratory people. In 1972 in *Papachristou v. City of
Jacksonville*,[3] the U.S. Supreme Court held that vagrancy ordinances were
unconstitutionally vague, and it limited cities' authority to criminalize a person because she or he was spending time unproductively. In the 1980s and
1990s homelessness increased and became more visible, but cities no longer
had vagrancy regulations on their books and instead drew on activity-
specific prohibitions. Homelessness was redefined as a problem that was
characterized in part by unwelcome public-space interactions.

CONSTRUCTING HOMELESSNESS AS A PUBLIC-SPACE PROBLEM

Today the discussion about homelessness takes place on many levels. Even
agreement on the extent of homelessness or a common understanding about
causes and potential solutions would not eliminate immediate sidewalk

effects at given moments. Homelessness is a national problem that was partly caused by inadequate federal housing programs and failed anti-poverty strategies. It is also a local problem that is caused when a person sleeps in a doorway. One discussion informs but does not eliminate the other.

Researchers have attributed the rise in homelessness since the 1980s to widespread deinstitutionalization of people who are mentally ill, cuts in welfare rolls, fewer manufacturing jobs, increased drug use, and escalating housing costs (for an analysis of these factors, see Jencks 1994). During this thirty-year period, the characteristics of the people who become homeless have also changed. Families, typically headed by single mothers, represent a growing percentage (ranging from 20 to 43 percent) of the total homeless population. Between one-third and one-half are girls and women, and African Americans are overrepresented. About 16 to 24 percent are currently employed. An estimated 25 percent are physically disabled, and about 20 percent are people fleeing domestic violence. Homelessness overall might be increasing. In 2003, Los Angeles reported a 15 percent increase in requests for emergency shelter by individuals and a 21 percent increase in requests by families (Tepper 2004).

More and more people became visibly homeless in the 1980s and 1990s at a time when municipalities were trying to attract middle-class consumers back to central cities. To do this, cities began targeting local disorder. Mayoral candidates like Rudy Giuliani in New York, Richard Riordan in Los Angeles, and Frank Jordan in San Francisco won elections with platforms that focused partly on street order (table 8.1). Activities associated with homelessness along with other minor infractions were the targets of "broken windows" policing strategies, which sought to reduce violent crime by eliminating minor disorderly behavior.

Sidewalk ordinances regulate many activities. Cities adopted ordinances that prohibit panhandling that was "aggressive" or that occurred at night, within ten feet of a bank entrance or an ATM machine, and near people as they left their cars. Cities nationwide prohibited loitering, camping, or sleeping in public. Eugene and Memphis started requiring beggars to obtain and carry licenses. New York barred sleeping in or near subways. In

Man sleeping in a doorstep, Alvarado Street, Los Angeles, California, 2005. Photograph by Renia Ehrenfeucht.

TABLE 8.1

Enactment of sit-and-lie ordinances in major U.S. cities

Year	City
1967	Los Angeles
1967	Miami
1975	Boston
1979	San Francisco
1980s	None
1992	Austin
1992	Olympia[a]
1993	Seattle
1995	Reno
1995	Las Vegas
1998	Philadelphia
2005	Denver
2006	Tucson
2006	Portland
2007	Olympia

Note:

a. The city of Olympia, Washington, enacted a pedestrian- and vehicle-interference law in 1993. This law was amended by ordinance in 2007 to prohibit sitting and lying in the downtown area during the day.

Cincinnati, it became illegal to sit or lay on sidewalks from 7 a.m. to 9 p.m. (Mitchell 2003). Seattle, New York, and Tempe enacted an array of ordinances prohibiting activities such as panhandling, sitting on the sidewalks, loitering, and sleeping in public spaces (Amster 2004; Gibson 2004; Duneier 1999). Even liberal California cities such as San Francisco, Santa Cruz, Berkeley, and Santa Monica passed antipanhandling and antihomelessness ordinances.

Cities have used ordinances against begging and loitering for more than a century, but in the 1990s they strengthened and enacted additional

Security officer speaking with sidewalk sitters, Seattle, Washington, 2007. Photograph by Jennifer Ruley.

public-space controls. When the National Law Center for Homelessness and Poverty (NLCHP) surveyed sixteen cities in 1993, a majority had enacted begging, public-speaking, or sitting ordinances that year (NLCHP 1993). In 1994, thirty-nine cities and counties adopted policies against loitering, begging, and sleeping in public, and twenty-six cities adopted antipanhandling ordinances. In 2003, every city surveyed had new public-space restrictions. Although no city surveyed had sufficient shelter space for everyone who asked for it, one-third of the cities had sitting or lying restrictions, and 16 percent had citywide bans on outdoor sleeping (NLCHP 1994, 2003). These ordinances have been amended repeatedly to reduce undesirable activities without overstepping constitutional boundaries. Table 8.2 lists examples of "sit and lie ordinances" from select cities. In addition, many cities discourage activities such as sitting or loitering through design features such as benches with dividers and railing on ledges.

Leonard Feldman has argued that reconfiguring vagrancy legislation into public-space ordinances is "a larger shift in the very constitution of the public sphere: from the productive public sphere and its preoccupation with idleness to the consumptive public sphere and its preoccupation with aesthetic appearance" (Feldman 2003, 29). People who lack homes have been troubling for both production and consumption. In the past, business leaders and industrialists worried that migratory workers would not work, and contemporary business leaders worry that people will not consume. Homelessness casts a pallor on recreational consumption because homeless people sometimes bother shoppers and discourage them from frequenting a given area. This is a nuisance for cities as they attempt to attract visitors and residents to central-city neighborhoods. The worry does not necessarily lead to a commitment to end homelessness because capitalist economies need economic disparities, surplus workers, and anxiety about losing status and security. As Mitchell (2003, 173) puts it, "The homeless and poor are desperately needed, but not at all wanted."

When Young (1990, 158) argues that a politics of difference allows for and requires treating people differently, she is not speaking directly to how people use public space or its role in political inclusiveness. Nonetheless, the right to use public space and make decisions about its use is a

TABLE 8.2

Content of site-and-lie ordinances in major U.S. cities

Year Enacted	City	Ordinance
1967	Miami	City of Miami Municipal Code section 37-3: Prohibits sleeping on streets, sidewalks, or public places or on the private property of another without the owner's consent
1979	San Francisco	San Francisco Police Code article 1, sections 22–24: Makes it unlawful to willfully and substantially obstruct the free passage of persons on any street, sidewalk, public passageway, or place
1992	Austin	Austin Municipal Code section 9-14-4: Prohibits sitting or lying on public sidewalks in the downtown business area; culpable mental state not required
1995	Las Vegas	Las Vegas Municipal Code section 10.47.020: Prohibits intentional obstruction of pedestrian or vehicular travel in areas that are open for pedestrian or vehicular travel
1995	Reno	Reno Administrative Code section 8.12.015(b): Prohibits sitting or lying on sidewalks in the downtown redevelopment district
1998	Philadelphia	Philadelphia Municipal Code section 10-611(1)(b)–(c), (2)(g)–(h): Prohibits sitting for more than one hour in any two-hour time period or lying on sidewalks in designated districts
2002 (modified 2006)	Houston	Houston Municipal Code section 40.16.40-352: Prohibits sitting or lying down on a public sidewalk or placing any article of bedding or personal item on a sidewalk between the hours of 7:00 a.m. and 11:00 p.m.
2005	Denver	Denver Municipal Code section 38-86.1: Prohibits any person from sitting or lying down on the public right of way in the downtown Denver Business Improvement District between the hours of 7:00 a.m. and 9:00 p.m.

TABLE 8.2
(continued)

Year Enacted	City	Ordinance
2005	Tucson	Tucson Municipal Code section 11-36.2(a): Prohibits sitting or lying down on a public sidewalk during the hours of 7:00 a.m. and 10:00 p.m.
2006	Portland	Portland Municipal Code section 14A.50.020, 030: Prohibits obstruction of public sidewalks in a designated downtown area or camping on public property or public rights of way
1993, amended in 2007	Olympia	Olympia Municipal Code section 9.16.180: Amended to prohibit sitting, lying down, selling things, or asking for money within six feet of a building downtown between 7:00 a.m. and 10:00 p.m.
Not available	Sacramento	Sacramento Municipal Code section 12.24.110: Prohibits any person, after ordered to move by a police officer, from walking, standing, lying, or placing an object on any portion of a street, sidewalk, or other public right of way in a way that blocks passage by another person or vehicle

Source: Online municipal codes for major U.S. cities.

fundamental dimension of public participation, and people must be able to use public spaces in ways that reflect their interests. Supporting basic needs becomes a priority when other options are unavailable.

Jeremy Waldron (1991, 296) has laid out a simple but fundamental defense of the right to sleep or sit in public: "Everything that is done has to be done somewhere. No one is free to perform an action unless there is somewhere he is free to perform it. Since we are embodied beings, we always have a location. Moreover, though everyone has to be somewhere, a person cannot always choose any location he likes. Some locations are physically inaccessible. And physical inaccessibility aside, there are some places one is simply not allowed to be." If a person is prohibited from doing what he must do to survive, he is prohibited from surviving (Waldron 1991).

Such arguments have formed a viable defense against outright bans on public sleeping. In the early 1990s, Santa Ana, California, tried to ban outright sleeping in all public spaces, but the ordinance was ruled to be unconstitutional (Takahashi 1998). In 2006, Los Angeles's prohibition on sleeping in all public spaces was also held unconstitutional. In both cases, the cities responded by delineating districts where public sleeping is allowed or banned. In Santa Ana, the city delineated an area where sleeping was prohibited, whereas Los Angeles defined an area where people can sleep during the night hours.

Although courts have upheld people's basic rights to panhandle, sleep, and sit in public spaces to differing degrees, these rights are severely limited. The negotiated positions—ordinances that strictly define where and how people can sleep—may limit outright prohibitions but still remove activities from their social and spatial contexts. If cities cannot deny people the right to sleep anywhere, they can still deny urbanites the opportunity to sleep whenever they need to or where they might be comfortable. By defining where and when people sleep, cities do not allow homeless residents the right to decide when or where they want or need to sleep, including how much privacy they seek and where they might be safe and quiet. We tend to agree with those who find these rights meager, even if necessary (Mitchell 2003).

Proponents of these regulations argue that restricting loitering and panhandling are necessary to ensure that public spaces are comfortable for people who are not homeless (Ellickson 1996; Kelling and Cole 1996). Public-space scholars have also delineated legitimate and illegitimate participants. For example, William H. Whyte (1980) advocated for places that encourage use and prompted cities to take back their public spaces from the "undesirables" that occupy them. According to Whyte, "The best way to handle the problem of undesirables is to make the place attractive to everyone else" (Whyte 1988, 158).

More recently, however, without addressing homelessness directly, Setha Low, Dana Taplin, and Suzanne Scheld (2005) have examined how large public spaces accommodate diverse uses. They have argued that

public-space planners must better accommodate discomfort, explicitly calling for practices that encourage diversity. Determining priorities for small
public spaces requires that cities must decide whose interests will be prioritized and who will need to adapt to these priorities.

Public-Space Responses to Homelessness in Three Cities

Public spaces are the first and often only sites where homeless and housed
residents interact, and these interactions and the public-space controls intended to govern them have numerous effects. Public-space interventions
force us to consider who causes harm to whom on the sidewalks and
whether people should be granted the use of sidewalks and other public
spaces as they see fit.

To examine these questions further, we focus on three cities—Boston,
Seattle, and Los Angeles—and draw on twenty-five interviews with municipal officials, homeless service providers, and business association representatives in these cities.[4] The homeless service providers were from shelters,
while the business representatives were involved in a formal business association. Both Seattle and Los Angeles have legislation that promotes business
improvement districts (BIDs). Boston has not enacted such legislation but
has business associations as well as numerous commercial corridors designated as Main Streets. The city officials we interviewed dealt directly with
homelessness programs and code enforcement. To complement the interviews, we also drew on newspaper accounts, reports, and other documenta-
tion about homelessness.

All three cities have regulations that govern street activities associated
with homelessness, but they have faced different issues (table 8.3). Los Angeles has the highest concentration of homeless population in the United
States and is the only city of the three with a skid row district. Boston and
Seattle no longer have similar identifiable districts but have areas where
people ask for money or sleep in public. Each city has been attempting to
revitalize its downtown neighborhoods since the 1980s, the period where
homelessness became increasingly visible on city streets. In these downtown

TABLE 8.3
Homelessness Ordinances: Los Angeles, Seattle, Boston

Year Enacted	Location	Prohibited Actions	Ordinance	Challenges to the Ordinance
1968	Los Angeles streets, sidewalks, or public ways	"No person shall sit, lie, or sleep in or upon any street, sidewalk, or public way."	Ordinance 137,269 added section 41.18d ("Loitering") to the Los Angeles Municipal Code.	On April 14, 2006, the Ninth Circuit Court of Appeals filed an opinion in *Jones v. City of Los Angeles* (case 04-55324), finding that the Eighth Amendment prohibits the city from punishing involuntary sitting, lying, or sleeping on public sidewalks that is in an unavoidable consequence of being human and homeless without shelter in the City of Los Angeles.
1975	Boston streets	"No person shall saunter or loiter in a street in such a manner as to obstruct or endanger travelers or in a manner likely to cause a breach of the peace or incite to riot."	Ordinance T14, section 286, added section 16–12.2 ("Loitering") to the City of Boston Municipal Code.	None

Year	Location	Ordinance	Provision	Outcome
1987	Seattle public places (areas generally visible to public view)	Seattle Municipal Code, 12A-12.015 ("Pedestrian Interference")	"A person is guilty of pedestrian interference if, in a public place, he or she intentionally obstructs pedestrian or vehicular traffic; or aggressively begs."	On December 6, 1990, in *Webster v. City of Seattle* (case 56959-2), this ordinance was upheld as constitutional by the Washington State Supreme Court after a challenge on the grounds of breadth and vagueness. The court concluded that the ordinance does not deny equal protection of the laws and upheld it. This finding reversed the prior findings by the Washington State Superior Court and the Seattle Municipal Court, which dismissed the charges in 1988.
1993	Seattle sidewalks in commercial districts	Ordinance 116885 S.1 added section 15.48.040 ("Miscellaneous Acts") to the Seattle Municipal Code.	"No person shall sit or lie down upon a public sidewalk or upon a blanket, chair, stool, or other object placed upon a public sidewalk, during the hours between 7 AM and 9 PM in the Downtown zone and Neighborhood commercial zones."	On March 18, 1996, in *Roulette v. City of Seattle* (case 94-35354), the Ninth Circuit Court of Appeals upheld a Seattle ordinance that had been challenged by homeless advocates and members of various political and social groups who stated that sitting or lying on the ground was a form of expression.

TABLE 8.3
(continued)

Year Enacted	Location	Prohibited Actions	Ordinance	Challenges to the Ordinance
1997	Los Angeles public places and within 15 feet of banks and automatic teller machines	"No person shall solicit, ask, or beg in an aggressive manner in any public place. All solicitation is prohibited within 15 feet of any entrance or exit of any bank, savings and loan association, credit union, or check cashing business during its business hours or within 15 feet of any automated teller machine during the time it is available for customer use."	Ordinance 171,664 added section 41.59 ("Prohibition against Certain Forms of Aggressive Solicitation") to the Los Angeles Municipal Code.	On December 19, 2000, City of Los Angeles Ordinance 173,705 amended the prohibition against certain forms of aggressive solicitation by deleting "restaurant" and "public transportation stops."

Sources: Los Angeles Municipal Code (searchable online through the city clerk to 1979 at http://cityclerk.lacity.org/ordinance/index.htm), Seattle Municipal Code, Boston Municipal Code (accessed at www.municode.com), Lexis Nexis.

neighborhoods, business owners are concerned when the street population interferes with business by crowding the sidewalks and making shoppers and workers uncomfortable.

In the 1980s, the city of Boston began revitalizing its Downtown Crossing area and created a pedestrian mall between two anchor department stores. The mall became a popular destination for many city residents, including those who were homeless. Since that time, tensions have arisen between the street population and other downtown street users. In response, the city established an Emergency Shelter Commission to address rising homelessness and integrate citywide efforts to obtain state and federal funds. A business association, the Downtown Crossing Association, was also established. At the time, homelessness appeared to be an emergency that would be resolved. Nearly thirty years later, homelessness is an ongoing problem. The 2004 City of Boston's one-night Homeless Census found 5,819 homeless people who mostly were sleeping in filled shelters. The census counted 299 people on the streets, up from 230 the previous year (Friends of the Boston Homeless n.d.). Unlike Seattle and Los Angeles, Boston has not initiated any systematic effort or ordinances targeting sidewalk and public-space use by people who are homeless, although in 1997 it enacted an antipanhandling ordinance that prohibited asking for money in an "aggressive" manner in any public place or asking for money within ten feet of a bank entrance or ATM.

In the 1990s, Seattle's downtown neighborhoods were rapidly revitalizing. Many large projects were constructed, including an urban mall and a symphony hall. A new public library opened in 2005. To address the problems that arose between visitors and the street populations, the city initiated a visible program that directly targeted street-level interactions through a series of public-space ordinances. The ordinances prohibit sitting and lying on sidewalks in downtown neighborhoods, and they also prohibit park use if a person has been cited for sleeping in the park previously. In response to ongoing problems, the Metropolitan Business Association developed an Ambassador Program that provides outreach and offers jobs to homeless people. The one-night count in King County, Washington, on January 27, 2006, found 1,946 people without shelter, 2,463 people in emergency shelters, and 3,501 people in transitional housing programs (Seattle/King County Coalition for the Homeless n.d.).

Los Angeles has more homeless residents than any other city in the nation. According to the Institute for the Study of Homelessness and Poverty, there are approximately 91,000 people who are homeless each night in Los Angeles County (including Pasadena, Long Beach, and Glendale, which do separate counts). Approximately 5 percent stay in skid row, where thousands sleep outside nightly. Next to skid row, skyscrapers loom in the new corporate downtown, while the city's older downtown neighborhoods retain many early twentieth-century brick and terracotta buildings and warehouses. Historic art deco theaters still line Broadway Street, and the small shops selling clothes, electronic, and household items command the second-highest rents per square foot in the county. The historic Central Market hosts grocery stands and small eateries, and the toy, fashion, and jewelry districts do steady trade.

Except for street-level retail businesses, the historic buildings were vacant until the 2000s, when developers started converting the buildings into lofts. The renovated units sell quickly, and their high prices have brought residents who feel uncomfortable being next to skid row. The southeastern part of downtown (known as Central City East) includes the flourishing garment, toy, and electronics districts but also presses against skid row (Wolch, Dear, Blasi, Flamig, Tepper, and Koegel 2007).

This economic vitality has squeezed skid row. The city has prohibited sleeping in public spaces, although the ordinance was modified to allow people to sleep in skid row at night. The city has enacted an ordinance that prohibits converting residential hotels to condominiums, but it also conducts sweeps along skid row streets.

PRESENTING DISCOMFORT AS HARM

Discomfort, not danger, makes homelessness incompatible with activities such as shopping and strolling along the sidewalks. Causing discomfort is not illegal, and U.S. society has not reached a legal or moral consensus about how to react to homeless people in public spaces. Cities and states prohibit activities that cause harm such as assault, battery, or property damage. In contrast, regulations that target homelessness address ordinary activities—spending time in public, resting, talking, asking for money, sitting on a bench, or sitting on a sidewalk. The difference lies in the way the activities are perceived.

The crux of the problem is determining who causes harm and who is being harmed. Margaret Kohn has argued that homelessness should cause discomfort even if people do not act in a threatening way to others. Witnessing suffering, such as the conditions in which homeless people live, "can and should cause dismay" (Kohn 2004, 172). As Kohn further discusses, our response to that suffering depends on whether we see harm in the suffering or the discomfort that seeing suffering causes.

On the sidewalks, people interact with those in different circumstances and much of the conflict around homelessness arises when people confront conditions that they do not want to take responsibility for. As one Los Angeles service provider explained, "Take the reality of Fourth and Main, for example, where you have people sleeping on the sidewalk and people trying to get in and out of Pete's, sort of a trendy bar and restaurant right at Fourth and Main. There is this clash, this collision course of forces where use of public space becomes the number one issue" (Los Angeles service provider interview).

Many public-space users feel uncomfortable when they encounter a homeless person, and business owners explain that groups of men or adolescents (not necessarily homeless) feel threatening to them and their customers. In Boston, a business representative explained that clusters of men, youth, and others loitering outside business entrances discourage customers from entering their stores (Boston business association interview), and another mentioned that groups of men in parks and other public spaces, especially when they also wash in the fountain and carry their belongings, intimidate the seniors living nearby (Boston business association interview).

Banning threatening behavior has been the justification for aggressive panhandling ordinances, which prohibit actions such as approaching someone in an aggressive manner or following or engaging people in conversation to ask for money. In Seattle, however, after experimenting with

Pete's, Fourth and Main Streets, Los Angeles, California, 2007. Photograph by Renia Ehrenfeucht.

various ordinances, a business association representative explained that aggressive panhandling mischaracterizes the problem. Shoppers and other street users can feel threatened simply because a person who appears homeless approaches them. Aggression between two panhandlers can intimidate other street users even if the aggression is directed elsewhere (Seattle business association interview).

Regulating discomfort depends on defining ordinances that are based on the subjective experiences of those being affected (those made to be uncomfortable). Ordinances such as loitering or aggressive panhandling privilege the affected person's experience. The Los Angeles municipal code, for example, defines *loitering* as standing in such a way that would "annoy or molest any pedestrian" or "obstruct or unreasonably interfere with the free passage of pedestrians" (Los Angeles Municipal Code 41.18). This gives authority to both the police and other users to move homeless people.

Because being homeless causes discomfort, people who appear homeless become troubling to those who see them. They may lead others to avoid parks or strips of sidewalks where homeless people are present (a fear and avoidance response) (Phillips and Smith 2004). Business owners fear that their customers will avoid an area if they feel uncomfortable, and both the discomfort and potential revenue loss are determined to cause harm.

EFFECTS OF PUBLIC-SPACE INTERVENTIONS

Public-space interventions have multiple effects and make daily life more difficult for people who are homeless. The ordinances do not address the problem of homelessness, but they force homeless residents to move within the region, prevent sleep or rest, and reduce sources of income. Assessing the effectiveness of public-space regulations, business association representatives had conflicting opinions. Ordinances and physical interventions are tools that business owners can use to move people from a particular spot, and some find this helpful for a specific area. Others argue that tightening public-space regulations does not resolve the problem.

The ordinances make daily life harder for people who are homeless. As one Los Angeles service provider described the situation, "It is bringing up a lot of stress. Without a formalized plan with some measurable, targeted outcomes in place, what we have with these initiatives that are popping up and led by different folks is a situation where people are being moved around without any idea of where they are going or where the resources are coming from to help them eliminate homelessness completely" (LA service provider interview). Another interviewee emphasized the stress and discomfort felt by the homeless who are "pushed into areas they don't know" (Los Angeles service provider interview).

Service providers in Los Angeles find that police tactics—such as issuing jaywalking tickets and asking if people are on parole without cause—harass homeless people (Los Angeles service provider interview; Los Angeles ACLU interview). At the same time, police departments are pressured by residents and merchants to "do something about the homeless." They experience significant pressure to move people who are homeless, even if they are engaging in nothing illegal (Los Angeles city official interview). Still, the police do not always enforce these ordinances. In 1993, the Los Angeles Homelessness Project of the University of Southern California found that many law enforcement departments have attempted to avoid criminalization of homelessness by not enforcing municipal ordinances against loitering, soliciting, aggressive panhandling, and sleeping or camping on the sidewalks.

Cities and business owners use formal and informal mechanisms to address immediate problems, but these have limited long-term effects. In Seattle, the city twice bulldozed homeless encampments in the Beacon Hill neighborhood (Tuinstra 2005). In Los Angeles, the downtown Central City Association pushed for the enactment of an antiencampment ordinance in 2002 to curb the number of people sleeping in tents and boxes in skid row (Rivera 2002). The city's Bureau of Street Services (BOSS) Investigation and Enforcement Division has removed homeless encampments. BOSS coordinates with the Los Angeles Homeless Services Authority (LAHSA), a public agency that is charged with responding to the city's homeless problem, to allow them to offer their services and ask people there to remove their belongings from the encampments before BOSS removes them. According to BOSS, people remove their belongings about half the time but return to the same spot regularly after an encampment is cleared (Los Angeles city official interview).

Although all parties agree that shelters and other services are necessary to alleviate homelessness, the service facilities affect the neighborhoods where they are located. Business association representatives in both Boston and Seattle explained that the shelters were good neighbors, but they also discussed the local effects of having services on a street. People line up and wait for shelters to open and meals to be served and must leave shelters in the morning with nowhere to go. They often linger on the sidewalks or parks in the neighborhood. When shelters transport their residents by bus to other areas, the neighborhoods where they are dropped off face a similar situation (Los Angeles service provider interview; Boston business association interview; Seattle business association interview). In this way, sidewalks become a point of contact between neighborhood residents and service agencies. Acknowledging the need for services does not eliminate site-specific conflicts.

Cities do not plan for people who are homeless. Many observers have examined municipal efforts to use soft-control design elements (such as benches with barriers between seats and rounded seating areas) to reduce access to ledges and prevent public sleeping and loitering (Davis 1991; Loukaitou-Sideris, Blumenberg, and Ehrenfeucht 2005). Although critics find such tactics unfair, many business associations favor such design interventions and find them effective at reducing local impacts (Boston business association interview; Los Angeles business association interview).

Service providers and business representatives emphasized the need for systematic solutions. As a Los Angeles service provider explained, "They need stable housing; they need affordable housing. They need income sources to stay in that housing.... There is no job creation, at least in living-wage jobs that can support individuals and families. Those jobs are actually going down" (Los Angeles service provider interview).

At best, ordinances or design interventions move people around locally, and any relief for one area creates a problem in another. In Seattle, for example, the ordinances are rarely used for arrests but instead are used as a tool to ask people who sit or lay on the streets to move (Seattle public

Clients outside the Midnight Mission, Los Angeles, California, Thanksgiving Day, 1975. Courtesy of the Los Angeles Public Library.

official interview). As a Los Angeles service provider argued, "Ordinances do not solve the problem. They just move people from encampments to another few blocks away. They are continually moved and they are not assisted" (Los Angeles service provider interview). Or as another service provider said, "The business community has put tremendous pressure on the Mayor's office, which in turn put the police out there. So the police do sweeps all the time and really have pushed homeless people out of skid row into other communities" (Los Angeles service provider interview).

No one argued that public-space ordinances address homelessness effectively because they simply push people from one area or neighborhood to the next. As one service provider in Los Angeles argued (Los Angeles service provider interview):

> Homelessness is a problem much bigger than the city of Los Angeles or the state of California. It is a national problem. Until we address the root issues of why we have the homeless issue to begin with, there is almost nothing that we can do that is effective at this level. We are trying to contain the problem and at least deal with the health issues associated with it and provide as much service as we can to those who are out there in need of service, but there's really not a solution that's going to be found at this level.

Each stakeholder addressed multiple aspects of these issues. Some service providers in Los Angeles were hopeful that media attention on homelessness in the downtown streets and sidewalks will increase the long-term commitment to reducing homelessness. As one argued (Los Angeles service provider interview):

> I think what downtown is experiencing is growing pains ... [I see] cities trying to recapture their downtowns. They are bringing in residents and loft conversions and condo conversions and businesses concentrating on tourism and making downtown the center of business again. This all puts pressure on the communities that have existed there for years.... For twenty years, skid row has been what it has been and, to use a phrase that I heard recently, "invisible within plain sight." ... With new eyes and new voices moving in, a new set of needs and concerns is also moving in.

In Los Angeles, further discussion might lead to more commitment to reduce street homelessness. The service providers echoed a hope that street-level conflicts could filter up because homelessness has become a problem for more people.

PUBLIC-SPACE RIGHTS AND NEEDS OF THE HOMELESS

We have argued that a fair response to conflicting uses in public spaces would take into account different groups' priorities for sidewalks and would privilege activities necessary for survival. We have also argued that the ordinances as enacted are unacceptably narrow. Openness—the freedom that people have to use public spaces based on individual interests within reason—is an integral public-space characteristic. In this section, we use the example of public sleeping to discuss why prohibitions are too limited and why retaining an element of independent choice is necessary for fair sidewalk regulations.

A city's moral authority to regulate public sleeping hinges on both the effects of public sleeping and the ways that the city conceives of homelessness. When other urbanites consider homelessness to be a choice or assume that homeless people have other places to spend time or meet basic needs, they might be less sympathetic to sharing public space. On the other hand, when city residents consider streets and parks to be the only viable spots for someone to sit or sleep, they might be sympathetic or at least tolerant. Because of this, many defend public sleeping and other activities associated with homelessness on the grounds that people who are homeless need access to public spaces to meet basic needs. However true this might be, the argument defines *basic needs* narrowly (a place to sleep but not the opportunity to choose where and when). Indeed, the constraints that the courts have placed on cities continue to give cities broad authority to limit unwanted activities.

The most convincing public-sleeping defense has been that because cities have fewer shelter beds than people who request them, they are required to allow people to sleep in public spaces. In Los Angeles, for example, as one service provider explained, "The reality is that we have 91,000 people who are homeless on any given night.... There are only 18,000 shelter beds in the entire system.... There is a huge gap between what is available and the need" (Los Angeles service provider interview). In another service provider's words, "There is pressure on housing, on shelters, and we don't have the resources that are necessary for people to move off the streets completely" (Los Angeles service provider interview). Similarly, in 2004, the Massachusetts Housing and Shelter Alliance reported that Massachusetts's shelters had been overflowing for over six years (Friends of Boston's Homeless n.d.).

Although cities nationwide have attempted to institute blanket regulations against public sleeping, these have been overturned in court. Los Angeles, for example, enacted an ordinance that prohibited sitting or sleeping on public streets and sidewalks "at all times and in all places," but in April 2006, the Ninth Circuit Court of Appeals held the ordinance unconstitutional in *Jones v. City of Los Angeles.*[5] According to the court, the ordinance violated the Eighth Amendment, barring cruel and unusual punishment, and held that the city cannot bar someone from sleeping on any public space in the city or sitting on a sidewalk everywhere and at all times if he or she has nowhere else to sleep or sit.

Even this opinion, however, is unacceptably narrow. Access to a shelter bed is only one factor in a decision that a person makes about where to sleep. The locations of shelters may not be close to where a homeless person wants to be. The shelters are not distributed evenly, and the number of beds available varies by area. In the Los Angeles area, "for example, skid row and Santa Monica have a ratio of about four homeless people to one bed, but in South LA it is fifty to one, and in the East San Gabriel Valley it is 137 to one" (Los Angeles service provider interview). A Los Angeles survey showed that with the exception of skid row, which draws its homeless population from different parts of the county and from other counties because of its large concentration of shelters and services, people living on the streets in other neighborhoods tend to come from the same locality. The same finding was consistent in Boston (Tepper 2004; Boston city official interview; Los Angeles service provider interview).

The conditions in shelters also discourage their use. Shelters do not offer private space, they have many restrictions, few accept heterosexual couples, they have strict hours, most demand sobriety, and they can be noisy and crowded. The rigidity of rules can make shelters feel like a prison, military camp, or hospital—a significant deterrent for many who have spent time in these institutions. Shelters can also be dangerous for gay and transgendered people. Most offer only a space to sleep with specific times for "lights out" and waking up. Even if a homeless person has a shelter available for the night, he or she has to spend time on public sidewalks and parks during the day. As a number of service providers indicated, shelters offer a temporary space inside and off the street for the night, which might be a best option for many, particularly in cold or wet weather, but not for everyone (Los Angeles service provider interview; Boston service provider interview).

Sleeping outside also is dangerous. People who live on the streets are robbed, attacked, sexually assaulted, and harassed by the police and private security guards (Los Angeles service provider interview; Boston city official interview). Because of these dangers, homeless people may sleep in spaces that are safer, either with others or in hidden spaces. In other words, people need the right to sleep in public spaces and to choose where in public they sleep.

Since the 1980s, people have set up cardboard shelters and tents along Los Angeles's skid row. Seattle has two tent cities in the county and one in the city. In all cities surveyed, people also sleep in doorways, in parks, and on benches. As one interviewee explained: "We went out and did a public hearing in Lancaster, and they were telling us of a teen sleeping in fox holes out in the desert. . . . People sleeping under the freeways, people using buses to sleep on, some homeless people—and this was years ago—would just go around and around on the bus out at LAX" (Los Angeles service provider interview).

The question of choice becomes a critical but difficult element. If the interests of homeless people must be prioritized, even when they might conflict with others, the parameters must be defined. Acknowledging homeless people's agency—the ability to reason and make decisions among the opportunities that they have—has become difficult because it has been conflated with the idea that people choose homelessness or at the very least make bad decisions that result in homelessness. Such arguments are usually put forth by those advocating for public-space controls. At the same time,

Cardboard shantytown, Sixth and Towne Streets, Los Angeles, California, 1987.
Photograph by Javier Mendoza, *Herald-Examiner* Collection. Courtesy of the Los Angeles
Public Library.

homeless advocates who cast the homeless as "free spirits" (Amster 2004) fall into the trap of suggesting that homeless people choose between homelessness and housing or between being inside or outside the mainstream society. In contrast, Duneier (1999) explores how people understand that they make decisions while simultaneously acknowledging that external factors (such as an inability to find work) affect those choices. The fact that people do not have extensive choices should not deny them the ability to make choices from limited opportunities.

CONCLUSION: WHOSE PUBLIC SPACES?

Homelessness is a public-space dilemma. People who are homeless sometimes disrupt other public-space activities and intimidate other street users—particularly in small urban spaces, such as sidewalks. At the same time, sidewalks support necessary activities, and just policies require treating different groups differently at times.

Homeless residents seek similar qualities in public spaces as people who possess private housing. During the day, they choose comfortable spaces with places to sit and protection from bad weather. If they panhandle, they want to be in areas that other people visit. At night, they want what other people want—some privacy and the freedom to sleep undisturbed. Although homelessness is a problem, public-space use for ordinary activities is not.

Homelessness raises a fundamental dilemma that cities face when they regulate public spaces. In small public spaces, cities must define priorities and determine whose interests are to be satisfied when activities conflict. If participating in small public spaces depends on not disrupting others and a person's living conditions disrupt people, then the situation precludes membership in such a public. City officials, service providers, and business representatives agree that the United States needs systematic solutions to homelessness. They have reached no consensus on how to prioritize activities on specific sidewalk stretches because the street conflict and not homelessness becomes the focus at any given moment. We argue, however, that those with fewer options should not be denied use of public spaces when their priorities conflict with those of others or when they make others uncomfortable. Instead, the fact that these residents are engaging in life-sustaining activities should ensure that their interests take precedent.

Kohn discusses three ways that scholars argue for homeless residents' rights, dividing the arguments into liberal, romantic, and democratic. She concludes that the democratic defense is the strongest. Seeing others makes urbanites better educated about the city in which they live and gives them a better basis for making decisions about social programs. Through their presence, people who are homeless are also in a better position to demand what they need (Kohn 2004, 167–188).

The liberal and romantic arguments also illuminate important points. The liberal critique of banning homelessness from public spaces is based on the argument that such prohibition attacks individual freedom. Homelessness, however, contradicts another cherished ideal of liberalism: private property ownership. Although the romantic view does not generally underlie scholarly arguments (there are exceptions; see, for example, Amster 2004), Kohn suggests that a romantic view offers an alternative to the dichotomy of a homeless person as victim or threat. It emphasizes a person's agency when confronting difficulties, both personal and structural, and it can create space on society's margins for different ways of living. It also allows people to make choices among the opportunities that they have at a given time rather than seeing a condition as an absolute choice to be either a marginal person or a failure. It thus introduces the possibility that public space can be used for survival—not as a place of last resort but as a step on a longer and varied journey.

Sidewalk as Urban Forest

In May 2006, Los Angeles Mayor Antonio Villaraigosa launched the city's Million Trees LA Initiative to plant a million new trees over the next several years (Million Trees LA n.d.). Other cities across the United States (including Denver, Chicago and Baltimore) have similar programs ("Hartford: General Benefits of Canopy" 2006; Meyer 2006; Slevin and Lyderson 2006) that envision sidewalks as part of an urban forest. This green vision for urban sidewalks aspires to create greener, healthier cities.

Trees offer many benefits that urbanites generally like, but planting and maintaining an urban forest has proven to be a formidable task. Urban forests require significant investment, and trees are rarely a priority for strained municipal coffers. Even with the political will behind the Million Trees LA Initiative, the program depends on partnerships with corporations and nonprofit agencies because the city cannot fund it alone. The initiative also depends on city residents to plant and care for the trees on both public and private land.

In this chapter, we discuss street trees and the public constituency for a vibrant urban forest—trees, plants, and accompanying wildlife—to demonstrate the complexities that surround sidewalk decisions. Street trees provide a useful opportunity for observing the actors, scales, and priorities that are essential to each decision about a stretch of sidewalk. In the previous chapters, we have discussed many conflicts that arise because of a fundamental public-space tension that occurs when diverse groups of people want different things from public sidewalks. Street trees are an excellent example because although they are generally desirable, urbanites sometimes have trouble reaching a consensus when they consider the details of an individual tree in a given location.

Street trees are located in the ambiguous area between buildings and the street for which abutting property owners share responsibility with the city. Benefits from the trees include cooling a house, shading a street, managing storm water, and reducing a city's overall heat or carbon production. Problems with individual trees affect abutting properties more than others. Trees are also unevenly distributed in cities, reflecting land-use patterns and structures of systemic inequality. Because they are provided in ways that require abutters to take responsibility and not all residents have the same resources or priorities, lower-income neighborhoods have fewer trees than wealthier areas. Urban tree providers must account for these differences as they develop programs to reflect the diverse people that populate U.S. cities.

To explore these issues, we interviewed fourteen representatives from urban-forest advocacy organizations and public agencies that are engaged in street-tree provision in Los Angeles and Miami. Inadequate funding and the lack of consensus about the importance of trees in urban infrastructure have hindered tree provision. These constraints make it necessary for other groups—residents and nonprofit agencies—to help develop the urban forest.

The History of Urban Forests

For centuries, the streets have been sites of urban environmental problems and solutions. In the nineteenth century, thick garbage and animal manure covered city streets, and by the late nineteenth century, cities nationwide were providing municipal services such as sewage and garbage collection to combat the filth. Street paving was a technique to make cleaning streets easier, and straight streets offered better ventilation (Winter 1993).

The functionality of trees cannot be separated from their symbolism. Tracing the history of the elm tree, Thomas Campanella has argued that "elm trees bore the very identity of the New England people" (2003, 10). For early New England towns, the planting of street trees provided shade and beauty but also humanized the streetscape, built an environment for people, and made the town a desirable place to live. By 1840, tree planting along streets and other public areas became increasingly common in New England (Campanella 2003, 83–98).

As U.S. cities grew swiftly in the mid-nineteenth century because of immigration and industrialization, the rapidly changing environment alarmed many urbanites. Fearful that this environment alienated residents from nature, late nineteenth-century park advocates sought to "bring nature back into the city" and called for parks, parkways, and street trees (Starr 1984). The melding of the country and the city and the development of urban forests was central to the ideology behind the design of parks and suburbs. Suburban streets were tree-lined, and parkways were planned to integrate circulation with nature. Reformers hoped that green cities would be therapeutic and able to uplift weary residents. In the early twentieth century, urban improvement societies advocated for tree-lined streets, and many tree-planting programs began at this time. For the hundreds of improvement societies that sprang up in cities across the nation during the City Beautiful era, tree planting and beautification of streets and public spaces were intended to build good citizens (Isenberg 2004).

For street trees, however, urbanization was harsh. In the 1880s, cities rapidly began installing infrastructure, and sidewalks became dominated by electric and telephone wires. Cables were sometimes strung from trees, and utility poles competed with trees for sidewalk space. Electric wires also burned trees, and falling branches damaged wires, leading to tree pruning or removal. Additionally, trees were damaged when streets were excavated to install or maintain urban infrastructure. Surface travel compacted the soil, constraining tree roots and impeding water infiltration, and horses were hitched and signs were posted to the tree trunks. When impervious asphalt replaced street pavers such as macadam, cobblestone, and bricks in the twentieth century, street trees received less water and fewer nutrients.

Environmental pollution led to poor health and short lives for street trees, and basic infrastructure was favored over beauty (Campanella 2003, 141–153).

As discussed previously, in the twentieth century, streets and sidewalks became increasingly viewed as single-use spaces—transportation corridors for efficient circulation rather than social, political, or natural spaces. Automobile transport took precedence over walking, and the benefits of street trees were devalued. Street-tree provision also followed an engineering rather than ecological approach. For many years, for example, few of the approved street trees in Los Angeles were native to the region (Bernier 2002). With decreasing municipal budgets, municipal bureaucracies started to view trees as a dispensable luxury.

By the late twentieth century, urban planners and municipal engineers no longer believed that a beautiful local environment alone could build good citizens, and concerns about public health and moral uplift were replaced with a focus on quality of life, long-term environmental quality, ecological sustainability, and environmental justice. Attention to these issues in recent decades has highlighted the potential for sidewalks as both healthful, enjoyable environments and sites that can possibly counter some problems associated with environmental pollution and global warming. These regional and global outcomes, however, come about by thousands of individual decisions, and street-tree providers must balance competing immediate interests and priorities. This raises numerous questions about who should make planting decisions, how many trees should be planted, what kinds of trees should be selected, and where they should be placed. To further complicate these questions, street trees are part of an urban forest that extends onto private property. Not surprisingly, the quality and size of the urban forest varies and reflects land-development patterns and neighborhood wealth.

DIVERSE INFLUENCES ON THE URBAN FOREST

THE IMPORTANCE OF TREES

Urban residents appreciate trees (Lohr, Pearson-Mims, Tarnai, and Dillman 2004; Gorman 2004). In a nationwide survey, residents identified shade and cooling, the calming effect of trees, and the reduction of dust and smog as trees' three most valued attributes (Lohr et al. 2004). Although feelings that trees are important to the quality of life varied by income (higher-income residents found trees more important), race, and ethnicity (white respondents ranked trees more important overall than African American and Asian American respondents did), and place of upbringing (people raised outside the city ranked trees as more important), all groups were overwhelmingly positive toward trees (Lohr et al. 2004).

Studies also suggest that contact with vegetation has psychological benefits. In Chicago, residents in the Robert Taylor Homes public-housing development who lived in buildings surrounded by more trees and grass reported fewer incidences of aggressive behavior than those in buildings surrounded by less vegetation (Kuo and Sullivan 2001).

Street trees offer environmental benefits that can help the city as a whole. The types of benefits that have been measured include energy conservation, ozone reduction, carbon sequestration, air-quality improvements, and storm-water management (Laverne and Winson-Geideman 2003; Maco and McPherson 2003). Environmental benefits also have immediate effects for city government and residents. Shade can decrease repaving costs (by reducing pavement fatigue, cracking, rutting, and other distress) (McPherson and Muchnick 2005) and reduce energy costs to residents (by cooling houses and decreasing the need for air conditioning).

Some scholars have argued that street trees increase the property values of adjacent properties. Indeed, a study examining the influence of trees on residential properties in Athens, Georgia, found that a large front yard tree was associated with a small increase (about 0.88 percent) in average house resale values (Anderson and Cordell 1988). Trees also improve the quality of the street experience. "If, in an American city, you wanted to make a major positive impact on an existing street and had a limited budget, you might well recommend planting trees as the way to get the most impact for your money," Allan Jacobs, former San Francisco planning director and professor of urban design, has argued (1990, 84).

Nevertheless, the general regard for trees does not mean that each tree benefits all residents. Street trees cause problems for abutting establishments. They shade gardens, drop fruit and leaves, and damage buildings during storms. Neighborhood residents bear the brunt of property damage and mess, and people's individual responses reflect past experiences. Individuals are less inclined to support new tree projects if trees have buckled their sidewalks, the fruit or flower drop has been messy, and trees were incorrectly pruned and therefore unhealthy or ugly (Northeast Trees interview; Los Angeles Conservation Corps interview, executive director; Citizens for a Better South Florida CSWD interview; Operation Green Leaves interview).[1]

Trees damage sidewalks. In Los Angeles, 4,000 of the 10,400 miles of sidewalks are cracked, mostly from tree roots (Los Angeles Bureau of Street Services interview, forester).[2] Cities are supposed to fix the damages that are caused by trees, but property owners experience the damages more than other users and also partially pay for repairs. One survey of eighteen California cities found that approximately $70.7 million was spent annually statewide to repair tree-root damage to sidewalks, gutters, and street pavement. Abutting property owners paid 39 percent of the sidewalk repairs and 17 percent of the gutter repairs. Because the survey was addressed to municipal arborists, it did not include additional money spent by individual property owners (McPherson 2000).

Trees that die must be replaced. Although Miami and Los Angeles can require property owners to replace a street tree that they remove, neither city has a policy for replanting trees, and many tree wells on sidewalks are empty. Donald Shoup (1996) has recommended that property owners be required to replace or add street trees in front of their property when they sell it, calculating that this will significantly increase the urban forest and cause only a limited burden for property owners.

Unlike residents, business owners do not always see the benefits of trees and occasionally want them to be removed. A survey of owners of commercial establishments found that many perceived the urban forest to be a nuisance or even a detriment to their businesses (Wolf 1998). Business owners do not want street trees to block their signage or reduce parking. In one study, researchers found that trees that provided a visual screen had a negative impact on office rental rates but that trees that shaded a building had a positive effect (Laverne and Winson-Geideman 2003).

Tree roots uplifting a sidewalk, Los Angeles, California, 2007.
Photograph by Anne McAuley.

Consumers, in contrast, responded favorably to street trees, ranking them as positive elements in revitalized inner-city business districts. Of the three scenarios presented (no trees, traditionally spaced street trees, and mixed vegetation), consumers ranked the "no tree scenario" the lowest and indicated that they would be willing to pay more for comparable goods in neighborhoods with trees (Wolf 2003). In a separate study, consumers and employees identified tree-lined street views more favorably than those with fewer trees (Wolf 2004).

In mixed-use neighborhoods, conflicts can arise between residents who want greener streets and merchants who do not want trees to block views to their establishments, hide their signs, crack the sidewalks in front of shop entrances, or restrict parking (Los Angeles Conservation Corps interview, executive director).

City engineers at times also want to remove trees that buckle sidewalks and damage underground infrastructure. Police officers and park managers have also opposed street trees when they block natural surveillance and good visibility of an area, fearing the trees might harbor criminal activity (Citizens for a Better South Florida, Community Science Workshop interview, director). The city as a whole and people beyond city boundaries would benefit if more trees grew throughout the region, but comprehensive policies to achieve this objective have been difficult to enact, partly because different municipal agencies have different aims.

Natural disasters also greatly affect the urban forest and people's perceptions of its value. In Miami, hundreds of trees were uprooted during Hurricane Andrew (Northeast Trees interview). This affected the neighborhoods when many trees caused property damage, and it also made residents fearful of planting more trees that might cause further damage (Northeast Trees interview; TREEmendous Miami interview).[3] The big trees offer the most benefits in terms of cooling the environment and reducing the heat-island effect, and yet they are the ones that frighten residents (Miami-Dade Department of Environmental Resource Management interview).[4] Providing the right tree species for a given space can circumvent some potential problems. An appropriate species should be determined by factors such as the width of the sidewalk where it will be planted or the overhead wires that might restrict its height (TreePeople interview).[5]

THE CHARACTERISTICS OF AN URBAN FOREST

Individual tree characteristics compound the complexity of street-tree provision. Factors that affect the vitality and quality of urban forests include tree quantity and species, their location and spacing, and the health of trees. A well functioning forest refers to how well the trees fulfill the objectives behind their planting and maintenance, including ecological benefits, aesthetics, property value or revenue increases, or protection from sun and rain.

Cumulative urban forests are extensive. The City of Los Angeles has over 10 million trees, and public agencies manage 2 million of these. The city has 700,000 street trees along 6,500 miles of road and over 10,400 miles of sidewalk. Each year, 5,000 new trees are planted, and 2,000 are removed (Los Angeles Bureau of Street Services interview, forester; Los Angeles Bureau of Street Services interview, arborist).[6] With a $1.2 million budget, the Miami-Dade County Right of Way Aesthetics and Assets Management Division planted approximately 1,500 trees in 2005. There are 52,000 trees in Miami-Dade County's Unincorporated Municipal Service Area (Miami-Dade Public Works correspondence).[7]

In addition to the number of trees, the type of trees also matters. Live oaks, for example, with wide, shady canopies frame the streets of New Orleans differently than the iconic palms of Los Angeles frame its streets. Measuring canopy coverage to determine the surface area covered by tree branches might better capture the urban forest's impact. A national tree organization, American Forests, suggests target canopy rates for various geographic regions and different parts of the city. It recommends 40 percent coverage for the East and Pacific Northwest and 25 percent for the dryer regions. The targeted coverage varies by the part of town. For example, it recommends 25 percent tree-canopy coverage in urban residential zones in areas east of the Mississippi and the Pacific Northwest and 18 percent in the Southwest and dry western regions. It recommends less coverage for central business districts (American Forests n.d.).

The national average coverage has been estimated at 27 percent (Million Trees LA n.d.), and both Los Angeles and Miami fall short of this figure. In Los Angeles, a recent tree-canopy analysis showed 18 percent canopy cover (Million Trees LA n.d.). Miami-Dade County has a canopy cover of approximately 10 percent, but Miami's last canopy analysis was

Palm trees offering little shade, Sunset Boulevard, Los Angeles, California, 2005.
Photograph by Renia Ehrenfeucht.

Canopied street, Coral Gables, Miami, Florida, 2006. Photograph by Renia Ehrenfeucht.

done in 1996 (Miami-Dade Department of Environmental Resource Management interview).

Not all trees are equally desirable. Some trees are considered weeds, and others are invasive species. In Miami-Dade County, as many as half the trees might consist of "invasive exotics" (Miami-Dade Department of Environmental Resource Management interview; Citizens for a Better South Florida, Community Science Workshop interview, director). These are detrimental to the urban forest because they tend to push out native species and even cause extinction of plants or animals (Citizens for a Better South Florida n.d.). In addition to differences in the canopy and therefore their resulting shading or cooling effect, trees vary significantly in their water uptake by species and size.

Determining the right tree for a given place depends on many factors. Trees grow at different rates, offer more or less shade, and grow to different heights, making some better suited for being close to power lines. Some species tolerate dry or wet conditions, cold weather, or high winds better than others. All these factors must be taken into account, depending on the geographic region and the particular location within an urban area (Northeast Trees interview; Miami-Dade Public Works correspondence).

In many cases, species native to the region have become preferable street trees, but this too is only one of many factors that determine the tree that is right for a given location. Street life is harsh even for native trees. Trees have different life spans, and some species can live for hundreds and even thousands of years. Street trees, however, have shorter lives due to the difficult urban conditions, and this is especially true for inner-city trees. Factors such as vehicle collisions, extreme temperatures, environmental pollution in the air and soil, and inorganic soils shorten the life of trees. Bad pruning, poor maintenance, compacted soil around tree roots, and impervious surfaces that reduce water infiltration also have negative effects (Miami-Dade Public Works correspondence; Northeast Trees interview). In some Los Angeles inner-city neighborhoods, trees live an average of only five years (P. Smith, personal communication with authors).

Tree form and overall appearance also matter. For decades, palm trees have symbolized Los Angeles, and cherry trees Washington, D.C. Seattle's flowering cherry and apple trees create pink and white confetti around the city each spring, and New Orleans' live oaks line its historic boulevards. However, cherry trees are small, and they offer little canopy as street trees. Palm trees do not provide much shade or protection from rain, and their fronds can cause damage during storms—factors important enough that even an image-conscious city like Los Angeles is turning toward other preferred species (Steinhauer 2006).

INEQUITABLE DISTRIBUTION OF TREES

Street trees can also be seen through an environmental-justice lens. Canopy analyses have confirmed what appears true when walking through neighborhoods: low-income neighborhoods have fewer trees than wealthy neighborhoods have. This finding is consistent with environmental-justice research that indicates that uneven local environmental quality is an important urban problem: environmental burdens fall disproportionately on people of color and those with low incomes, and wealthy neighborhoods receive more amenities.

In Los Angeles, a survey of council districts showed that tree-canopy coverage varied from as low as 5 percent to as high as 37 percent (Million Trees LA n.d.). Council districts with high numbers of low-income and minority residents (council districts 1, 13, and 14) are "tree-poor." Council districts with a high percentage of industrial uses also have fewer trees (Northeast Trees interview; Million Trees LA n.d.). In Miami, the canopy in some neighborhoods is as low as 1 percent. Areas that sustained damage during Hurricane Andrew in 1992 have the lowest percentages, but real estate development and citrus canker have also killed many trees (Miami-Dade Department of Environmental Resource Management interview).

In general, Miami's low-income neighborhoods are also tree-poor. Wealthy neighborhoods such as Coral Gables have canopy coverage as high as 40 percent, but in low-income neighborhoods canopies can be as low as 2 or 3 percent (Operation Green Leaves interview; TREEmendous Miami interview; Citizens for a Better South Florida, Community Science Workshop interview, director; Citizens for a Better South Florida interview).[8]

Streets with few trees, South Los Angeles, California, 2007. Photograph by Anne McAuley.

Using digitized aerial photographs, Nik Heynen (2006) examined changes in the urban canopy of Indianapolis from 1962 to 1993 and found that his model (which included household income, percentage of household-income change, percentage of rental properties, and percentage of change in land use as independent variables) explained 49 percent of the change in tree canopy, and household income was the only statistically significant variable. Land-use change and proportion of rental versus owner-occupied housing were not found to be significant. Heynen also found a 66 percent decrease in trees along transportation corridors with a 23 percent decline in canopy overall.

Low-income neighborhoods have fewer trees for many reasons. They usually include multifamily properties, which typically have less green space than houses in neighborhoods with large residential lots. In inner-city neighborhoods, fewer trees are planted on the small lots or along apartment buildings that cover much of the parcel (Northeast Trees interview).

Low-income areas such as South L.A. and Little Haiti in Miami are indeed underserved. At the same time, residents with very low incomes have priorities other than tree provision (Los Angeles Conservation Corps interview, conservation programs director; Northeast Trees interview; Operation Green Leaves interview; The Grove Treeman Trust interview).[9] Because cities do not have the capacity to provide and maintain all the street trees, the responsibility falls on abutting property owners. Residents in areas with owner-occupied housing are more likely to plant and maintain trees. In low-income areas, many absentee property owners do not invest in the neighborhood (Miami-Dade Department of Environmental Resource Management interview; The Grove Treeman Trust interview). Poor inner-city neighborhoods also often have poor air quality and other environmental hazards that can hurt trees.

Without public investment, ensuring adequate and high-quality maintenance is difficult (Parks for People interview).[10] Street-tree maintenance does not only involve watering and caring for trees but also fixing the sidewalks and public infrastructure damaged by them. Municipal professionals can reduce the damage from street trees by paving in ways that accommodate them. These range from using more adaptable paving materials (such as rubber sidewalks or pavers) or meandering the sidewalk around the tree roots. This does not happen often, and the lack of resources and maintenance further discourages tree planting in underserved urban areas.

THE PUBLIC'S DIVERSE PRIORITIES AND PREFERENCES

A viable urban forest depends on the trees that are healthy and well chosen, but urbanites have differing priorities and preferences, and the incorporation of diverse interests into tree programs is challenging. Empirical evidence has consistently found that landscape and park-use preferences vary by race and ethnicity (Elmendorf, Willits, and Sasidharan 2005; Loukaitou-Sideris 1995). Managers of large urban parks have been attempting to plan for the activities of diverse groups (Low, Taplin, and Scheld 2005), and some cities have been strategizing about how to respond to the different needs of new residents (Sandercock 2003). The issues are to understand variable desires and needs (and more research is needed to identify different social preferences for trees and landscaping) and also the ways to provide people with what they want even though neighborhoods do not have comparable resources and time to contribute.

On the sidewalks, street trees are located in the ambiguous area between the property line and the curb and are partially the property owners' responsibility. The sidewalk's location associates it with both private property and the public realm, and municipalities share the costs of and responsibilities for the trees with residents and tree-providing organizations. Individual property owners benefit from reduced energy costs, comfort, and beauty. In some areas, old trees create a canopy over the enclosed, shaded streets and contribute to the street's beauty and prestige. When sidewalks are used primarily for strolling, street canopies and falling leaves add to the charm and cause few problems. But the presence of street trees can also conflict with other intended uses, especially in neighborhoods with narrow sidewalks and little open space. In such dense neighborhoods, trees may reduce play areas and shade yards (Northeast Trees interview).

Physical urban elements have symbolic and functional value. Residents differ in their preferences for tree types and public-space designs. Recent immigrants want familiar trees or fruit trees from other regions (Miami-Dade Department of Environmental Resource Management interview; The Grove Treeman Trust interview). In many cases, residents are attached to existing trees and oppose efforts to remove them, even if the trees cause problems to the sidewalks or the roadway. At other times, however, residents become frustrated when the city preserves a tree that is buckling or littering the sidewalk (Los Angeles Bureau of Street Services interview, forester). When Citizens for a Better South Florida interviewed residents in Little Havana about their preferences, many people preferred paved patios to treed yards (Citizens for a Better South Florida interview).

Street-tree providers—the public agencies and the advocacy organizations—try to accommodate people's preferences since residents are more likely to care for a tree they want (The Grove Treeman Trust interview). Because trees require certain conditions to thrive, however, even if an organization intends to provide street trees to serve community needs, the choice of the "right" tree is more complicated than giving residents the trees they desire. For example, fruit trees are popular in many neighborhoods, but they do not offer a good tree canopy or shade. In Los Angeles, the city does not allow fruit trees on public properties and instead offers shade trees as part of its free-tree programs (Northeast Trees interview; Operation Green Leaves interview).

Tree health depends on the local climate and soil conditions. Despite being in the southern part of the country, Miami and Los Angeles have only five common trees on their recommended tree lists. A city's climate might not suit a given tree, and conditions in one neighborhood differ from another. Therefore, a desirable tree in a person's previous neighborhood might cause unanticipated problems in a new area. Jacarandas, for example, are beautiful but messy when they flower for a month each year and therefore may not be desirable on a narrow street in a dense neighborhood. Certain tree species are not resistant to specific weather conditions. In Miami, the strong winds and rains during hurricanes can uproot trees (Miami-Dade County Department of Resource Management n.d.; Operation Green Leaves interview; Citizens for a Better South Florida, Community Science Workshop interview, director; Northeast Trees interview).

Ongoing care and maintenance are the biggest challenges (Miami-Dade Department of Environmental Resource Management interview). Neither Miami nor Los Angeles has adequate funding to maintain all trees, and urban forestry has been a relatively low municipal priority (Northeast Trees interview). It takes little to kill a young tree, and to make tree-planting programs succeed, residents need to learn how to care for trees. Trees can suffer from both too much water and too little water, need fertilizer and long-term care, and must be pruned correctly, but many residents do not know how much and how often to water a tree or will not see the tree's care as a priority (Miami-Dade Department of Environmental Resource Management interview; Citizens for a Better South Florida, Community Science Workshop interview, director). To make a tree-planting program work, residents must do more than agree to it or state explicitly they want trees; they also need to commit to maintaining them (Northeast Trees interview). More people from wealthy neighborhoods participate in these programs than those from low-income areas (Los Angeles Conservation Corps interview).

Making the programs cost in terms of time or money can help ensure that people are committed to the trees they plant. In Miami's Adopt-a-Tree program, residents can spend two or three hours waiting to get their trees, and participants must go through a training process that explains the basics of planting and long-term maintenance (TREEmendous Miami interview; Miami-Dade Department of Environmental Resource Management interview). The Los Angeles Conservation Corps requires people present a site plan to show where they will plant the seven trees that they can receive (Los Angeles Conservation Corps interview, conservation programs director). In Fresno, California, residents who planted their own trees were more satisfied with the outcomes. They felt a sense of ownership over street trees, and the satisfaction that accompanies resident involvement in tree planting may instill a greater sense of responsibility for tree maintenance that will decrease tree mortality (Sommer, Learey, Summit, and Tirrell 1994).

PROVIDERS OF THE URBAN FOREST

A healthy urban forest requires a collective understanding about the needs of the trees and the contributions that a healthy forest will make. Public interests, however, are varied and reflect multiple and sometimes incompatible priorities. Three critical actors in tree provision—the municipal agencies responsible for street trees, nonprofit tree organizations, and city residents—have multiple albeit overlapping interests (tables 9.1 and 9.2).

PUBLIC AGENCIES

Many public agencies affect the urban forest, and each agency has many goals. Some are vested in the ecological benefits to the city that trees provide and the quality of the streetscape, and others are responsible for sidewalk maintenance and safety or concerned about the liability if a problem arises. Both Miami and Los Angeles, as well as the other three cities that we look at in this book, have tree master plans (table 9.3).

In Los Angeles, the Department of Public Works has the authority to issue permits to plant, prune, or remove trees that are located on Los Angeles streets, even those in front of private residences (Los Angeles Municipal Code section 62). The Urban Forestry Division of the Los Angeles Bureau of Street Services (in the Public Works Department) maintains trees, landscapes the public right of way, and recycles green waste (Los Angeles Bureau of Street Services interview, arborist). The county-level Department of Environmental Resources Management (DERM) oversees the street trees in Miami's public rights of way. The City of Miami's Parks Department plants, maintains, and trims all trees in the city's public parks. In the City of Miami, the director of the Department of Public Works requires citizens to pay for permits to trim, prune, plant, or remove trees from public land (City of Miami Code section 3.17).

Public agencies work to replace and preserve the tree canopy. The Los Angeles Department of Public Works can require that residents replace trees that they damage or remove (LAMC section 62), even if the abutting property owner has bought, planted, and maintained the tree. When new subdivisions are built in Los Angeles, developers might be required to plant trees in public streets. Public Works will maintain the trees, but the developer pays for five years of maintenance (LAMC section 62). In Los Angeles, when the city removes trees, it replaces them on a two to one basis, and when it repairs the sidewalk, the city plants trees in all vacant sites. But

TABLE 9.1
Tree-planting stewards: Who plants, maintains, and sustains the urban forest

Actions	Boston	Los Angeles	Miami	New York	Seattle
Tree planting					
Public departments	Parks Department	Bureau of Street Services (Urban Forestry Division)	Department of Environmental Resource Management (County) Miami Green Commission	Department of Parks and Recreation New York Tree Trust	Office of Sustainability and Environment
Nonprofits	Boston 4-H Urban Stewards Boston Natural Areas Network Eagle Eye Institute Earthworks Franklin Park Coalition YouthBuild	Los Angeles Conservation Corps Northeast Trees Parks for People Tree People	A Better South Florida Florida Native Plant Society Grove Treeman Trust Operation Green Leaves Treemendous Miami	Environmental Action Coalition Greening for Breathing Sustainable South Bronx	Friends of P-Patch Open space Advocates Plant Amnesty Seattle Tilth

Tree maintenance	Parks Department	Urban Forestry Division	Department of Parks (city) Department of Environmental Resources Management (county)	New York Tree Trust	Office of Sustainability and Environment
Watering	Property owner	Property owner	Property owner	Property owner	Property owner
Available planning guidelines					
Recommended tree list	×	×	×	×	×
Right trees for right space	×	×	×	×	×
Spacing	×	×	×	×	×
When to plant	—	—	×	×	—
How to plant	×	×	—	×	×
Maintenance and watering	×	×	×	×	×

209

TABLE 9.2
Overview of tree planting in five cities

Actions	Boston	Los Angeles	Miami	New York	Seattle
Street tree oversite and maintenance	Boston Parks Department Massachusetts Department of Conservation and Recreation	City Bureau of Street Services (Urban Forestry Division)	Miami-Dade County Department of Environmental Resource Management City of Miami Public Works	New York City Department of Parks and Recreation New York Tree Trust (program of Parks and Recreation and the City Parks Foundation)	Office of Sustainability and Environment Urban Forest
Free tree programs	Yes. Boston Parks Department offers free trees to residents (one-year backlog)	Yes. Department of Water and Power offers up to seven free trees to residential utility customers	Yes. Miami-Dade Adopt-a-Tree Program provides trees and training to eligible residential properties	Yes. Parks and Recreation Department offers free trees to residents (one-year backlog)	Yes. Department of Neighborhoods provides free trees to groups of five or more residential households agreeing to care for trees.
Recommended tree species list.	Limited list available through the Parks Department	Detailed list available plus information on when and where to plant	Detailed list available on recommended and invasive tree types	Detailed list available plus information on when and where to plant	Detailed list available plus information on tree sizes and where to plant

Estimated tree canopy cover	29% (2006)	18% (U.S. Department of Agriculture Forest Service, PSW Research Station, Center for Urban Forest Research)	10% (1996) (American Forests)	21% (2004) (American Forests)	18% (1992) (Department of Transportation)

TABLE 9.3

Street tree master plans: Identifying urban forest priorities

	Boston	Los Angeles	Miami	New York	Seattle
Plan name	Growing Boston Greener	Million Trees LA	Miami Street Tree Master Plan	Initiative for Plant 1 Million Trees	Seattle Master Street Tree Plan
Dates	2001–2020	2007–2020	2006–2020	2007–2017	1990–1999
Canopy coverage goal	35%, adding 100,000 trees	1 million new trees	30%	1 million new trees in next 10 years	40%
Target date for coverage goal	2020	2020	2020	2017	None stated
Implementing agencies	Boston Urban Forest Coalition (public, private, and nonprofit partners)	Urban Forestry Division in partnership with six nonprofit partners	None stated	Mayor's Office Department of Parks and Recreation	City Arborist Department of Transportation
Educational component	None stated	None stated	None stated	None stated	City arborist offers classes

Online planting information

Links to nonprofit organizations |

Sources: For Boston, http://www.na.fs.fed.us/urban/ucf_status2001_frames/urban_resources_p63_68.htm; for Los Angeles, http://www.milliontreesla.org; for Miami, http://www.miamidade.gov/image/reports.asp; for New York, http://forestry.about .com/b/b/256604.htm; for Seattle, http://www.seattle.gov/transportation/mastertreeplan.htm.

even the Urban Forestry Division of the Bureau of Street Services focuses more on maintenance than planting, and no agency has the resources to plant trees throughout the city (Los Angeles Bureau of Street Services interview, forester; Los Angeles Bureau of Street Services interview, arborist).

To encourage more tree planting, city agencies develop programs to give free trees to residents. Miami-Dade County DERM administers an Adopt-a-Tree program to encourage tree planting, and in 2006, 13,000 trees were adopted through the program. The program targets single-family and duplex residential properties. Since beginning the program, the county has distributed 83,000 trees (giving approximately 17,000 per year) (DERM n.d.). The Los Angeles City Department of Water and Power separately runs the Trees for a Green LA program, which provides up to seven free trees to residential utility customers (Los Angeles Conservation Corps interview, conservation programs director).

NONPROFIT TREE PROVIDERS

To implement the adopt-a-tree programs, cities partner with nonprofit organizations. For example, Miami-Dade County partners with nonprofit organizations such as TREEmendous Miami, which has a mission to "protect, preserve and plant trees in Miami-Dade County" (TREEmendous Miami interview). TREEmendous Miami works with the county on the Adopt-a-Tree program and offers property owners up to two free trees a year. The program encourages tree planting to replenish the canopy but also educates property owners about choosing the right tree for a given space, energy conservation, tree care, and tree maintenance. Not everyone is physically able to plant trees, and TREEmendous Miami also plants trees for seniors and people with disabilities who would otherwise not be able to participate (TREEmendous Miami interview).

Planting programs take many forms, and each provider organization may have distinct objectives. Organizations such as TREEmendous Miami focus primarily on distributing and planting trees. Others use planting trees to teach environmental stewardship, and some encourage neighborhood youth to become involved with environmental revitalization efforts to teach job skills, neighborhood pride, and environmental stewardship.

Most tree organizations target areas with few trees. In Los Angeles, TreePeople works to involve people to "heal the urban environment" and focuses on underserved communities. Parks for People works to resolve the "open space crisis" in Los Angeles, focusing again on underserved communities. Northeast Trees wants to "restore nature's services in resource-challenged communities." And the Los Angeles Conservation Corps organizes conservation and service programs that employ at-risk youth. In Miami, Operation Green Leaves focuses on Little Haiti, Treeman Trust plants trees in Coconut Grove, and TREEmendous Miami facilitates tree planting throughout the city, focusing on underserved neighborhoods (Operation Green Leaves interview; Citizens for a Better South Florida CSWD interview; TREEmendous Miami interview; The Grove Treeman Trust interview; Northeast Trees interview; Parks for People interview).

Advocacy programs serve neighborhoods while fulfilling other goals. Citizens for a Better South Florida has multilingual environmental programs and a native plant nursery, and Operation Green Leaves combats deforestation in Haiti while encouraging tree planting in Miami. Miami's Treeman Trust also promotes the use of native species. The Los Angeles Conservation Corps collects native seeds, has a nursery, and does other habitat restoration (Citizens for a Better South Florida, Community Science Workshop interview, director; The Grove Treeman Trust interview; Operation Green Leaves interview; Los Angeles Conservation Corps interview, conservation programs director). Both cities also have greening programs to create destination urban corridors and park improvements. In Miami, the city has developed a comprehensive plan to develop the Miami River Greenway, and Los Angeles grassroots organizations are working with the city to redesign the Los Angeles River (Parks for People interview).

In Los Angeles, TreePeople and Northeast Trees have made the provision of street trees a central component of their struggle for a better environment. Street trees are part of those organizations' objective to build civic capacity in order to restore the natural environment and "identify and steward the kind of environmental improvements that the community wants.... The purpose is to both develop the knowledge and commitment to ensure that trees and other improvements receive needed care but also to develop leadership and civic capacity to make environmental improvements" (Northeast Trees interview).

Youth-oriented organizations use tree planting and other environmental improvement projects to involve youth in organized activities that simultaneously improve neighborhoods and teach job skills. Youth are also conduits of information to parents, particularly in communities with high immigrant populations. Los Angeles Conservation Corps, a nationwide nonprofit that is based on the New Deal conservation corps, plants tree, improves trails, restores natural habitats, and develops community gardens. Northeast Trees also teaches environmental stewardship to youth, and its mission includes environmental improvements (such as building parks in resource-poor communities, watershed rehabilitation including stream restoration, and other water-quality projects that can both contribute to local environmental quality for residents and broader environmental improvements). Other street-tree programs are part of projects that have multiple purposes, such as getting youth involved in after school activities (Los Angeles Conservation Corps interview; Northeast Trees interview).

NEIGHBORHOOD ORGANIZATIONS AND RESIDENTS
In addition to nonprofits, neighborhood organizations also take the initiative in planting trees. Civic groups and homeowner associations regularly ask municipal agencies to plant trees (Miami-Dade Public Works correspondence). To support resident-initiated activities in Los Angeles, the Office of Beautification (through the Department of Neighborhood Empowerment) offers neighborhood matching grants that can be used by neighborhoods for tree planting. The more involvement the residents have in the choice and location of trees, the more invested they become (Northeast Trees interview).

Finally, in addition to municipal agencies, nonprofits, and neighborhood groups, property owners of adjacent establishments have often a role to play in the provision of street trees. The ambiguity that surrounds the maintenance and responsibility of sidewalks, coupled with questions about liability and the accrued benefits and problems from street trees, have motivated some municipalities to request abutting property owners to agree before any new tree can be planted on the sidewalk. In Los Angeles, the city requires that abutting property owners commit to watering the trees before the city issues a permit to allow trees to be planted. This hurdle can penalize central-city neighborhoods with a high degree of absentee owners because the property owner, not a tenant, must agree to maintain the trees. This also can be difficult for commercial properties when the business owners lease their storefronts (Northeast Trees interview).

CONCLUSION

Street trees have historically served different functions. They add a natural element to high-traffic urban settings, provide aesthetic improvements, and contribute to the status and prestige of wealthy neighborhoods. Recently, advocates have also emphasized the regional environmental benefits of trees, and a number of groups are working to provide trees on city streets and to address scarcity in poor urban neighborhoods.

A high-quality urban forest is one in which street trees and other elements serve desired functions. These outcomes vary greatly in scale, from citywide cooling and storm-water retention to reducing an individual's energy bills. Trees offer greater benefits when they grow throughout the city, but without a public commitment, cities will not fund planting, regular maintenance, and long-term care. Individual preferences, immediate local benefits and concerns, long-term citywide benefits, the goals of the organizations involved in street-tree planting, and financing mechanisms for supply and maintenance all become factors in street-tree provision.

Numerous parties are involved in planting and maintaining trees. Trees are part of the right of way, an infrastructure element that affects the city, the region, the neighborhood, and the abutting property, and yet they are within the area over which property owners are responsible. This raises two important issues for public space and the development of public interests for shared spaces. The urban forest is a shared project, and the benefits accrue from its totality more than from individual trees. Nonetheless, residents' diverse interests are an important part of the urban forest's creation and upkeep because they are integral to its success and health and because different social groups have different needs and priorities. The urban forest also must be equitable. Providing trees and improving sidewalk aesthetics will require public investment. Unless cities direct more funds to poor inner-city neighborhoods, citywide benefits will be limited, and green visions will materialize only where residents can afford it.

V

Regulation and Control

Conflicts over competing uses motivate municipalities to regulate sidewalks. These controls—how they are worded and how they are enforced—raise delicate questions: In practice, whose interests have priority, and whose should have priority? Should comfort be a litmus test or even a factor when deciding which activities should be allowed or excluded? How can cities balance diverse interests when some interfere with others, both symbolically and physically? Will municipalities sacrifice justice when seeking vitality?

Since the nineteenth century, U.S. cities have sought to regulate their public spaces, but public-space controls have neither alleviated discomfort nor encouraged sidewalk activity. Even when regulations manage to change or "clean up" a small area, they do so at a cost. They move undesirable activities or exclude undesirable people, which has unintended consequences: it can shift troubling activities from one place to another with fewer controls, or it can deaden a sidewalk stretch by unintentionally eliminating the good with the bad.

Because public spaces come with a presumption of openness, regulations require justification. In searching for control, neighborhoods often begin to equate disorder with danger, as we explore in chapter 10. Visible sex work is an example. It conflicts with the image of a desirable and safe neighborhood, and the associated effects cause direct discomfort. But the genuine conflicts between those who use the sidewalks to procure business and those who want to eliminate this business do not make the sidewalks dangerous. Nevertheless, invoking danger helps solidify a "problem" that can be eliminated, but it also reduces the discussion about more complicated social conditions and alternatives. Since absolute control of public space is impossible, even if the incidences of panhandling or sex work decline, the perception that there is a problem might not. If public spaces appear more dangerous, whether or not they actually are, intervention becomes justified.

Acknowledging that those who use sidewalks for economic survival or daily subsistence should have access does not automatically define where these activities should take place. Some people and neighborhoods have the power to exclude undesirable uses, which leads areas with less influence to shoulder undesirable sidewalk activities. Public-space controls therefore pose a dilemma: How do we plan for public-space activities that some find unwelcome without privileging influential property interests over less influential areas? Allowing zones of relative tolerance in certain areas or containing undesirable uses protects some groups of residents and businesses better than others.

Cities have used numerous tools for controlling public spaces, but they lack a coherent framework, as we discuss in chapter 11. Municipalities depend on two constructs to govern sidewalks. First, the pedestrian as the primary user remains conceptually important in sidewalk regulation, and cities rely on a 'logic' of unimpeded movement (Blomley 2007a, 2007b). Few U.S. sidewalks, however, have so many pedestrians that other uses need to be suppressed. Obstruction of movement is not an objective assessment. Instead, "obstructive" activities are viewed as such if they negatively affect adjacent properties. Therefore, the second construct is that sidewalks are linked to abutting properties. Abutting interests govern sidewalk use, even when they are mediated through city policies.

Some city policies attempt to eliminate, contain, or prohibit controversial activities. They often confuse public space as a social entity (through which people develop relationships, articulate interests, and live shared and varied lives) with the conception of public space as a physical entity (which can be controlled). Municipal attempts to privatize sidewalks or purge them from the "unholy" and "unwashed" citizens make them ineffective places to educate urbanites about a city's various publics and issues. Cities respond to activities through a lens that assumes the primacy of movement and adjacent property rights, and other people's interests are negotiated through this vision. City actions are as much incremental reactions as proactive attempts to purify public space.

Diverse residents want to eliminate prostitution, public drug use, and visual disorder in the form of graffiti, litter, and abandoned property, and these concerns deserve public attention and discussion. Responding to such issues and local conflicts with increasing public-space controls, however, will resolve very little. It might divert attention from systemic problems, including entrenched poverty, lack of well-paid employment, and educational opportunities. It also divides residents into those who can be planned for and those who must be planned against, and in doing so, it creates more legitimate and less legitimate urbanites. Perhaps most important, however, municipal efforts to control public spaces are rarely effective. Cities need innovative approaches to integrate diverse activities and contradictory goals and continue the process of making space for multiple publics.

Controlling Danger, Creating Fear

Urban public spaces offer opportunities for interactions with unfamiliar people and unexpected experiences. For many, they seem to teem with danger, deviance, and vice. Responses to these concerns result in definitions of appropriate behavior and acceptable people, the identification of those who fit in and those who do not, and the justification of sanctioned controls.

People feel fear or cause anxiety as they go about their daily business. A homeless person on the sidewalk may cause discomfort. People of color walking in a white neighborhood may invoke fear. Unaccompanied children are seen to be at risk, and women are warned not to walk alone at night. Even middle-class men, who might feel the most freedom in the city, identify parts of the city where they will not go.

Still, danger attracts as it repels, and the unknown and possible brush with danger makes urbanity exciting. This can be true for both women and men, and some groups (such as adolescents) make friends and find privacy in public spaces (Wilson 1991; Chauncey 1994; Valentine 1996). Middle-class adults also find satisfaction in forays into illicit zones. Thus, absolute order does not appeal even to those who seek it.

The desire for safety and order poses fundamental challenges to public spaces, however. The process of seeking safety and order in effect (not necessarily by intent) gives some people more legitimacy to make claims than others. Some groups become those whose interests are being protected, and others those to be protected against. This dichotomy denies some members of the public legitimacy because they and their activities are defined as disorderly or dangerous. In disputes over sidewalk activities, people not connected to property are perceived as the intruders and therefore have fewer claims to an area's sidewalks.

While many urbanites agree with municipal agendas seeking to make streets and sidewalks safe, attempts to reduce discomfort may have also undesirable effects. The process of justifying the regulations helps create the problem that it purports to solve, and therefore striving for safety may instead help engender fear. Barricading streets to block transients and crime, for example, may result in the stigmatization of a neighborhood and cause further anxiety among residents. Thus, controls and regulations may work against their explicit outcome.

STREET DANGER AS A RECURRING THEME

Cities have historically been perceived as violent places that are filled with vice and other dangers but that also provide freedoms that facilitate desirable social changes. Much danger and diversity has been experienced on public streets and sidewalks. The danger that is associated with violent crimes has often been conflated with discomfort from prostitution, drunkenness, and drug use as well as incivilities that challenged social expectations.

In the aftermath of the Civil War and in response to social unrest and various incidents of disorder, municipalities enhanced their professional police forces (Monkkonen 1981). In the nineteenth century, police officers dealt mostly with public disturbances that were brought about by drunkenness, boisterousness, and minor public misconduct. Most arrests were of disorderly drunk men who were held and released the following morning. For police officers to retain their authority, residents had to believe that they were following impartial laws and were not simply tools of wealthy residents who wanted to control the activities of the poor. The legitimacy of the police came not from the law but from the legitimacy bestowed by those who had to follow the law (Winter 1993, 50–64). Behind policing strategies lay a conviction that ordinary citizens desired safe and orderly streets and that most people who used the streets were not inherently criminal. The worry that street crime was increasing was recurrent, and demand for more policing followed.

Although crime had identifiable victims and culprits, many public activities that caused concern were uncivil or disorderly rather than criminal (such as vices like street prostitution). As we have discussed previously, women became suspect and inherently a cause for concern when walking alone at night (Winter 1993, 173–189; Wilson 1991; Baldwin 2002).

Social distinctions were fragile and had to be maintained through daily repetition. Because of this, city streets became the sites of everyday politics for equality, and many have recognized the importance of these challenges to the moral order. As already discussed, a "minor" infraction of a social convention (such as an African American who refused to step off the sidewalk when near a white sidewalk user) was not an inconvenience but a threat that at times sparked riots because it signaled broader social disagreement. This incivility challenged social status and norms.

By defining what constituted uncivil or inappropriate behavior, middle-class residents could differentiate themselves as well as justify outside intervention, either of their own through preventive societies or by the government (Gilfoyle 1994). The children who were visible as they worked and played "became a subject for public hand-wringing" and reformers' intervention (Baldwin 2002, 593). Keeping children off the street became a defining aspect of middle-class culture, and children who played and worked in public became symbols of neglect who needed protection.

In the nineteenth century, as more people socialized on city streets, the night became strongly associated with crime and vice (Baldwin 2002). Based on a middle-class culture that was being built on the ability for people to separate themselves from the dark, dirty streets, residents feared violence but also a mix of danger and social impropriety. A separation of spheres developed in the nineteenth century and took physical form in the suburbs where residents could selectively engage in public realms. Commercial leisure became gradually common for both working- and middle-class residents, and the streets were increasingly left to working-class women and men.

Neither danger nor disorder prevented middle-class residents from frequenting areas seen as marginally proper. Indeed, the ability to cross that boundary became a source of middle-class pleasure. Vacations to Atlantic City, for example, demonstrated one's entrance to the white middle class, but these same vacationers sought danger and exoticism along the city's Midway. Visiting casinos, risqué shows, and African American nightclubs were another dimension of their newfound white middle-class identity (Simon 2004, 45–62).

Vice districts both challenged and upheld propriety. In the late nineteenth century, reformers attempted to contain visible prostitution (Gilfoyle 1994), and sex districts became a solution to pervasive vice. These districts often overlapped with ethnic neighborhoods such as Harlem in New York or Chinatown in Los Angeles, and they drew visitors from around the city. The policies meant to contain vice contributed to diversity in these districts, as all forms of perceived vice and deviance were separated from zones of respectability.

Such districts were not only centers of vice. Sex districts were also more tolerant of interracial and interethnic coupling. Some of this took place within the context of economic exchange, but in these neighborhoods, residents were more tolerant of different ethnic backgrounds. Ethnic diversity did not necessarily challenge social norms because racial differences were exploited, and white prostitutes could command higher fees (Wild 2005, 121–147; Mumford 1997). Nonetheless, these districts that tolerated vice and nonnormative relationships formed a boundary against which respectability was measured. These districts were troubling because they destabilized the very boundaries that they helped create and that white urbanites worked to maintain.

These moral boundaries defined people's appropriateness through their association with areas of the city and with the activities that took place there. The dangerous street was no place for women and children, and therefore by definition, those out on the street were not respectable. Deferential behavior or segregated space was necessary if a shared space like a streetcar or sidewalk had to be cooccupied. The boundaries of propriety were maintained by fear—fear of losing status for some, fear of violence for others—yet the fear was never strong enough to completely eliminate unsettling activities.

Efforts to contain vice highlight an important tension: some individuals' rights come into conflict with social norms, and this elicits regulation. Historically, however, challenges to discriminatory social relationships have led to a more just society, and perceptions of what is proper or improper change. In the battle over inclusion in public spaces, some claim participation as legitimate members of the polity, and this battle wages within the definitions of what constitutes public danger and disorder.

The Danger and Disorder Connection

Overlapping constructs of race, sex, danger, and deviance pervade urban discussions about public disorder and danger. Crime has generally been a salient urban issue. A significant body of literature has attempted to identify the causes of crime, the factors that affect increase or decrease in crime, and the effects of crime on different aspects of urban life (Ferraro 1994; Levitt 2004). Outcomes include decreased sense of well being, restricted activities, and influences on decisions such as housing choice.

Fear of crime is associated with crime rates, and researchers differentiate perceived risk (a cognitive assessment) from fear (an emotional response) when they explore the effects of crime and the sources of information about crime and danger (Lane and Meeker 2003). Perceptions of risk invoke fear, and people with different demographic characteristics have varying levels of fear of crime. Women, people of color, seniors, and urban residents fear crime more than those who do not fall in these categories (Miethe 1995). People of color report more fear of victimization and crime, but young men (who are most likely to experience violence) are not the most fearful, which suggests that many factors affect what is perceived to be risk and whether this translates into fear (Lane and Meeker 2003). As Rachel Pain (2001) has highlighted, the relationship between social identities and fear of crime has been dichotomized: young people are both threatened and threatening, people of color are both victims and offenders, men both provoke fear and are fearless, and women are both fearful and passive.

Fear and perceived risk affect urbanites in different ways and may lead people to utilize precautionary measures and strategies. These include adopting certain behaviors to avoid interaction; choosing specific routes, travel patterns, and public places over others; completely avoiding streets and activities deemed to be unsafe; and in some instances staying behind locked doors, barred windows, or even gated communities (Loukaitou-Sideris 2005). In general, fear makes people (particularly certain groups such as the elderly) avoid public spaces or use them less (Miethe 1995; Ferraro 1994; Loukaitou-Sideris 2006).

Urban critics such as Jane Jacobs (1961) have proposed that dense urban areas are safer because people watch what goes on and watchful residents control neighborhoods. Empirical evidence supports this idea, and in at least one city, population density was negatively correlated with violent crime (Christens and Speer 2005). Some land uses—including parks, playgrounds, and businesses—increased perceptions of community danger, but these were not significant when levels of crime were controlled (Wilcox, Quisenberry, and Jones 2003).

Danger and fear are problematic, but what causes fear is less certain. Criminologists explain that perceived risk and fear of crime do not represent "mathematical functions of actual risk but are rather highly complex products of each individual's experiences, memories, and relations to space" (Koskela 1997, 304). Fear is affected by the dynamics of physical and social settings, but it is also influenced by parental and societal warnings and media accounts (Loukaitou-Sideris 2005). Cities have tried to address street crime, but even decreasing crime rates have not resulted in commensurate reductions in fear (Silverman and Della-Giustina 2001). Urban residents learn about crime through the media, which focuses on high-profile events more than statistics, so even if the incidences of crime decline, a well-publicized event will cement danger in people's minds. Additionally, discomfort can contribute to feelings of danger, and reducing crime alone may not create a local environment that feels safe (Silverman and Della-Giustina 2001).

Although crime and fear of crime are problems, incivility is more prevalent than threats to safety or property. Incivilities—"infractions of the moral order that sustains public life"—can negatively impact the "quality of life," a notion that encompasses a variety of subjective factors that influence perceptions about well being (Dixon, Levine, and McAuley 2006, 187). Civility has important social functions. Respectful interactions "enable citizens to have rewarding social interactions, enjoy ontological and physical security and to develop social networks sustained by trust. These in turn support a wider social sphere characterized by peaceful coexistence, prosperity and inclusion" (Phillips and Smith 2003, 86). Incivility nonetheless is not the same as danger.

Even if they are not dangerous, spaces of travel expose people to incivility. In one study, three out of four incivility incidents were reported in "utilitarian" spaces including public transport (19 percent), streets (18 percent), sidewalks (12 percent), and supermarkets (10 percent). In contrast, incivility was less common in "expressive" public environments such as pubs and nightclubs (6 percent), beaches and parks (3 percent), sports venues (3 percent), and movie theaters (3 percent) (Phillips and Smith 2003). Surveys of transit riders waiting at bus stops in Los Angeles showed that people felt fear and that safety was a prominent concern, especially among women (table 11.1). Incivilities such as drunkenness, obscene language, and groping were commonly mentioned (Loukaitou-Sideris 1999). Kelling and Coles (1996) have argued that incivilities have increased in the last few decades as courts have privileged individual rights of people who are homeless or are loitering over those of communities seeking to control disorderly behaviors. However, with no benchmarks to measure previous levels of incivility, it is difficult to determine whether such incidents have increased.

According to Ralph B. Taylor (2001, 95–104), the "incivilities thesis" has taken five distinct paths that attempt to link disorder with crime:

- Fear of crime indicates a general urban anxiety and focuses on what might be behind the fear that people feel.

- Incivilities suggest that public agencies or neighborhood organizations have been unable to control areas effectively and therefore increase residents' risk of victimization.

- Residents express most fear when both incivilities and crime rates are high, but if one or the other is not, residents will be less fearful. This suggests that each is distinct but they interact.

TABLE 10.1

Problems that bus riders believe take place at bus stops (N = 212)

Perceived Problem	Responses		Total
	Men	Women	
Panhandling	87	94	181
	(48.1%)	(51.9%)	
Drunkenness	76	103	179
	(42.5%)	(57.5%)	
Vandalism	78	63	141
	(55.3%)	(44.7%)	
Obscene language	55	75	130
	(42.3%)	(57.7%)	
Drug use or sales	54	41	95
	(56.8%)	(43.2%)	
Verbal or physical threats[a]	42	53	95
	(44.2%)	(55.8%)	
Pickpocketing	45	48	93
	(48.4%)	(51.6%)	
Jewelry snatching	40	44	84
	(47.6%)	(52.4%)	
Robbery	38	35	73
	(52.1%)	(47.9%)	
Violent crime[b]	9	13	22
	(40.9%)	(59.1%)	

Source: Author's survey of bus riders in the ten most dangerous Los Angeles bus stops (Loukaitou-Sideris 1999).

Notes:

a. Physical threats are primarily groping.

b. Violent crime is primarily aggravated assault or murder.

- Wesley Skogan (1990) has explored the effects of urban disorder, arguing that disorder or incivilities can facilitate neighborhood decline.

- James Q. Wilson and George L. Kelling (1982) causally linked crime and disorder in their "broken windows" thesis, which suggests that disorder indicates that local control is weak, residents who are surrounded by disorder become increasingly hesitant to intervene or use public spaces, the withdrawal of residents from neighborhoods leads to decreased informal control and increased disorder, and eventually violent crime increases.

Wilson and Kelling's influential hypothesis justifies attending to minor civil offenses (such as panhandling, graffiti, and public drunkenness) and allows those who are ambivalent about prohibiting these activities to take action against them. Their "broken windows" hypothesis focuses on the role of both social and physical incivilities as a subject of inquiry and articulates connections that others have made (Lewis and Maxfield 1980). It has been the basis for community-policing strategies in cities such as New York, Chicago, Seattle, Baltimore (Kelling and Coles 1996), and Los Angeles.

Empirical evidence for the causal relationship between disorder and violent crime has been mixed. A 1990 national analysis of forty neighborhoods in six cities suggested that crime, disorder, and fear were associated (Skogan 1990), but a subsequent reevaluation of these data cast doubt on the original findings (Harcourt 1998). In the case of adult entertainment, officials in cities such as New York have claimed that their zero-tolerance policing practices reduced sex work; however, sex-industry changes that have decentralized it spatially and allowed online solicitation might also explain the decreasing size of urban adult entertainment districts (Ryder 2004).

Unlike Wilson and Kelling, who sought to establish a causal connection between incivility and crime, Skogan (1990) questioned whether incivilities and disorder contribute to neighborhood decline. This raises two questions: who is being uncivil to whom (that is, who generates disorder, and who must be protected), and in what ways do public spaces contribute to perceptions of disorder? The more complex question, however, is determining what lies behind perceptions of danger and disorder. Much incivility research has focused on observable elements (such as loitering groups of youth or men, people who are homeless, graffiti, garbage, and broken windows), and only recently have scholars attempted to evaluate fleeting incivilities (such as rude interactions) (Phillips and Smith 2006). Some have argued that incivility or disorder research is unproductively narrow because researchers tend to take a normative view that disorder is negative, assume a common understanding of what constitutes disorder, ask narrow questions about the effects of and responses to incivility, and study stereotypically "bad" neighborhoods. Phillips and Smith (2006) propose that we will better understand responses to incivility by focusing on incivility and not only on neighborhoods that appear to have high levels of incivility.

Reducing incivility, disorder, and crime appears to be a laudable objective because doing so improves urbanites' quality of life and sense of well being. When Sampson and Raudenbush (2004) asked "What makes disorder a problem?," however, they found that when visual disorder was held constant, neighborhood demographics (specifically a large number of low-income and nonwhite residents and visitors) caused people of different incomes and ethnicities to perceive the neighborhood as disorderly. The presence of African American men was also positively associated with perceptions of high crime rates (Quillian and Pager 2001).

Kefalas (2003) offered further evidence that the need for order stems from what Alain de Botton (2004) has termed "status anxiety"—the fear of losing what we have and seeing ourselves as worse off than others. She found that residents in a white, lower-middle-class Chicago neighborhood paid attention to removing graffiti, mowing unkempt lawns, and disrupting groups of loitering youth. Their attention to visual disorder was associated with a need to maintain the community, even though some residents would have moved to a suburb if they could have afforded it. Although residents maintained the physical environment, they were projecting the encroaching disorder on the low-income African Americans who lived nearby.

Municipalities respond to urbanites' fears of disorder by regulating, controlling, and eliminating feared elements and activities from public streets and sidewalks. They privilege the complaints of residents and business owners, often at the expense of other street users. Some wealthy citizens have ensured local security by gating neighborhoods, privatizing streets, and employing private guards for their protection (Newman 2001; Low 2003). Indeed, in recent decades, affluent communities around the country have sealed their streets and public spaces from outsiders. In low-income neighborhoods, as well, residents view public-space controls as their defense from gangs, drug traffickers, prostitutes, and other dangerous people (Leavitt and Loukaitou-Sideris 1994).

Some cities develop safe zones around tourist destinations (Neill 2001). Vice districts and tourist destinations serve similar functions: they let people know where to find entertainment. These containment techniques also attempt to protect tourists and others from those who are considered dangerous.

This search for order has targeted certain individuals (such as prostitutes, drug traffickers, and panhandlers) to protect others. The concentration of prostitution in vice districts or homelessness in skid-row areas helps hide undesirable individuals and their activities from other residents and visitors, but it does little for the people who live in neighborhoods where these activities are contained. Public-space regulations differentiate among different groups of sidewalk users but also have different effects on different neighborhoods.

DANGER, DISORDER, AND LEGITIMATE USERS

The United States has always had an ambivalent attitude toward activities such as sex work and drug and alcohol use, which are perceived as dangerous when they take place in public spaces. Because they are illegal and stigmatized, such activities make an area disorderly. In this section, we discuss primarily street prostitution, although the ordinances (those that established drug-abatement zones) that target individuals who repeatedly engage in drug use have similar effects. One effect is that street prostitutes who are defined as disorderly lose their status as legitimate public space users. As a condition of probation, women and men convicted of prostitution cannot enter the abatement zones without defending their presence. These individuals are prohibited. The presence of prostitution or drug sales in an area stigmatizes a neighborhood by association.

Maintaining public health has been the primary justification for prohibiting prostitution, but other reasons include protecting minors from being coerced into prostitution, preventing organized crime, protecting the women and men working as prostitutes, and protecting the sanctity of the family. In a few places (such as in the state of Alabama), prostitution is a loitering offense, and remaining in public places to engage or solicit another person to engage in prostitution or other deviate sex is prohibited. In most states, however, prostitution is prohibited outright, regardless where it occurs (Posner and Silbaugh 1996, 155–187).

Street prostitution comprises only a small part of the sex trade. It is the most dangerous form of sex work for the workers involved, and because of its visibility, it receives disproportionate attention from police officers and neighborhood residents. In many European countries, the sale of sex is not prohibited even if associated public acts are unlawful. In Spain, prostituting oneself is not criminalized, but pimping is, and in Britain, prostitution is not illegal although soliciting, running a brothel, procuring, living on "immoral earnings," and curb-crawling are (O'Neill and Barberet 2000). The regulations can be so onerous that it can be virtually impossible to avoid breaking the law in the act of selling a lawful service (Hubbard 1999).

In the case of prostitution, illegality justifies denying public-space users rights to protection and safety. Prostitution- and drug-abatement zones are intended to target repeat offenders, and in the early 2000s, numerous cities in Florida established "prostitution-free zones" that repeat offenders must avoid as a condition of probation. The first was established in Fort Lauderdale in 1995, and other cities such as Miami Beach followed, designating eighteen blocks of South Beach as a "hooker-free zone" (Moser 2001, 1101).

In the summer of 2003, Miami implemented "Prostitution Mapping," which was designed to eliminate prostitution (Miami 2004). The city worked with the police department to designate as prostitution zones four areas frequented by prostitutes. If someone is convicted of prostitution, the person can go to jail or, as a part of a probationary sentence, agree to stay away from the designated zone for three to six months unless they live, work in legal employment, conduct legitimate business, or engage in other personal affairs not related to prostitution. The person would also have to justify his or her reason for being in a prostitution zone—that is, the person must demonstrate that she or he has "legitimate business." Those who engage in prostitution regardless of whether they participate in the mapping program are subject to arrest and conviction.

Describing "Prostitution Mapping" as a best practice at the United States Conference of Mayors, Miami's mayor Manny Diaz was quoted as conflating the reduction of crime with improvements in the appearance of streets: "The mapping system is just one way Miami continues to work to reduce crime and improve the appearance of our streets and neighborhoods." He further suggested that cutting down on prostitution will reduce many other offenses: "By working to eradicate prostitution in the city, we are cutting down on the drug use, violence and other offenses that are tied to this one crime." Police chief John Timoney agreed: "We're trying to quite literally clean up the city aesthetically. We're trying to make it look safe, feel safe and be safe" (U.S. Conference of Mayors n.d.). By 2004, when Mayor Diaz gave the State of the City address, 500 people had been "arrested and mapped" and the program, which began in the Upper Eastside had been extended to Little Haiti, Flagami, and Little Havana (Miami 2004). The city drew on the "broken windows" hypothesis when it enacted the zones and argued that reducing visible disorder in the form of street prostitutes would reduce other crimes.

Antiprostitution ordinances differ from sit-and-lie ordinances that target homeless individuals. The sit-and-lie ordinances target activities. Because not everyone must sleep in a public space to survive, these ordinances address individuals categorically, but they do not bar individuals when they are not engaging in prohibited activities. In the case of drug-free or prostitution-abatement zones, individuals who have been convicted of these offenses are either prohibited outright from entering a designated zone altogether or, in other cases, prohibited if they cannot provide an explicit justification for their presence, such as paid work. Their legal public participation is restricted, and their right to simply walk, meet with friends, or be present on a certain street or sidewalk becomes contested. The basis for these ordinances and the sit-and-lie ordinances are similar in that they are designed to protect others' "quality of life" from the perpetuators of disorder.[1]

In the early twentieth century, people were defined as vagrants when they engaged in repetitive undesirable activity, and vagrants could be cited for vagrancy even if they were not engaged in an illegal activity at the time of the citation. In 1972, in *Papachristou v. City of Jacksonville*,[2] the U.S. Supreme Court held that vagrancy ordinances were unconstitutional and based its argument on the ordinances' history of addressing people's former relationships to work and their attempts to tie transitory people to the land. The logic that some people become vagrants has returned in prostitution-abatement ordinances, and individuals can be cited for a repetitive activity even if they are not engaged in an illegal action at the moment of the citation. The legality of such zones has been questioned (Moser 2001) because they effectively banish people who are engaged in street prostitution (Sanchez 2004).

Zones of safety engender fear of unsafe areas. Vice zones operate similarly and simultaneously create areas of relative tolerance where people know that they are allowed to seek sex. At the same time, criminalizing activities such as sex work and drug use concentrates these activities and stigmatizes the areas in which they occur.

Associating sex work with criminality endangers people who work in prostitution because they get less police protection and creates a sense that these women and men deserve violence. It also underlies the ordinances that curtail ordinary access to public space. Someone who engages in an illegal activity is no longer granted the same level of access to public participation.

Casting some individuals as illegitimate public-space users affects these individuals. Streetwalking can be dangerous because women work at night in public places, carry cash, and visit isolated places with strangers. Even if they record information (such as a license plate number) when a person victimizes them, they work in public spaces where they are in danger of retaliatory violence if they report the incident to the police. Even in countries where prostitution is legal, it is often stigmatized, and women who work in prostitution receive less protection from the police against victimization (O'Neill and Barberet 2000).

In an Urban Justice Center report (2003, 34–48) about street prostitution in New York, the women and men interviewed reported that they regularly were harassed and even cited by police officers when they were not working—for example, when waiting to have their hair done, when walking out of a store with groceries, or when talking with a friend. If someone was "a known prostitute in a known prostitution area," her daily activities became suspect, and simply being in public legitimated harassment. Women who worked on the streets rarely reported violence against them to the police because they knew that the police would do nothing for them and in some instances would not even take a report of the crime (Urban Justice Center 2003). At the same time, the stigma affects other areas of a prostitute's life. As one woman reported, she would rather work indoors because "it's safer. And I don't get to be seen by the cops, the neighbors, my family."

Women of color are disproportionately represented in street prostitution. Because both clients and managers prefer white and light-skinned women, other areas of the sex industry (such as strip clubs) have low informal quotas for women of color (Chapkis 2000). Transgender women also have few options in sex work and are more likely to work on the street (Urban Justice Center 2003). If the purpose is to help people leave sex work, the ordinances might be having the opposite effect. New York's attention to street offenses in the mid-1990s moved many street prostitutes off the streets, and men and women began to work inside. One of the unintended consequences of this shift was that many women began to see prostitution as more of a career rather than a way to make money temporarily, with implications for the length of time they work in this field and their ability to transition to other employment afterward (Murphy and Venkatesh 2006).

Residents often identify incivilities as undesirable public activities such as public drunkenness or prostitution. Examining attitudes toward alcohol drinking on public streets, Dixon, Levine, and McAuley (2006) asked interviewees why an alcohol ban was enacted. Participants referred to situational improprieties and not fear of or reduction in crime. Analyzing campaigns against prostitution in two cities and the grievances put forth by neighborhood residents in newspaper articles, Weitzer (2000) found that the tangible neighborhood incivilities, not morality or social or economic factors, drove these anti-street-prostitution campaigns. Residents complained about disorderly conduct (arguing, fighting, public sex, and public partying), unhygienic and unsightly paraphernalia (condoms and syringes), public-health risks, harm to children (through public sex, direct solicitation of children, and children's observation of solicitations), and harassment by customers of women who did not engage in sex work. These negative outcomes were believed to hurt local merchants and contribute to neighborhood decline (Weitzer 2000).

Such conflicts are not solely about neighborhood disorder or decline. Campaigns to clean streets and sidewalks and to keep neighborhoods safe from bad neighbors are also about defining a cause by which people can define their identity (Bauman 1999). Prostitution creates a bad neighbor and causes panic about urban life. It gives residents a cause that they can unite around to define propriety against another group whose members are conceived of as outsiders.

In the neighborhood antiprostitution campaigns that Weitzer (2000) examined, activists framed the problem of neighborhood incivilities as one where the community was besieged by outsiders (prostitutes, johns, pimps, and prostitute-rights organizations). To these activists, prostitution was not a victimless crime but harmed residents' quality of life. Although on occasion neighborhoods do fight against indoor prostitution establishments, the majority of activism is typically against street prostitution (Weitzer 2000). Phil Hubbard (1998) found that community protests in Birmingham (United Kingdom) constructed ideas about community in opposition to immoral prostitutes. By giving primary consideration to the desire of one part of the community—residents and business owners—and drawing on fears of strangers and outsiders, people engaging in street prostitution have lost their status as legitimate public actors who can engage in public spaces on the same terms as others. Those connected to property are legitimate, and the stranger-resident dichotomy defines who is disorderly and against whom civility can be measured.

Policing prostitution has been expensive for cities. Each year, over 90,000 arrests are made for prostitution-law violations, and more people are arrested under loitering and disorderly conduct laws. About 90 percent of these arrests take place in cities. The largest sixteen U.S. cities spent an average of $7.5 million on enforcing such laws in 1985, but more than twenty years later none of this appears to have reduced street prostitution (Weitzer 2000, 159–160). At best, regulations and their selective enforcement might contain street prostitution in a particular area or displace street prostitution away from an area (Weitzer 2000, 160). Even in Nevada, where brothels are legal in counties with low populations, street prostitution flourishes in Las Vegas and Reno, where it is prohibited (Weitzer 2000).

In summary, incivilities and vice in public spaces generate urban anxieties and conflicts over sidewalk use. Movements against street prostitution and other vices are fights over the boundaries of respectability, where the identities of "respectable" citizens are counterpoised against the identities of those who deviate from social norms. Those who are not connected to property are more likely to be defined as outsiders and lose status as legitimate public space users.

CONCLUSION

Fear pervades urban life and public spaces. Sidewalks, like other public spaces, entail the possibility of danger and even violence. They can be disorderly and expose people to uncomfortable encounters. For this reason, cities and urban residents have attempted to minimize disorder by legislating certain uses and users away from public sidewalks. Defining legitimate public activities is also a form of deciding legitimate public actors.

In attempting to make sidewalks orderly, comfortable, and safe, municipalities face two problems. They run the risk of eroding the public sphere by justifying ordinances that deny some people's rights to increase other peoples' comfort. The critical, underlying questions are what constitutes "excessive" or "normal" and who gets to define it. Second, the process of achieving safety may magnify fear by creating a vicious circle. Fear can encourage behavioral modifications that discourage public-space use, further making public spaces appear more dangerous because they are less familiar. In addition, withdrawing from public space leads to fewer eyes on the street and therefore more danger. In the process of protecting themselves, urban residents become more scared of the city they inhabit.

If disorder instigates discomfort, and suggests something is wrong, then we *ought* to be having a discussion about the moral order that governs our public daily life. If an underlying cause of discomfort is the violation of "moral rules that govern social relations in public," then the explicit discussion should be about these rules and their beneficiaries (or victims) (Dixon, Levine, and McAuley 2006, 187). In diverse cities, the individual rights of some to participate in public spaces might indeed violate others' sense of comfort. This is certainly true on urban sidewalks that urbanites must learn to share.

Municipalities in Control

Few cities have a coherent framework for governing sidewalks.[1] Because sidewalks are provided and maintained as transportation facilities, cities are authorized to control other activities that may take place on them. A city's objectives in providing and regulating sidewalks might appear to be obvious. A city's economic interests—growth and development—encourage public-space controls that support an economic-growth agenda (Peterson 1981; Logan and Molotch 2007). This interest in public-space controls is present even when the underlying economic concerns shift. After examining regulations that were intended to control homelessness, for example, Feldman (2004) argued that municipal ordinances reflect a shift from a concern about production to a concern about consumption.

In some districts (such as business improvement districts), interested parties control defined public spaces to benefit a subset of users and to exclude some people. Indeed, privatized spaces have long been designed by their private owners to be accessible to users who are categorically, if not personally, known. Municipal governments often borrow some of these "hard" and "soft" control practices (Loukaitou-Sideris 1993) to control sidewalks in certain neighborhoods. Hard control practices (regulations, laws, and policing) have been visible and controversial, but soft control practices (designs and landscapes that gentrify or deemphasize the sidewalk) also help attract certain sidewalk users and filter out others.

Privatization implies a coherent system for regulating sidewalks and street networks—one that intends to make spaces function more like private spaces. Privatization is more evident in some city areas (those associated with "prime" commercial space and economic activity) than others. It generally is hard to identify an integrated framework of sidewalk control that applies citywide, and privatization would not accurately describe it. Nevertheless, municipal policies and ordinances assume a link between sidewalk space and abutting property interests—particularly those properties that are engaged in economic activities. Rather than incorporating a vision for a desirable "public" as privatized spaces do, most policies simply associate an area with the abutting properties.

In this chapter, we discuss some of the strategies that cities use to govern public spaces. We draw on (1) a survey of the municipal codes and general plans of the ten largest California cities (Los Angeles, San Diego, San Jose, San Francisco, Long Beach, Fresno, Sacramento, Oakland, Santa Ana, and Anaheim) and (2) research on the five cities discussed in preceding chapters (Los Angeles, Seattle, Boston, Miami, and New York). In studying the California survey, we evaluated the municipal codes and general plans for regulations that affected sidewalk use and categorized them by issue (such as vending, panhandling, use by abutting businesses, and public protest). Because uniform information about sidewalks was not always available, we also interviewed planners and public works officials.

SIDEWALKS AS AN INTERMEDIARY ZONE

Municipal policies that govern sidewalks are fragmented. Sidewalks are part of a public roadway system, and people have the right to use them. Nevertheless, their maintenance is the responsibility of both the city and the adjacent property owner. This creates ambiguity, but also helps explain why abutters' concerns are privileged.

The ten California cities examined here have basic requirements for providing sidewalks. Sidewalks are required with new developments, and cities set minimal standards. As shown in table 11.1, the minimum pedestrian right of way is typically four to five feet, with a total right-of-way sidewalk requirement usually ranging from eight to ten feet to give space

TABLE 11.1
Sidewalk standards by municipality

City	Minimum Number of Feet	Commercial Minimum Number of Feet	Designated Pedestrian Areas
Anaheim	4	b	Yes
Fresno	4	8 to 10	Yes
Long Beach	4	8.5 to 10	Yes
Los Angeles	5	10	Yes
Oakland	6	b	Yes
Sacramento	4.5	6	Yes
San Diego	5	10	Yes
San Francisco	4	a	Yes
San Jose	4	10	Yes
Santa Ana	5	8 to 10	Yes

Notes:
a. No standards available from planning, zoning, engineering, or public works departments.
b. No standards available from planning departments.

for landscaping. In some cities, the minimum is the only standard.[2] In Long Beach, for example, the municipal code requires that a sidewalk be provided along each side of the street, and new developments must minimally provide four-foot sidewalks (Long Beach Municipal Code n.d.).

Many of the cities surveyed, however, have developed extensive guidelines to provide more pedestrian-friendly public environments. San Diego, for example, has published a *Street Design Manual* to guide street and sidewalk design (San Diego 2002), and in the "urban parkway" design alternatives, sidewalk width can be as wide as twenty feet for the sidewalk and landscaping strip. In the Los Angeles General Plan, sidewalk widths including a landscape strip range from five to seventeen feet (Los Angeles 1999). The San Francisco General Plan specifically discusses pedestrian-oriented policies (San Francisco 1995). When cities designate

pedestrian-oriented districts, they intend sidewalks to accommodate outdoor seating and require specific elements, including specialty paving, more
extensive and varied landscaping, and designed news racks, trash receptacles,
and lampposts.

Although cities envision sidewalks as interconnected transportation
systems and only some as specific destinations, in each city we surveyed,
the abutting property owners are responsible for sidewalk maintenance and
have to keep sidewalks clear of obstructions. This clearly attaches the sidewalk to the abutting property.

Municipal responsibility about sidewalks does not disappear, however.
After they learn about a problem, cities are liable for accidents that occur on
the sidewalks. Municipal authorities can make the property owner repair the
sidewalk, or they can repair sidewalks and assess the cost to the adjacent
property owners. Because they could be held liable, regardless of who is responsible, cities make temporary improvements to sidewalks to reduce the
risk of accidents. When street-trees damage sidewalks, cities pay for repairs.[3]

Liability is not a minor concern. Trip-and-fall ·accidents are the most
common sidewalk claims brought against municipalities. In Los Angeles, approximately 600 to 700 claims are filed each year, but the city is not always
liable. Even in small cities, such as West Hollywood (which is two square
miles), twenty-four claims were filed in 2001.

From 1911 to 1978, Los Angeles property owners were responsible for
the upkeep of sidewalks. In 1978, the city took over the responsibility for
upkeep but ran out of money for repairs after two years, when it sought
unsuccessfully to make property owners repair sidewalks. The city initiated
a street-improvement project to maintain its streets and sidewalks, but
according to one official, limited funding for the program has meant that
the city is between forty and sixty years behind in street and sidewalk
repair.[4]

SIDEWALKS AND THE PROPERTIES ABUTTING THEM: A GOVERNING FRAMEWORK

Cities use multiple strategies to govern sidewalk behavior, including local
ordinances, development incentives, land regulations, and design practices.

In commercial districts, cities collaborate with private entities or develop public-private partnerships with business associations and corporations.

Cities draw on four primary control strategies. They deemphasize public sidewalks by developing and encouraging developers to build introverted spaces and walkways. They privatize sidewalks by facilitating business improvement districts and fencing. They beautify or gentrify neighborhood districts with an emphasis on sidewalk uses such as street cafés, bakeries, flower shops, and public art. Finally, they enact land-use strategies and regulations aimed to contain activities in specific areas or constrain the manner they take place. As table 11.2 indicates, all ten California cities use some of these strategies to control their sidewalks.

These strategies suggest that that there is a guiding relationship even if a coherent governing structure for sidewalk control is absent.[5] Cities use these techniques in different combinations with variable objectives. Although mechanisms differ, each strategy primarily considers the interests of abutting properties. No multifaceted public realm is envisioned or planned for.

DEEMPHASIZING SIDEWALKS

Urban sidewalks appeared disorderly when central cities were facing economic decline and losing both sales-tax revenues and corporate offices to outlying suburban areas in the 1960s and 1970s. In the late 1970s, municipal governments in many U.S. cities began encouraging privatized public space by turning over its production, management, and control to the private sector and giving incentives to developers to provide public spaces. As downtowns were rebuilt in the 1980s and 1990s, developers designed plazas, shopping paseos, and galleries that were open for public use (Loukaitou-Sideris 1993). Developers and municipal planners considered such plazas amenities for downtown workers, making downtowns enjoyable for users who did not want to confront the presumably dangerous streets.

Plazas and other privately provided public spaces avoid the street. Design decisions turn private plazas inward and orient them away from the sidewalk. Design techniques include enclosing the plaza with walls that hide and protect plaza users from sidewalk denizens, using blank façades to separate private from public spaces, and placing major entrances to plazas off

Table 11.2

Sidewalk control strategies in California cities

Strategy	Means of Control	California Cities
Deemphasis of sidewalks	*Design:* Drastic separation of sidewalk from surrounding space (such as sunken plazas, skywalks, and enclosing walls)	Los Angeles, Sacramento, San Diego, San Francisco
Gentrification and beautification of sidewalks	*Regulatory ordinance:* Designation of pedestrian-oriented district *Land-use strategy:* Allow only specific land uses *Landscape design:* Create upscale streetscape	Anaheim, Fresno, Long Beach, Los Angeles, Oakland, Sacramento, San Diego, San Francisco, San Jose, Santa Ana
Privatization of sidewalks	*Enabling legislation for business improvement districts:* Private security *Design:* Fencing	Fresno, Oakland, Los Angeles, Sacramento, San Diego, San Francisco, San Jose
Taming sidewalk behavior	*Regulatory ordinances:* • Containing activities to particular districts (such as vending) • Prohibiting stationary activities (such as sitting, sleeping) • Requiring activity permits (for parades, demonstrations, special events) • Regulating activities (such as panhandling, alcohol consumption)	Anaheim, Fresno, Long Beach, Los Angeles, Oakland, Sacramento, San Diego, San Francisco, San Jose, Santa Ana

private parking structures rather than off the sidewalk. These efforts negate the public environment and deemphasize the sidewalk as a connecting element between a plaza and other urban spaces.

Underground and overhead spaces—sunken plazas and skywalks—also distance their users from the street. This has created what Trevor Boddy calls the "analogous city" (Boddy 1993) or a city of contrived urban spaces that keep out the poor and undesirable. Because private plazas, skywalks, and other similar spaces are not intended to serve all urbanites (on the contrary, they are designed to separate people), critics have condemned them as exclusive and highly controlled (Sorkin 1992; Loukaitou-Sideris and Banerjee 1993).

Sunken or elevated plazas are common. Some plazas in California (such as Seventh and Fig, Security Pacific Plaza, and California Plaza in downtown Los Angeles; One Hundred First Plaza and Crocker Center in San Francisco; and Horton Plaza in San Diego) separate their consumers from the nuisances of public sidewalks (noise, traffic, and other people) (Loukaitou-Sideris and Banerjee 1998).

Skywalks also give pedestrians alternatives to the sidewalk. In downtowns throughout the United States, cities such as Minneapolis, St. Paul, Detroit, and Cincinnati have built pedestrian bridges to connect new high-rise towers into a network that lead people from their underground garages to their office cubicles without having to set foot outside.[6] Although initially touted as a means to protect users from the snow, sleet, and ice of harsh northern climates, skywalks quickly appeared in cities with mild weather, including Miami, Dallas, Charlotte, Los Angeles, San Francisco, and Santa Cruz. In Los Angeles, skywalks interlink parts of the downtown core around the Bonaventure Hotel.

In downtown San Francisco, the skywalks of the Embarcadero protect upscale pedestrians from the street's dangers by offering an exclusive array of retail services above ground. These second-story corridors, often aligned with retail shops and services, offer a "surrogate street" (Whyte 1988) that retains some desirable public elements but screens out undesirable or unsafe components. From the city's perspective, these techniques can have both positive and negative effects. They shield some people from others, but

Sunken downtown plaza, Seventh Street and Fig Plaza, Los Angeles, California, 2002.
Photograph by Anastasia Loukaitou-Sideris.

Downtown skyways, Los Angeles, California, 2003. Photograph by Renia Ehrenfeucht.

they also can have a "deadening effect" on sidewalk life and may contribute to the decline of street-level retail and property values, an outcome counter to a city's interests (Robertson 1993).

PRIVATIZING SIDEWALKS

Privatized plazas and alternative pedestrian routes are possible only for large developments and buildings. Many residents and visitors enjoy sidewalks that are lined with small businesses and the sense of urbanity that a street offers. In the 1990s, private-public space controls were extended to the sidewalk within specific business improvement districts in an attempt to rebuild a textured urban core. BIDs are public-private partnerships that are enabled by the state, enacted by municipal governments after petitions from property owners, and governed by the city's regulations and a governing board (Houstoun 1997, 21).[7] Property or business owners within such districts pay additional taxes or assessments that are returned to the association to spend on services or capital improvements (Houstoun 1997). Municipalities sometimes provide seed money to help spur BID development (Howard 2000). The city of Los Angeles, for example, encourages BID development by marketing the districts and by providing start-up funds and consultants to interested business groups (Dickerson 1999).

In the last twenty years, more than a thousand BIDs have been created in more than forty states, more than 120 of them in California (Sinton 1998; Muller 2006). Seven cities of the California survey have enthusiastically adopted BIDs, and four of the five cities we looked at in this book also have BIDs. Only Massachusetts has not enabled BIDs, but some business associations in that state told us that they thought BIDs would be useful. Los Angeles has become a BID hotbed, with over twenty active zones formed since 1995 and many more on the drawing board. This rate is paralleled in New York, and San Diego has a BID Council comprised of nineteen BIDs that presently include 12,000 businesses. The Council's Web site claims that San Diego's program is "the largest in California and the most active in the nation." San Francisco, Sacramento, San Jose, and Fresno have concentrated their BID efforts primarily in their downtown areas.[8] Oakland's first BID was established along Lakeshore Avenue on the edge of Lake Merritt.

The common services that are offered by BIDs are additional security, street cleaning and maintenance, and streetscape improvements such as specialty trash cans, benches, and landscaping.[9] BIDs are often interested in improving a limited public realm and eliminating sidewalk activities that are disruptive to business. Elizabeth Jackson, president of the International Downtown Association, attributes the popularity of BIDs to the "incredible effectiveness in cleaning up cities and reducing anti-social behavior" (quoted in Sinton 1998). Business owners and merchants want to clean up their sidewalks from perceived nuisances, which range from trash to unwanted people such as street vendors and panhandlers. Municipal governments are also content to pass the responsibility and cost of control to private hands and pockets.

Despite their popularity, BIDs have been controversial because of the additional level of control that cities allow private business associations to exercise over sidewalks and other public spaces. Private security guards, accountable only to their employers, patrol the sidewalks and informally welcome some users and discourage others. Although security guards must abide by laws, the increased attention that they pay to particular areas ensures that those areas are less comfortable for nontargeted users. In these cases, cities agree that abutting businesses should be able to determine what constitutes "unacceptable" behavior and who is desirable. In Los Angeles, the controversy reached the courts when twelve homeless people filed suit against three security companies and their employers for violation of their civil rights (Dickerson 1999).

Another form of sidewalk privatization comes through the fences that surround outdoor seating spaces that are adjacent to restaurants and cafés. Some cities require businesses to enclose outdoor seating, and California state law stipulates that alcohol can be served only in enclosed areas. In most California cities, many restaurants, cafés, and eateries enclose parts of their sidewalks. In downtown San Diego, for example, more than 100 fenced-off business areas are found on public sidewalks (Ford 2000).

Private security guards, Downtown Center Business Improvement District, Los Angeles, California, 2003. Photograph by Renia Ehrenfeucht.

Sidewalk cafés have been a celebrated part of urban life since the sidewalks of nineteenth-century Paris enticed residents and visitors with the urban vibrancy of their cafés, flower shops, and boutiques—all extending onto the sidewalk (Oldenburg 1989). Whereas in Paris the private space of the café blends seamlessly into the public space of the sidewalk, in U.S. cities, fences create an abrupt border. Indeed, critics have charged that cities are allowing private interests to extend their control over public space (Ford 2000). Staeheli and Thompson (1977, 33) describe an area on the Hill District near the campus of the University of Colorado, Boulder: "not only was the private space in front of the business ... clearly marked, but the fences that enclosed sitting areas posted signs that limited activity in the public space beyond. At first, the signs warned passers by not to sit on fences or tie the dogs to them. As time passed, however, the signs attempted to regulate behavior on the sidewalk and street. These signs warned against skateboarding, loitering, and other forms of 'inappropriate behavior.'"

In extreme cases, local governments actually pass the ownership of the sidewalks to the private sector. For example, in Las Vegas, the county has allowed some casino resorts to keep sidewalks in private hands instead of dedicating them to the public, hoping that the property owners will be able to control activities better than the county does (Blumenberg and Ehrenfeucht 2008).

BEAUTIFYING SIDEWALKS

When cities and businesses redesign spaces for a consuming public, they often target leisure consumers. Since the 1990s, municipalities have revitalized, beautified, and gentrified old commercial streets to draw upscale shoppers back into their jurisdictions. In their attempts to "turn around" decaying streets, many cities have reinvented their main streets around an entertaining shopping experience (Banerjee, Giuliano, Hise, and Sloane 1996).[10]

When cities develop pedestrian districts, they use ordinances and design interventions to create areas that are conducive to shopping and that have restaurants, coffeehouses, boutiques, bookstores, and other desirable uses. Cities also attempt to create arts districts that will support galleries, museums, and other complimentary activities. Architectural and landscape design creates a desirable atmosphere for the leisure consumer.

Cities are directly involved in these improvements by installing public art, street furniture, and decorative lighting; funding building façade improvements; and offering incentives to convert old warehouses into trendy restaurants and shops. Design guidelines can suggest a theme and ensure that development is consistent in scale and massing. The type of merchandise, parking rates, and atmosphere of luxury tend to discourage the nonconsuming public (or at least those who are less likely to become consumers). Design acts as a subtle but effective screening process to ensure consistency between sidewalks and abutting businesses and to extend the sidewalks as part of the abutting businesses.

The most acclaimed models of this strategy in Southern California are Santa Monica's Third Street Promenade and Old Town Pasadena's Colorado Boulevard, two street segments that are among the most popular commercial destinations in the region (Banerjee et al. 1996). Hoping to repeat the economic success of these two streets, the city of Los Angeles has designated pedestrian retail districts along Ventura Boulevard in the San Fernando Valley, Sunset Boulevard in Hollywood, and the Boardwalk in Venice, among others.

Proponents of these efforts have specific leisure consumers in mind and can threaten existing businesses. After the Los Angeles city council approved a plan to beautify more than four miles of Ventura Boulevard and limit allowable retail uses, existing business owners argued that they were being driven out of the area. The preliminary list of allowable retail businesses was expanded to include beauty salons, barber shops, pharmacies, and copying businesses (Kondo 2000). A $7.3 million plan for the renovation of the Boardwalk in Venice began despite resistance from merchants, street vendors, and street performers who worried the plan would gentrify the area and drive out some of its current users (Maher 1995; Gliona and Abram 1998).

Other cities in our survey have also beautified commercial street segments. Long Beach has gentrified Pine Avenue by inviting well-known retail chains (such as Crate and Barrel and Z Gallerie) and including a

Sidewalk improvement, Santa Monica Boulevard, West Hollywood, California, 2002.
Photograph by Renia Ehrenfeucht.

multiscreen theater complex. Sacramento has redeveloped a four-block area known as Old Sacramento with restaurants, shops, and a museum following a themed design that evokes the city's cowboy roots. San Diego's Gaslamp District has become a leisure destination with over eighty restaurants, clubs, theaters, and galleries. By pursuing strategies to gentrify streets, cities indirectly attempt to blend sidewalks with upscale retail and create a safe, urban experience.

TAMING SIDEWALKS

Cities have also pursued regulations that restrict unwanted activities. As we have discussed, cities enact ordinances that regulate sidewalk uses such as street vending, street homelessness, loitering, and panhandling (table 11.1), but they are limited in what they can prohibit. Without authority to determine what is permissible, cities instead draw on two land-use strategies to determine where, when, and how activities may occur. They segregate unwanted activities into separate districts and restrict stationary uses.

Because cities cannot eliminate most activities, they seek to contain locally undesirable uses in areas deemed more appropriate. Historically, most unwanted sidewalk uses were allowed in officially designated districts or indirectly sanctioned in certain low-income neighborhoods and immigrant areas where city officials turned a blind eye. Prostitution was limited to red-light districts (Howell 2000; Weitzer 1999), and social services such as residential hotels, shelters, and soup kitchens were concentrated in skid rows (Rossi 1989; Foscarinis 1996). Cities have attempted to relegate public protests to designated zones and to limit the time, place, and manner of speech and expressive activities. In the case of street vending, cities have established street vending districts or public markets.

When an activity occurs on the street, cities have drawn on what Nicholas Blomley (2007a) has referred to as "traffic logic," which assumes the primacy of unimpeded movement. Examples of sidewalk regulations from Seattle, Boston, New York, Miami, and Los Angeles are included in table 11.3. Cities put constraints on the manner in which activities are conducted rather than prohibiting activities outright, and many ordinances are designed to ensure that an activity does not interfere with walking.

Vending carts in MacArthur Park Vending District, Los Angeles, California, 2003.
Photograph by Renia Ehrenfeucht.

TABLE 11.3
Selected sidewalk ordinances in five cities

Boston Municipal Code	Los Angeles Municipal Code	Miami Municipal Code	New York Administrative Code	Seattle Municipal Code
Vending				
Chapter 16-2. Hawkers and peddlers: Requires a local license for vending produce, goods, wares, and merchandise; requires an additional permit for vending in a designated district	Chapter 4.2.42.00(m). Establishment and management of special vending districts: Allows merchandise and food vending by permit in special districts; currently no active districts in the city	Chapter 39-28: Prohibits food, beverage, and merchandise vending without a permit; special vending guidelines apply on certain streets	Title 20-2.27. General vendors: Requires a license for vending of items other than books, pamphlets, and magazines; caps the number of licenses issued Title 17-3.2. Food vendors: Restricts pushcarts to certain sidewalks and locations within the sidewalk	Chapter 15.17.005. Vending and display in public places: Prohibits the display or selling of goods, wares, merchandise, or services in a public place Chapter 15.17.010. Areas where mobile vending is restricted: Other than vending on foot of newspapers, pamphlets, and programs or when licensed at an event, prohibits peddling from a public place while walking, moving from place to place, or using a mobile cart or vehicle

Sitting and sleeping

16-19.1. Use of public grounds: Prohibits sitting or lying on grassed land, benches, and monuments in public grounds and gardens	4.1.41.22. Loitering—river bed: Prohibits camping, lodging, making or kindling a fire, washing or bathing, sleeping, laying any bed or any blanket, quilt, straw, or branches for the purpose of resting or sleeping thereon or remaining or loitering in the official bed of the Los Angeles River	37-3. Sleeping on streets, sidewalks, etc.: Prohibits sleeping on any street, sidewalk, or public place	Zoning ordinance 37-06. Nighttime closing of existing public open areas: Allows the Planning Commission to authorize nighttime closure of plazas, plaza-connected open areas, and residential or urban plazas if such closing is necessary for public safety, among other possible reasons	Chapter 15.48.040. Sitting or lying down on public sidewalks in downtown and neighborhood commercial zones: Prohibits sitting or lying on a public sidewalk or on a chair, blanket, stool, or other object placed on a sidewalk in the designated zones between 7 a.m. and 9 p/m/ (see also "Loitering")
16-12.2. Loitering: Prohibits loitering if it obstructs or endangers travelers	4.1.41.18. Sidewalks, pedestrian subways—loitering: Prohibits standing in or on sidewalks in a way that annoys or molests pedestrians or unreasonably interferes with pedestrians' free passage	No specific ordinances	No specific ordinances	Chapter 12A.12.015. Pedestrian interference: Prohibits obstruction in a public place of pedestrian or vehicular traffic, meaning to walk, stand, sit, lie, or place an object in a way that blocks passage by another person or a vehicle or requires another person or a driver to take evasive action to avoid physical contact

TABLE 11.3
(continued)

Boston Municipal Code	Los Angeles Municipal Code	Miami Municipal Code	New York Administrative Code	Seattle Municipal Code
No specific ordinances	4.1.41.59. Prohibition against certain forms of aggressive solicitation: Prohibits soliciting, asking, or begging in an aggressive manner in any public space; must remain at least 15 feet from bank entrances and ATMs	No specific ordinances	Title 10–1. Public safety: Prohibits aggressive soliciting, asking, or begging within 10 feet of an entrance to a bank or check-cashing facility during business hours and from any ATM machine	Chapter 12A.12.015. Pedestrian interference: Prohibits aggressive begging that intends to intimidate (meaning make a reasonable person feel fearful or compelled) another person into giving money or goods

Under the assumption that movement is the primary purpose of a street, cities have limited stationary activities and required vendors to move regularly. For example, the city of Anaheim has passed a law requiring pushcart merchants to change locations every ten minutes, and in 1994 the city of Santa Ana enacted an ordinance that prohibits food vendors from remaining in any location for more than thirty minutes (Nalick 1995). Supporters of these ordinances argue that they are necessary to ensure traffic safety and eliminate loitering—therefore keeping people in motion—as well as prevent unfair competition (Hernandez 1994).

Beyond vending, cities such as Los Angeles, San Jose, and Santa Ana have enacted restrictions on other stationary sidewalk activities. In these cities, individuals are prohibited from sitting, lying, or sleeping on any street, sidewalk, or other public way. Proponents justify these broad restrictions in the name of unimpeded pedestrian circulation.

Advocates for homeless people and for civil liberties argue that these laws allow the police to harass the homeless and violate their civil rights (Foscarinis 1996; Miller 1995; Millich 1994; Takahashi 1998; Mitchell 2003). Many municipal bans on sidewalk activities have been declared unconstitutional (Teir 1998), and this has furthered shaped the mechanisms or strategies by which control can be achieved. For many who are involved in keeping the streets free from obstructions, these laws and procedures simply regulate sidewalk behavior and focus on pedestrian movement as the purpose for sidewalks (Blomley 2007a, 2007b). Nonetheless, some argue that these regulations serve as a pretext for eliminating unwanted uses, particularly those by ethnic minorities and the indigent (Foscarinis 1996; Kopetman 1986).

CONCLUSION

No coherent framework of policies and ordinances governs urban sidewalk activities. Instead, cities employ techniques that regulate land uses and use design to make some activities more acceptable and to filter out others. Regulatory authority rests with multiple city agencies (such as planning and public works departments) that issue codes and guidelines for sidewalk design and uses. This fragmented regulatory authority results in varied—and sometimes contradictory—regulatory strategies.

Rather than offering a vision for an inclusive, diverse public realm, these strategies associate sidewalks with abutting properties, and cities take steps to ensure that property interests are met, even at the price of serving some people better than others. Many control techniques are implicit and occur outside the regulatory realm. They come about through building designs, street improvements, and the deferring of responsibility to private entities such as BIDs. Both hard control practices that use regulations and laws and soft control practices using design and landscaping ultimately determine the sidewalk's users and uses.

Revisiting Public Space and the Role of Sidewalks

What role is played by urban sidewalks in the early twenty-first century? After the 2001 World Trade Center attacks, Anthony Vidler argued that streets and sidewalks continue to be sites "of interaction, encounter and the support of strangers for each other; the square as a place of gathering and vigil; the corner store as a communicator of information and interchange. These spaces, without romanticism and nostalgia, still define an urban culture" (Vidler 2001, quoted in Mitchell 2003, 3).

But what do they define? Urban observers have interpreted the street as an important site of democracy, and this assumption needs to be further examined. At certain exceptional moments, people still take to the streets and feel united with those they find there. Common causes and concerns can bring people together, and urban sidewalks have provided the space for people to unite—whether to cope with a tragedy such as a terrorist attack or a beloved president's assassination, respond to violence, or demand the end of a war. Through these ephemeral acts, urbanites express grief or joy, insert group identities, and present demands to their government.

The more numerous daily sidewalk encounters are also important and continue to be a way for people to negotiate conflicting interests. Through these actions and reactions, urbanites live ordinary lives, debate issues of broad concern, and learn about others. Such activities are not uniquely public, however, and they also unfold in parochial and private realms. Nevertheless, the public realm of the sidewalk serves as a visible site for contestation and conflict. Despite a hundred-year preoccupation with turning the sidewalk into an orderly space for unobstructed movement, widely varying activities are still contested on these narrow strips.

As a conclusion, we briefly outline some critical questions about public space and the public sphere—questions about public spaces of the future and constructs about public space trends that need complementary or challenging explanatory frameworks. We then turn to the multiple actors who affect inclusion or exclusion from public spaces and the role of state intervention.

QUESTIONS

We need to know more about public relationships in a global, media-centric era. How important are public-space activities, and what effects do they have? How and where do people meet, learn about others, and make demands on their government? How do different urbanites understand public culture? What do they value? What do they fear?

Many scholars have offered useful directions for future thinking. Drawing from Sandercock (2003), we might ask how cities can better integrate immigrants, given that multiple public-space conflicts arise around vending and day-labor sites. Streets are shared spaces, and controls—formal and informal—are inevitable and necessary for an enjoyable and functional public realm. But from Mitchell we might ask, "what *sort* of order is best for the city—and for whom? Who will have the right to the city?" (Mitchell 2003, 228; italics in original). The controls we use and the logic behind them are also important, and drawing from Blomley (2007a, 2007b), we seek to understand the logic that underlies a city's approach to sidewalk use and the ways that it operates. Whose interests are served? Whose rights are protected? Who is being planned for, and who is being excluded? Following Phillips and Smith (2006), we might explore what makes incompatibilities incompatible. We could also shift the focus from studying public spaces to asking where and how people engage in activities considered public. How sidewalks relate to other spaces deserves further examination, as does the relationships among varying public institutions and the changing private and parochial realms.

Constructs

The moments of interaction that take place on sidewalks are complex and include more than the immediacy of the interaction. Crossing paths with people in different circumstances tells us about both the city and ourselves. Individually, we find that we accept poverty, feel powerless to change our or others' circumstances, or fear that we too might fall onto hard times. We might worry that problems that plague other parts of the city, the country, the world, or simply another neighborhood will encroach on us, and we may wish to render them invisible.

Conflicts over public encounters and interactions have been debated in numerous ways, and we discuss four here. Two influential frameworks are privatization and the claim for individual rights. The first describes a process by which public spaces become more like private spaces, and the second focuses on rights of individuals in public. Quality-of-life claims and safety are two frameworks that attempt to insert an experiential or emotional component. Both seek to explain tangible and intangible responses and violations, although safety also embeds an explicit public interest. All four frameworks are useful and help explain the complexity of public spaces.

Privatization

Privatization is an influential hypothesis that includes numerous distinct trends. It suggests a withdrawal from public life and an increased emphasis on privacy. As privately owned and managed public spaces have proliferated, public activities are associated with spaces that foster consumerism, such as malls, shopping plazas, and destination streets. To the extent that municipal governments contract out previously public services, give private entities control of publicly owned spaces, or regulate public spaces to compete with private public spaces, they participate in the process of privatization. Individuals participate by frequenting privately managed spaces and by selecting gated and other secured residential communities. Critics have argued that privatized public spaces threaten diversity and democracy by siphoning people and activities away from public sidewalks and toward more private and protected territories. Privatized spaces are nonetheless popular.

More generally, the public/private distinction has been fruitful for public-space scholars, but its limitations are equally great. Information about the world comes through public media such as the Internet, television, and radio but might be absorbed and experienced in private spaces. Conversely, private telephone conversations and other intimate interactions also take place in public. The public/private distinction seems decreasingly accurate because public and private actions intertwine and spaces mean different things for different people. As we have argued, however, the distinction is not irrelevant and should not be disregarded until we have a better formulation. We also need a more complex understanding of people's encounters in the wide variety of places that they engage with those outside their immediate circles.

RIGHTS

In contrast to privatization as a process, rights focus on individuals. Asserting rights allows for ranking claims to public spaces, and to some degree rights preempt other concerns. Specifically, rights are claims in the face of state action, and for this reason, they have received much attention by legal scholars. Defenders of access to public space have often drawn on constitutional rights—from freedom of speech to prohibitions on cruel and unusual punishment—to other legal defenses such as interpreting prostitution-free zones as banishment. Although rights preempt a city's regulatory ability, municipalities also adapt to constraints, reformulate their responses, and fine-tune their ordinances to achieve desired outcomes without violating basic liberties. Rights safeguard democratic practices and thus are critical but also limited. It is a meager victory to win the right to beg, to sit on a sidewalk, or to speak so that the audience can hear.

QUALITY-OF-LIFE ISSUES

When people appear disruptive or activities become unwanted, the problem contains both tangible and intangible elements. People become uncomfortable and may evoke "quality-of-life" claims. Indeed, much tension around the acceptable uses and users of sidewalks and other public spaces is generated because of such claims. The quality of urban life and space is more than a simple list of objective assessments, such as the quality of paving, number of street trees, or number of benches. Residents and urban planners make more vague "quality-of-life" claims based on subjective assessments of well-being, comfort, and safety. Rights are constraints against such claims. At times, however, privatization has allowed some people to seek spaces where they are more likely to feel comfortable.

The desire of individuals and neighborhood groups to enhance their quality of life and sense of well-being may have both positive and negative impacts on the openness and vibrancy of public spaces. Improving physical neighborhood characteristics, providing trees, and supporting businesses make neighborhoods more livable. But some people also interfere with others' sense of well-being, and the notion incorporates a significant degree of qualitative self-assessment. Because of this, quality-of-life claims may privilege the experience of those with more influence.

Although public-space providers listen and invoke quality-of-life concerns, this notion nonetheless poses significant challenges. Street trees, planters, decorative lighting, or sidewalk cafés may enhance some people's feelings of well-being, and conversely, graffiti, litter, panhandling, and street vending can diminish it. However, restrictions on vending and panhandling, for example, can hurt the well-being of those engaging in these activities, and physical improvement can also be used to determine who is welcome or not.

SAFETY AND SECURITY

Safety has become a quality-of-life concern, as well, but it has a legitimate public purpose. Local governments have the authority to take action to keep urbanites safe and secure. Safety can determine the type of activities that are allowed or prohibited, but often it is the presumption of a lack of safety rather than a clear presence of danger that guides state controls and actions. Articulating a concern for safety or security is powerful, nonetheless, and can have immediate effects. Event permits can be denied, cities can enact ordinances that prohibit panhandling in the evening, and loiterers get moved along. In the post 9/11 era, dangers can be generally evoked and often go unexplained. Demands for safe and secure public spaces usually trump other goals that involve their communicative, political, or social aspects.

ACTORS

All four constructs influence people's actions and claims. Each definable public-space issue involves many people who have multiple objectives. In some cases, the motivations of powerful actors may be easy to identify. Multinational corporations, for example, may want to avoid challenges to their labor practices or environmental violations. But why do the goals of one actor foster agreements among other actors with different goals? Why would the sanctity of a World Trade Organization meeting, for example, outweigh the dissenters' decision to disrupt the event, even when the dissenters draw attention to problems at a magnitude of human-rights abuses?

A partial explanation lies in the multiple scales that each public interaction embodies. Although many agree that poor work conditions are wrong and environmental devastation is unsustainable, the protest event also closes streets, disrupts daily activities of those who reside, work, or shop in the area, creates discomfort, and may even invoke fears for personal safety.

Cities and their municipal professionals—traffic engineers, city planners, building-and-safety officials—represent important actors in the determination and regulation of public-space uses. Cities try to mediate among incompatible uses on sidewalks and in other public spaces. Restrictions on the time, place, and manner of activities—words associated with First Amendment rights but appropriate for describing a variety of public-space controls—have been a primary technique for doing this. But activities are not always transferable to different times, places, and manners, and regulations meant to mediate can be prohibitive. Rights at the very least protect some aspects of basic subsistence and communication, but they do not provide a vision for a better way forward.

In recent decades, local groups—neighborhood councils, business improvement districts, and homeowner associations—have sought to define and control sidewalk uses and other neighborhood public spaces. Although some fear that civic engagement is declining, others look at such activities as hopeful indicators of civic renewal.

In response to the modernist top-down planning and destructive urban-renewal policies in the 1960s and 1970s, urban planners and designers have advocated for community-based planning and participatory design. Community-based visions have many positive outcomes. But to praise local actions as a true exercise of grassroots democracy overlooks who gets included and excluded from participation. Notions of neighborhood and community effectively privilege those who own real estate over those who do not own property. Even positive outcomes result in policies and programs that are more responsive to resident interests. Some neighborhoods also have more influence than others. Without acknowledging the need for a greater vision of equity, neighborhood-based responses will likely benefit more resource-rich than resource-poor neighborhoods.

Ultimately, the interplay of different actors over different public-space activities and rights hinges on the issue of inclusion and exclusion. Cities pass ordinances and selectively enforce them to prohibit or contain certain activities. They use hard control practices through policing to ban certain sidewalk users, as well as soft controls such as outdoor seating, landscaping, and other design details to encourage some users at the expense of others. Individuals or neighborhood groups seek to exclude other people and activities for many reasons. Residents may be personally uncomfortable but also fear property damage or economic loss from the stigma associated with another person.

These moments of public interaction reflect larger issues and debates. A lack of control and the inability to protect oneself from the intrusion of unwanted interactions, people, or knowledge—or exciting but rapid change or uncertainty—might motivate people to seek exclusion. Thinkers such as Jane Jacobs or William H. Whyte were comfortable in seeking exclusion of some through encouraging active use by others. But we respectfully disagree that exclusion should be the intent of an active public realm.

WHAT DO WE WANT FROM PUBLIC SPACES?

As planners, we cannot help but ask "What do we want from public spaces?" If we envision an engaging urban public realm, what would it look like? What spaces and policies might facilitate it?

As history shows, public spaces have never been just, access has never been universal, and systematic solutions for public spaces have never been meant to integrate the priorities of all users. Urbanites, nonetheless, have fought for justice, demanded access, and adapted themselves to urban life and space according to their interests. Although complete participation or access to public space has not and cannot be fully realized, Nancy Fraser (1992) tells us that societies that provide opportunities and places for contestation and conflict come closer to the ideal than those that seek a homogenized public sphere.

Anxiety and possibility intertwine in urban public spaces. Opportunity among unknowns has drawn people to cities. If we seek security to such a degree that we remove the possibility of chance encounters, spontaneous interaction with strangers, and conflict, we eliminate a quality for which we turn to public spaces. Public-space controls, in fact, rarely make people feel safer. On the contrary, the processes used to justify state action—narratives of danger and harm—might undermine our sense of well-being by amplifying incompatibilities among activities that ultimately we cannot and do not necessarily want to control.

The trend of the last decades has been to segregate, contain, and enclose uses, homogenize urban form, and prohibit anything that falls outside a narrow cadre of activities. In a post-9/11 era, this is not likely to change, yet as residents and urban designers and planners, we need to be more vigilant to ensure that sidewalks remain accessible and open, even if this means some potential danger and conflict. Municipal regulations and sidewalk design must balance the needs of a diverse public, and people need to be able to integrate without assimilating.

Attempts to design and regulate sidewalks must balance competing, even incompatible activities. We are challenged with formulating and envisioning a just city. This requires acknowledging the complexity of the task ahead—the real incompatibilities, the unpleasantness we advocate for, the uncertainty that most might feel but few want to live with—but urbanites are up to it. The passion that cities invoke will accept nothing less.

NOTES

CHAPTER 2

1. Sidewalks were mentioned in the Laws of the Indies, ordinance 115, which implies that sidewalk planning was familiar in Spain in the late sixteenth century (Crouch, Garr, and Mundigo 1982).

2. In the early 1880s, improvements were accepted by a resolution that was made after completion and recorded in the city's *Compiled Ordinances and Resolutions* (vol. 2, *1878–1884*; vol. 3, *1884–1887*); resolutions 216 (1884), 309 (1884), 311 (1885); ordinances 176 Old Series (O.S.), 3052 New Series (N.S.), 6811 N.S., 6825 N.S., 8450 N.S., 10382 N.S., 12830 N.S.

3. *Compiled Ordinances and Resolutions* (vol. 2, *1878–1884*; vol. 3, *1884–1887*; vol. 4, *1887–1889*); ordinances 176 O.S., 3052 N.S., 6811 N.S., 6825 N.S., 8450 N.S., 10382 N.S., 12830 N.S.

4. *Marini v. Graham*, 67 Cal. 130, 132 (1885).

5. Ordinances 55 O.S., 56 O.S., 163 O.S., 203 O.S., 244 O.S., 253 O.S., 288 O.S., 985 N.S., 6387 N.S., 12026 N.S., 12556 N.S., 14041 N.S., 16449 N.S., 19553 N.S., 41903 N.S.

6. Los Angeles City Countil minutes (vol. 15, pp. 105, 123, 419; vol. 21, pp. 263, 331, 353, 401); ordinances 55 O.S., 56 O.S., 253 O.S., 4790 N.S.

7. Los Angeles City Council minutes (vol. 15, pp. 105, 123, 419; vol. 21, pp. 263, 331, 353, 401); ordinances 55 O.S., 56 O.S., 253 O.S., 4790 N.S.; Los Angeles City Council minutes (vol. 15, pp. 419, 753–754; vol. 19, p. 328; vol. 21, pp. 263, 353); ordinance 163 O.S.

8. Ordinances 1132 N.S., 4833 N.S., 4990 N.S., 6189 N.S., 26595 N.S.

9. Ordinances 1642 N.S., 4833 N.S., 19704 N.S., 19385 N.S.; Los Angeles City Council minutes (vol. 80, p. 571).

10. Los Angeles City Council minutes (vol. 26, p. 772); petitions 778, 789 (1888).

11. Police Judge reports (1898); Police Department Annual Reports for the years ending June 30, 1912, June 30, 1913, June 30, 1915, and June 30, 1916.

12. Today sidewalks continue to be maintained and often provided by abutting land owners, even though municipalities are perceived as being legally responsible for them.

CHAPTER 4

1. For African Americans in the early days of the republic, the Fourth of July celebration did not hold much meaning. Freedom was celebrated through an alternative calendar of feasts that related to their own African past and culture (Fabre 1994). Such celebrations were initially held secretly in black churches but eventually became more public, took to the streets, and offered a counterceremony to mainstream Fourth of July parades (Regis 1999, 493).

CHAPTER 6

1. This description of the 2000 Democratic National Convention in Los Angeles was drawn from Alvord and Woodyard (2000), Purdum (2000), Woodyard and Alvord (2000), and Teachey (2000).

2. The discussion in this section is drawn from Ehrenfeucht and Loukaitou-Sideris (2007).

3. *Hague v. Committee for Industrial Organization (CIO)*, 307 U.S. 496 (1939).

4. *Shuttesworth v. Birmingham*, 394 U.S. 153 (1969). This case challenged the constitutionality of a Birmingham, Alabama, ordinance that required a permit for street parades or demonstrations and required those seeking a permit to disclose the purpose of the demonstration. According to the ordinance, the government could refuse a permit on the basis of possible threats to public welfare, health, decency, safety, peace, good order, morals, or convenience. Using this ordinance, the city police arrested participants marching in a peaceful demonstration on Birmingham sidewalks and protesting the denial of civil rights to African Americans (Janiszewski 2002).

5. *Forsyth County, Georgia v. Nationalist Movement*, 505 U.S. 123 (1992).

6. *United States v. Kokinda*, 497 U.S. 720 (1990).

CHAPTER 7

1. This section was drawn from Ehrenfeucht and Loukaitou-Sideris (2007).

2. Interview with Sean Basinski, director, Street Vendor Project, New York, October 31, 2005.

3. Interview with Tom Cusick, president, Fifth Avenue Merchant Association, New York, October 31, 2005.

4. This number was estimated by Sean Basinski, director of the Street Vendor Project. Others believe that the number of vendors in New York City is possibly 14,000 people.

5. For example, vendors of print material are protected by the First Amendment.

6. Interview with Jen Hensley, assistant vice president, Alliance for Downtown New York, October 21, 2005.

7. Interview with Mark Wurzel, general counsel, Grand Central Partnership, New York, October 24, 2005.

8. Interview with Gary Harris, chief investigator, City of Los Angeles Bureau of Street Services, November 10, 2005.

9. Petitions should contain the signatures of at least 20 percent of business owners and 20 percent of area residents within a 500-foot radius of a proposed vending area.

10. Interview with Joe Colletti, executive director, Institute of Urban Research and Development, Los Angeles, November 30, 2005.

11. Interview with Sandi Romero, owner, Mama's Hot Tamales, MacArthur Park, Los Angeles, August 12, 2006.

CHAPTER 8

1. The term *skid row* was coined from a road that was lined by lodging establishments for migratory men in late nineteenth-century Seattle. The road was a path for timber companies that skidded logs down the hill to the waterfront for shipment (Ford 1998).

2. The origin of the word *hobo* is not confirmed. Some believe that it comes from the greeting "ho-boy" or the term "hoe-boy," which meant "farmhand," but other interpretations also exist.

3. *Papachristou v. City of Jacksonville*, 405 U.S. 156 (1972).

4. For chapter 8, we interviewed twenty-five city officials, homeless service providers, and business association representatives in Seattle, Boston, and Los Angeles between October 2005 and September 2006. In each city, the homeless service representatives were from shelters. The business representatives were involved in a business improvement district in Los Angeles and Seattle or an official business association in Boston, which did not have BID enabling legislation. The city officials that we interviewed dealt directly with homelessness programs and code enforcement. To ensure that respondents could discuss the issues honestly, we include no identifying information. To allow comparisons,

the references in the chapter refer to the city and the type of organization the interviewee represented.

5. *Jones v. Los Angeles*, 04-55324 (April 2006).

CHAPTER 9

1. Interview with Northeast Trees, Los Angeles, July 19, 2006; interview with Los Angeles Conservation Corp., executive director; interview with Citizens for a Better South Florida, director of the Community Science Workshop, untaped, September 28, 2006; interview with Operation Green Leaves, Miami, untaped, October 24, 2006.

2. Interview with Los Angeles Bureau of Street Services, forester with the Urban Forestry Division, Department of Public Works, Los Angeles, August 16, 2006.

3. Interview with TREEmendous Miami, September 8, 2006.

4. Interview with Miami-Dade County Department of Environmental Resource Management, September 8, 2006.

5. Interview with TreePeople, Los Angeles, Forestry Division, August 25, 2006.

6. Interview with Los Angeles Bureau of Street Services, arborist with the Urban Forestry Division, Mar 23, 2006.

7. Email correspondence with Miami-Dade County Public Works Department, Right-of-Way Aesthetics and Assets Management Division, June 13, 2006.

8. Interview with Citizens for a Better South Florida, Miami, education manager, October 24, 2006.

9. Interview with Los Angeles Conservation Corp., conservation programs director, September 1, 2006; interview with The Grove Treeman Trust, Miami, November 4, 2006.

10. Interview with Parks for People, a division of the Trust for Public Land, Los Angeles, August 17, 2006.

CHAPTER 10

1. Seattle drew on a similar logic when it prohibited those cited for sleeping in parks from later using the parks.

2. *Papachristou v. City of Jacksonville*, 405 U.S. 156 (1972).

CHAPTER 11

1. This chapter is primarily drawn from Loukaitou-Sideris, Blumenberg, and Ehrenfeucht (2005).

2. This is consistent with American Association of State Highway and Transportation Officials (AASHTO) guidelines, which recommend a minimum clear sidewalk area of four feet, with the entire border area eight feet (AASHTO 1990). In commercial areas, the recommended minimum is four to eight feet or greater. AASHTO also recommends sidewalks on each side of the street, with the clear area as far from the roadway as possible.

3. In rare occasions, such as in Santa Monica, California, the Public Works Department makes the repair, and the abutting property owners are responsible for half of the cost.

4. Sidewalk repair is a big issue for Los Angeles. Former mayor Richard Riordan was considering allocating funds from an expected tobacco industry lawsuit settlement for sidewalk repairs. When the city was found liable in a series of lawsuits against police misconduct, funds from the tobacco judgment were hastily earmarked to cover the cost of the police settlements.

5. Kohn (2004, 11) has proposed treating public space as a cluster concept ("a term that has multiple and sometimes contradictory definitions"), with three components—ownership, accessibility, and intersubjectivity. Although here we speak about cities' tools, we were influenced by this notion when trying to make sense out of disjointed and often ineffective attempts to guide sidewalk use and users.

6. Minneapolis was the first city to initiate a system of skywalks in its downtown in 1962.

7. Enabling legislation was passed in California in 1994.

8. Two very active business improvement districts in San Francisco are the Telegraph Ave. BID (formed in 1998 and encompassing 19 blocks and 187 businesses) and the Union Square BID (formed in 1999 and encompassing 10 blocks and 191 businesses). The Downtown Sacramento Partnership is a coalition of BIDs that covers 65 blocks and represents 525 businesses in the downtown area. The Downtown Improvement District in San Jose represents more than 1,800 businesses (Sinton 1998).

9. Ten different business improvement district functions are identified as maintenance, security, consumer marketing, business recruitment and retention, public-space regulation, parking and transportation management, urban design, social services, visioning, and capital improvements (Houstoun 1997).

10. The National Trust for Historic Preservation has created the National Main Street Center. Since 1980 the Center has offered incentives and training to communities around the country to revamp their historic commercial areas.

References

Abrams, Garry. 1992. "We're Doing OK: Selling Dolls in LA." *Los Angeles Times*, January 26, 1992, E1.

"Advice 'On the Half Shell.'" 1882. *Los Angeles Times*, June 28, 3.

Aitken, Stuart, and Chris Lukinbeal. 1998. "Of Heroes, Fools, and Fisher Kings: Cinematic Representations of Street Myths and Hysterical Males." In Nicholas Fyfe, ed., *Images of the Street: Planning, Identity and Control in Public Space* (141–159). London: Routledge.

"All Along the Line." 1897. *Los Angeles Times*, December 28, 7.

Alvord, Valerie, and Chris Woodyard. 2000. "Armies of Officers Stand between Dems, Protesters." *USA Today*, August 17, 2000, 8A.

American Association of State Highway and Transportation Officials (AASHTO). 1990. *A Policy on Geometric Design of Highways and Streets*. Washington, DC: American Association of State Highway and Transportation Officials.

American Civil Liberties Union (ACLU) Washington. 2000. "ACLU Challenges Seattle's WTO No-Protest Zone." Press Release, March 7. Available at http://www.aclu-wa.org/LEGAL/WTO-Lawsuit.Release.3.7.00.html. Accessed on February 15, 2006.

American Civil Liberties Union (ACLU). 2005. "Appeals Court Finds Government May Have Violated Rights of WTO Protesters in Seattle." June 1. Available at http://www.aclu.org/FreeSpeech/FreeSpeech.cfm?ID=18408&c=86. Accessed on February 15, 2006.

American Public Works Association. 1976. *History of Public Works in the United States 1776–1976.* Chicago: American Public Works Association.

American Society of Civil Engineers. 1990. *Residential Streets.* 2nd ed. New York: American Society of Civil Engineers.

Amster, Randall. 2004. *Street People and the Contested Realms of Public Space.* New York: LFB.

Anderson, L. M., and H. K. Cordell. 1988. "Influence of Trees on Residential Property Values in Athens, Georgia (U.S.A.): A Survey of Actual Sales Prices." *Landscape and Urban Planning* 15: 153–164.

Anderson, Nels. 1923. *The Hobo: The Sociology of the Homeless Man.* A study prepared for the Chicago Council of Social Agencies under the direction of the Committee on Homeless Men. Chicago: University of Chicago Press.

Austin, Regina. 1994. "An Honest Living: Street Vendors, Municipal Regulation, and the Black Public Sphere." *Yale Law Journal* 103(8): 2119–2131.

Baldwin, Peter C. 1999. *Domesticating the Street: The Reform of Public Space in Hartford, 1850–1930.* Columbus: Ohio State University Press.

Baldwin, Peter C. 2002. "'Nocturnal Habits and Dark Wisdom': The American Response to Children in the Streets at Night, 1880–1930." *Journal of Social History* 35(3): 593–611.

Ball, Jennifer. 2002. *Street Vending: A Survey of Ideas and Lessons for Planners.* Washington, DC: American Planning Association.

Banerjee, Tridib, Genevieve Giuliano, Greg Hise, and David Sloane. 1996. "Invented and Re-invented Streets: Designing the New Shopping Experience." *Lusk Review* 2(1): 18–30.

Barna, Mark. 2002. "Cast of Street Characters Brings Promenade to Life." *Associated Press State and Local Wire*, May 21.

Barthes, R. 1986. "Semiology and the Urban." In M. Gottdiener and A. Lagopoulos, eds., *The City and the Sign: An Introduction to Urban Semiotics* (87–98). New York: Columbia University Press.

Bates, Frank G. 1912. "Village Government in New England." *American Political Science Review* 6(3): 367–385.

Bauman, Zygmunt. 1999. *In Search of Politics*. Stanford, CA: Stanford University Press.

Beazley, Harriot. 2002. "'Vagrants Wearing Make-Up': Negotiating Spaces on the Streets of Yogyakarta, Indonesia." *Urban Studies* 39(9): 1665–1683.

Bell, David. 1995. "Perverse Dynamics, Sexual Citizenship and the Transformation of Intimacy." In David Bell and Gill Valentine, eds., *Mapping Desire: Geographies of Sexualities* (304–317). New York: Routledge.

Benjamin, Walter. 1999. *The Arcades Project*. Cambridge, MA: Harvard University Press.

Berestein, L. 1995. "Wheeling and Dealing: Street Vendors Risk Citations and the Ire of Other Merchants as They Try to Eke Out a Living." *Los Angeles Times*, February 2, J12.

Bernier, Anthony Allyre. 2002. *The Sidewalk Metropolis: Street Furniture and Pedestrian Public Space in Twentieth-Century Los Angeles*. Ph.D. dissertation, Department of History, University of California, Irvine.

Blomley, Nicholas. 2007a. "Civil Rights Meets Civil Engineering: Urban Public Space and Traffic Logic." *Canadian Journal of Law and Society* 22(2): 55–72.

Blomley, Nicholas. 2007b. "How to Turn a Beggar into a Bus Stop: Law, Traffic and the 'Function of Place.'" *Urban Studies* 44(9): 1697–1712.

Bluestone, Daniel M. 1991. "'The Pushcart Evil': Peddlers, Merchants, and New York City's Streets, 1890–1940." *Journal of Urban History* 18(1): 68–92.

Blumenberg, Evelyn, and Renia Ehrenfeucht. 2008. "Civil Liberties and the Regulation of Public Space: The Case of Sidewalks in Las Vegas." *Environment and Planning A* 40: 303–322.

Boddy, Trevor 1993. "Underground and Overhead: Building the Analogous City." In Michael Sorkin, ed., *Variations on a Theme Park: The New American City and the End of Public Space* (123–245). New York: Noonday Press.

Boocock, S. S. 1981. "The Life Space of Children." In S. S. Keller, ed., *Building for Women* (16–43). Lexington, MA: Lexington Books.

Boski, Joseph. 2002. "Responses by State Actors to Insurgent Civic Spaces Since the WTO Meetings at Seattle." *IDPL* 24(4): 363–381.

Boyer, Christine. 1983. *Dreaming the Rational City: The Myth of American City Planning.* Cambridge, MA: MIT Press.

Brand, Anna. 2006. *Renegotiating Democracy in Public Space.* Master's thesis, University of New Orleans, Department of Planning and Urban Studies.

Brasseaux, Carl A. 1980. "The Administration of Slave Regulations in French Lousiana, 1724–1766." *Louisiana History* 21: 139–158.

Brickell, Chris. 2000. "Heroes and Invaders: Gay and Lesbian Pride Parades and the Public/Private Distinction in New Zealand Media Accounts." *Gender, Place and Culture* 7(2): 163–178.

Bromley, Ray. 2000. "Street Vending and Public Policy: A Global Review." *International Journal of Sociology and Social Policy* 20(1/2): 1–28.

Brown-May, Andrew. 1998. *Melbourne Street Life: The Itinerary of Our Days.* Australian Scholarly/Arcadia and Museum Victoria.

Bulwa, Demian. 2005. "Pride Parade Celebrates Causes from Equal Rights to Spanking." *San Francisco Chronicle*, June 27, B1.

Burnstein, Daniel. 1996. "The Vegetable Man Cometh: Political and Moral Choices in Pushcart Policy in Progressive Era New York City." *New York History* 77(1): 47–84.

Bzowski, Frances Diodato. 1995. "Spectacular Suffrage; or How Women Came Out of the Home and into the Streets and Theaters of New York City to Win the Vote." *New York History* 76: 57–94.

Campanella, Thomas J. 2003. *Republic of Shade: New England and the American Elm.* New Haven: Yale University Press.

Casillas, Elsa. 2005. *The MacArthur Park Vending District: An Experiment in Street Vending.* Master's thesis, University of California, Los Angeles.

Catling, H. W. 1986–1987. "Archaelogy in Greece." *Archaeological Reports* 33: 3–61.

Chapkis, Wendy. 2000. "Power and Control in the Commercial Sex Trade." In Ronald Weitzer, ed., *Sex for Sale: Prostitution, Pornography, and the Sex Industry* (181–202). New York: Routledge.

Chauncey, George. 1994. *Gay New York: Gender, Urban Culture and the Making of the Gay Male World 1890–1940.* New York: Basic Books.

Christens, Brian, and Paul W. Speer. 2005. "Predicting Violent Crime Using Urban and Suburban Densities." *Behavior and Social Issues* 14: 113–127.

Chudacoff, Howard, and Judith Smith. 2005. *The Evolution of American Urban Society.* Upper Saddle River, NJ: Pearson/Prentice Hall.

Citizens for a Better South Florida. n.d. Available at http://www.abettersouthflorida.org/jplants.html. Accessed on September 19, 2006.

"The City's Legal Responsibilities and Powers." 1918. *American City* 19(2) (August): 145.

"The City's Legal Responsibility and Powers." 1919. *American City* 20(2) (February): 193–195.

———

Clifton, Alexandra Navarro. 2003. "Iraq War Bill Includes Millions for Trade Conference in Miami." *Palm Beach Post*, November 4, 7B.

Cohen, Lizabeth. 1996. "From Town Center to Shopping Center: The Reconfiguration of Community Marketplaces in Postwar America." *American Historical Review* 101: 1050–1081.

Cole, David. 1986. "Agon at Agora: Creative Misreadings in the First Amendment Tradition." *Yale Law Journal* 95: 857–905.

Comfort, Louise 2001. *Rapidly Evolving Response Systems in Crisis Environments: An Analytical Model.* Working Paper 2001-6, Graduate School of Public and International Affairs, University of Pittsburgh.

Coombe, Rosemary. 1995. "Interdisciplinary Approaches to International Economic Law: The Cultural Life of Things—Anthropological Approaches to Law and Society in Conditions of Globalization." *American University Journal of International Law and Policy* 10 (Winter): 791–835.

Crawford, Margaret. 1999. "Blurring the Boundaries: Public Space and Private Life." In John Chase, Margaret Crawford, and John Kaliski, eds., *Everyday Urbanism.* New York: Monacelli Press.

Cresswell, Tim. 1991. *Tramp in America.* London: Reaktion.

Cross, John. 2000. "Street Vendors, Modernity, and Postmodernity: Conflict and Compromise in the Global Economy." *International Journal of Sociology and Social Policy* 20(1/2): 29–51.

Crouch, David. 1998. "The Street in the Making of Popular Geographic Knowledge." In Nicholas Fyfe, ed., *Images of the Street: Planning, Identity and Control in Public Space* (160–175). London: Routledge.

Crouch, Dora, P., Daniel J. Garr, and Axel I. Mundigo. 1982. *Spanish City Planning in North America.* Cambridge, MA: MIT Press.

Cunningham, C., and M. Jones. 1999. "The Playground: A Confession of Failure?" *Built Environment* 25A: 11–17.

Dailey, Jane. 1997. "Deference and Violence in the Postbellum Urban South: Manners and Massacres in Danville, Virginia." *Journal of Southern History* 63(3): 553–590.

Davis, Mike. 1990. *City of Quartz: Excavating the Future in Los Angeles.* London: Verso.

Davis, Mike 1991. "A Logic Like Hell's: Being Homeless in Los Angeles." *UCLA Law Review* 39 (December): 325–332.

Davis, Tim 1995. "The Diversity of Queer Politics and the Redefinition of Sexual Identity and Community in Urban Spaces." In D. Bell and G. Valentine, eds., *Mapping Desire: Geographies of Sexualities.* New York: Routledge, 284–303.

de Botton, Alain. 2004. *Status Anxiety.* New York: Pantheon Books.

De Certeau, M. 1993. "Walking in the City." In S. During, ed., *The Cultural Studies Reader.* London: Routledge.

Deutsche, Rosalyn. 1996. *Eviction: Art and Spatial Politics.* Cambridge, MA: MIT Press.

Dickerson, Marla. 1999. "Small Business, Enterprise Zone, Zones of Controversy: Improvement Districts Spur Revival—and Division." *Los Angeles Times*, January 20, A1.

Dixon, John, Mark Levine, and Rob McAuley. 2006. "Locating Impropriety: Street Drinking, Moral Order, and the Ideological Dilemma of Public Space." *Political Psychology* 27(2): 187–206.

Domosh, Mona. 1998. "Those 'Gorgeous Incongruities': Polite Politics and Public Space on the Streets of New York City." *Annals of the Association of American Geographers* 88(2): 209–226.

Doyle, Bertram Wilbur. 1937. *The Etiquette of Race Relations in the South: A Study in Social Control.* Chicago: University of Chicago Press.

Duany, Andres, Elizabeth Plater-Zyberk, and Jeff Speck. 2000. *Suburban Nations: The Rise of Sprawl and the Decline of the American Dream.* New York: North Point Press.

Duneier, Mitchell. 1999. *Sidewalk.* New York: Farrar, Straus and Giroux.

Ehrenfeucht, Renia. 2006. "Constructing the Public in Urban Space: Sidewalks, Streets and Municipal Regulation in Los Angeles, 1880–1940." Ph.D. dissertation, University of California, Los Angeles.

Ehrenfeucht, Renia, and Anastasia Loukaitou-Sideris. 2007. "Constructing the Sidewalks: Municipal Government and the Production of Public Space in Los Angeles, California, 1880–1920." *Journal of Historical Geography* 33: 104–124.

Einhorn, Robin L. 1991. *Property Rules: Political Economy in Chicago, 1833–1872.* Chicago: University of Chicago Press.

Ellickson, Robert C. 1996. "Controlling Chronic Misconduct in City Spaces: Of Panhandlers, Skid Rows, and Public Space Zoning." *Yale Law Review* 105(5): 1165–1248.

Elmendorf, William F., Fern K. Willits, and Vivod Sasidharan. 2005. "Urban Park and Forest Participation and Landscape Preference: A Review of the Relevant Literature." *Journal of Arboriculture* 31(6): 311–317.

Fabre, Genevieve. 1994. "African-American Commemorative Celebrations in the Nineteenth Century." In Genevieve Fabre and Robert O'Meally, eds., *History and Memory in African-American Culture* (72–91). New York: Oxford University Press.

Feldman, Leonard C. 2004. *Citizens without Shelter: Homelessness, Democracy, and Political Exclusion.* Ithaca: Cornell University Press.

Ferraro, K. F. 1994. *Fear of Crime: Interpreting Victimization Risk.* Albany: State University of New York Press.

Finnegan, Margaret. 1999. *Selling Suffrage: Consumer Culture and Votes for Women.* New York: Columbia University Press.

"Florists Are Again Making War on Flower Vendors." 1908. *Los Angeles Record*, February 27, 5.

Fogelson, Robert. 1993. *The Fragmented Metropolis: Los Angeles, 1850–1930.* Berkeley: University of California Press.

Ford, Larry. 1998. *Cities and Buildings: Skyscrapers, Skidrows, and Suburbs*. Baltimore: John Hopkins Press.

Ford, Larry. 2000. *The Spaces between Buildings*. Baltimore: John Hopkins Press.

"For the Homeless." 1896. *Los Angeles Times*, September 20, 25.

Foscarinis, Maria. 1996. "Downward Spiral: Homelessness and Its Criminalization." *Yale Law and Policy Review* 14: 1–62.

Franck, Karen, and Stevens, Quentin. 2007. "Tying Down Loose Space." In Karen Franck and Quentin Stevens, eds., *Loose Space* (1–34). London: Routledge.

Fraser, Nancy. 1992. "Rethinking the Public Sphere: A Contribution to the Critique of Actually Existing Democracy." In Craig Calhoun, ed., *Habermas and the Public Sphere* (109–142). Cambridge, MA and London: MIT Press.

Friends of Boston's Homeless. n.d. "2004 City of Boston Homeless Census." Available at www.fobh.org/census.htm. Accessed on August 30, 2005.

Fyfe, Nicholas R. 1998. "Introduction: Reading the Street." In Nicholas Fyfe, ed., *Images of the Street: Planning, Identity and Control in Public Space* (1–10). London: Routledge.

Gardner, Brooks Carol. 1995. *Passing By: Gender and Public Harassment*. Berkeley: University of California Press.

Geist, Johann F. 1983. *Arcades: The History of a Building Type*. Cambridge, MA: MIT Press.

Genini, Ronald. 1974. "Industrial Workers of the World and Their Fresno Free Speech Fight, 1910–1911." *California Historical Quarterly* 53(2): 100–114.

Gibson, Timothy A. 2004. *Securing the Spectacular City: The Politics of Revitalization and Homelessness in Downtown Seattle*. Oxford: Lexington Books.

Gilfoyle, Timothy J. 1994. *City of Eros: New York City, Prostitution, and the Commercialization of Sex, 1790–1920*. New York: Norton.

Gliona, John, and Susan Abram. 1998. "Council Bans Freestyle Vendors in Venice." *Los Angeles Times*, April 2, A1.

Goffman, Erving. 1980. *Behavior in Public Places*. Westport, CT: Greenwood. Originally published in 1969.

Goheen, Peter G. 1993. "The Ritual of the Streets in Mid-Nineteenth-Century Toronto." *Environment and Planning D: Society and Space* 11: 127–145.

Goheen, Peter G. 1994. "Negotiating Access to Public Space in Mid-Nineteenth Century Toronto." *Journal of Historical Geography* 20(4): 430–449.

Gorman, James. 2004. "Residents' Opinions on the Value of Street Trees Depending on Tree Location." *Journal of Arboriculture* 30(1): 36–44.

Gorov, Linda. 2000. "Campaign 2000 / The Democratic Convention / Protests; Mixed Messages Compete to Be Heard." *Boston Globe*, August 15, A18.

Gotham, Kevin Fox. 2002. "Marketing Mardi Gras: Commodification, Spectacle and the Political Economy of Tourism in New Orleans." *Urban Studies* 39(10): 1735–1756.

Groth, Paul. 1994. *Living Downtown: The History of Residential Hotels in the United States*. Berkeley: University of California Press.

Harcourt, Bernard. 1998. "Reflecting on the Subject: A Critique of the Social Influence Conception of Deterrence, the Broken-Windows Theory, and Order Maintenance Policing New York Style." *Michigan Law Review* 97: 291–389.

"Hartford: General Benefits of Canopy, Commons on Canopy Decline in U.S." 2006. *Hartford Courant*, September 24, C2.

Hemmens, Craig, and Katherine Bennett. 1998–1999. "Out in the Street: Juvenile Crime, Juvenile Curfews, and the Constitution." *Gonzaga Law Review* 34: 268–327.

Hernandez, Greg. 1994. "Vending Permit Hold May Be Extended." *Los Angeles Times*, December 19, B2.

"Heroic Attempts in Detroit to Regulate Pedestrian Traffic." 1929. *American City Magazine* 40 (January): 183.

Hershkovitz, L. 1993. "Tiananmen Square and the Politics of Place." *Political Geography* 12: 395–420.

Heynen, Nik. 2006. "Green Urban Political Ecologies: Toward a Better Understanding of Inner-City Environmental Change." *Environment and Planning A* 38: 499–516.

Hickey, Georgina Susan. 1995. "Visibility, Politics, and Urban Development: Working-class Women in Early Twentieth-Century Atlanta." Ph.D. dissertation, University of Michigan.

Hoffman, Abbie. 1968. *Revolution for the Hell of It.* New York: Dial.

Houstoun, Lawrence. 1997. *BIDs: Business Improvement Districts.* Washington, DC: Urban Land Institute.

Howard, Bob. 2000. "Valley Business: A BID for Change." *Los Angeles Times*, March 28, B6.

Howell, Ocean. 2001. *The Poetics of Security: Skateboarding, Urban Design, and the New Public Space.* Available at http://bss.sfsu.edu/urganaction/ua2001/ps.html. Accessed on March 3, 2008.

Howell, Phillip. 2000. "A Private Contagious Diseases Act: Prostitution and Public Space in Victorian Cambridge." *Journal of Historical Geography* 26(3): 376–402.

Hubbard, Philip. 1998. "Sexuality, Immorality and the City: Red-light Districts and the Marginalisation of Female Street Prostitutes." *Gender, Place and Culture* 5(1): 55–72.

Hubbard, Philip. 1999. *Sex and the City: Geographies of Prostitution in the Urban West.* Brookfield, VT: Ashgate.

Hunt, Alan. 2002. "Regulating Heterosocial Space: Sexual Politics in the Early Twentieth Century." *Journal of Historical Sociology* 15(1): 1–34.

Hunt, Felix. 1912. "A Practical Detail of City Planning." *American City Magazine* 7 (November): 411–415.

Isenberg, Alison. 2004. *Downtown America: A History of the Place and the People Who Made It*. Chicago: Chicago University Press.

Ith, Ian. 2001. "Court Vindicates City's WTO Riot Measures: Judge Says Schell Acted Appropriately." *Seattle Times*, October 31, A1.

Jackson, Peter. 1998. "Domesticating the Street: The Contested Spaces of the High Street and the Mall." In Nicholas Fyfe, ed., *Images of the Street: Planning, Identity and Control in Public Space* (176–191). London: Routledge.

Jacobs, Allan. 1990. "In Defense of Street Trees." *Places* (Winter): 84–87.

Jacobs, Allan, Elizabeth Macdonald, and Yodan Rofé. 2002. *The Boulevard Book*. Cambridge, MA: MIT Press.

Jacobs, Jane. 1961. *The Death and Life of the Great American Cities*. New York: Random House.

Janiszewski, Jonathan. 2002. "Comment: Silence Enforced through Speech: Philadelphia and the 2000 Republican National Convention." *Temple Political and Civil Rights Law Review* 12: 121–139.

Jencks, Christopher. 1994. *The Homeless*. Cambridge, MA: Harvard University Press.

Jones, O. 2000. "Melting Geography: Purity, Disorder, Childhood, and Space." In S. Holloway and G. Valentine, eds., *Children's Geographies: Playing, Living, Learning* (29–47). London: Routledge.

Kates, Steven M., and Russell W. Belk. 2001. "The Meanings of Lesbian and Gay Pride Day: Resistance through Consumption and Resistance to Consumption." *Journal of Contemporary Ethnography* 30(4): 392–429.

Kazin, Michael, and Steven J. Ross. 1992. "America's Labor Day: The Dilemma of a Workers' Celebration." *Journal of American History* 78(4): 1294–1323.

Kefalas, Maria. 2003. *Working Class Heroes: Protecting Home, Community and Nation in Chicago*. Berkeley: University of California Press.

Keith, M. 1995. "Shouts of the Street: Identity and the Spaces of Authenticity." *Social Identities* 1(2): 297–315.

Kelley, Robin D. G. 1993. "'We Are Not What We Seem': Rethinking Black Working-Class Opposition in the Jim Crow South." *Journal of American History* 80: 75–112.

Kelling, George, and C. Coles. 1996. *Fixing Broken Windows: Restoring Order and Reducing Crime in Our Communities*. New York: Free Press.

Kennedy, Elizabeth Lapovsky, and Madeline D. Davis. 1993. *Boots of Leather, Slippers of Gold: The History of a Lesbian Community*. New York: Penguin Books.

Kettles, Gregg. 2004. "Regulating Vending in the Sidewalk Commons." *Temple Law Review* 77(Spring): 1–46.

Kinser, Samuel. 1990. *Carnival, American Style: Mardi Gras at New Orleans and Mobile*. Chicago: University of Chicago Press.

Kohn, Margaret. 2004. *Brave New Neighborhoods: The Privatization of Public Space*. New York: Routledge.

Kondo, Annette. 2000. "Panel OKs Updated Boulevard." *Los Angeles Times*, July 26, B4.

Kopetman, Roxana. 1986. "Back off Ban on Vendors, City Advised." *Los Angeles Times*, October 8, B1.

Koskella, H. 1997. "Bold Walk and Breakings: Women's Spatial Confidence versus Fear of Violence." *Gender, Place, and Culture* 4(3): 301–319.

Kostof, Spiro. 1992. *The City Assembled: The Elements of Urban Form through History*. New York: Brown.

Kowinski, Severini. 2002. *The Malling of America: Travels in the United States of Shopping*. Philadelphia: Libris.

Kugelmass, Jack. 1993. "'The Fun Is in Dressing Up': The Greenwich Village Halloween Parade and the Reimagining of Urban Space." *Social Text* 36: 138–152.

Kuo, Frances E., and William C. Sullivan. 2001. "Aggression and Violence in the Inner City: Effects of Environment via Mental Fatigue." *Environment and Behavior* 33(4): 543–571.

La Corte, Rachel. 2003. "Miami Ready for Free Trade Protesters." *Associated Press Archive*, November 14. Available at www.ap.org. Accessed on July 25, 2008.

Lane, Jodi, and James W. Meeker. 2003. "Ethnicity, Information Sources, and Fear of Crime." *Deviant Behavior: An Interdisciplinary Journal* 24: 1–26.

Laverne, Robert J., and Kimberly Winson-Geideman. 2003. "The Influence of Trees and Landscaping on Rental Rates at Office Buildings." *Journal of Arboriculture* 29(5): 281–290.

Law, Lisa. 2002. "Defying Disappearance: Cosmopolitan Public Spaces in Hong Kong." *Urban Studies* 39(9): 1625–1645.

Lawrence, Denise. 1982. "Parades, Politics, and Competing Images: Doo Dah and Roses." *Urban Anthropology* 11(2): 155–176.

Leavitt, Jacqueline, and Anastasia Loukaitou-Sideris. 1994. "Safe and Secure: Public Housing Residents in Los Angeles Define the Issues." In *Future Visions in Urban Public Housing: An International Forum*. Cincinnati, OH: Conference Proceedings.

Lederman, Robert. January, 1998. "Why New York City Still Illegally Arrests, Harasses and Persecutes Street Artists." *The Ethical Spectacle*. Available at http://www.spectacle.org/198/art.html. Accessed on September 31, 2006.

Lees, Loretta. 1998. "Urban Renaissance and the Street: Spaces of Control and Contestation." In Nicholas Fyfe, ed., *Images of the Street* (236–253). London: Routledge.

Levitt, Steven D. 2004. "Understanding Why Crime Fell in the 1990s: Four Factors That Explain the Decline and Six That Do Not." *Journal of Economic Perspectives* 18(1): 163–190.

Lewis, Dan A., and Michael G. Maxfield. 1980. "Fear in the Neighborhoods: An Investigation of the Impact of Crime." *Journal of Research in Crime and Delinquency* 17 (July): 160–189.

"Liability Concerning Sidewalks." 1918. *The American City* 18(1): 32.

Lipsitz, George. 1988. "Mardi Gras Indians: Carnival and Counter-Narrative in Black New Orleans." *Cultural Critique* 10: 99–121.

Locklear, William R. 1972. "The Anti-Chinese Movement in Los Angeles. In Roger Daniels and Spencer C. Olins, Jr., eds., *Racism in California: A Reader in the History of Oppression* (92–104). New York: Macmillan Company.

Lofland, Lynn H. 1973. *A World of Strangers: Order and Action in Urban Public Space*. New York: Basic Books.

Lofland, Lynn H. 1998. *The Public Realm: Exploring the City's Quintessential Social Territory*. New York: Aldine de Gruyter.

Logan, John R., and Harvey L. Molotch. 2007. *Urban Fortunes: The Political Economy of Place*. Berkeley: University of California Press.

Lohman, Jon. 1999. "'It Can't Rain Every Day': The Year-Round Experience of Carnival." *Western Folklore* 58(3–4): 279–298.

Lohr, Virginia I., Caroline H. Pearson-Mims, John Tarnai, and Don A. Dillman. 2004. "How Urban Residents Rate and Rank the Benefits and Problems Associated with Trees in Cities." *Journal of Arboriculture* 30(1): 28–35.

Long Beach, City of. n.d. *Long Beach Municipal Code*. Long Beach, CA. Ordinance 20.36.130.

Lopez, Robert J. 1993. "Pushcart Power; Frustrated by Policy Crackdowns, Vendors United to Legalize Their Meager Livelihoods. Next Month, Their Six-Year Struggle Comes before the City Council." *Los Angeles Times*, July 25, A14.

Los Angeles. 1899. City Council Minutes. Vol. 57, p. 256.

Los Angeles. n.d. City Council Minutes. Vol. 10, p. 595.

Los Angeles. 1901. City Council Minutes.

Los Angeles. 1903. City Council Minutes. Vol. 21, pp. 264–265.

Los Angeles. 1903. City Council Minutes. Petition 1202, September 15.

Los Angeles. 1908. City Council Minutes. Vol. 76, pp. 233, 252–253.

Los Angeles. 1999. *Los Angeles General Plan*. Chapter VI. Los Angeles, CA.

Los Angeles Police Commission. 1890. Minutes. January 8, January 15.

Los Angeles Police Department. 1901. *Annual Report for year ending 30 June 1901*.

Los Angeles Police Department. 1902. *Annual Report for year ending 30 June 1902*.

Los Angeles Police Department. 1913. *Annual Report for year ending 30 June 1913*.

Los Angeles Police Department. 1915. *Annual Report for year ending 30 June 1915*.

Los Angeles Police Judge Reports. 1893. *Annual Report for 1893*.

Los Angeles Police Judge Reports. 1897. *Annual Report for 1897*.

Lou, Raymond. 1990. "The Anti-Chinese Movement in Los Angeles, 1870–1890." In Robert Asher and Charles Stephenson, eds., *Labor Divided: Race and Ethnicity in United States Labor Struggles, 1835–1960* (49–62). Albany: State University of New York Press.

Loukaitou-Sideris, Anastasia, 1993. "Privatisation of Public Open Space: The Los Angeles Experience." *Town Planning Review* 64(2): 139–167.

Loukaitou-Sideris, Anastasia. 1995. "Urban Form and Social Context: Cultural Differentiation in the Meaning and Uses of Neighborhood Parks." *Journal of Planning Education and Research* 14(2): 101–114.

Loukaitou-Sideris, Anastasia. 1999. "Hot Spots of Bus Stop Crime: The Importance of Environmental Attributes." *Journal of the American Planning Association* 65(4): 395–411.

Loukaitou-Sideris, Anastasia. 2002. "Regeneration of Urban Commercial Streets: Ethnicity and Space in Three Los Angeles Neighborhoods." *Journal of Architectural and Planning Research* 19(4): 334–350.

Loukaitou-Sideris, Anastasia. 2005. "Is it Safe to Walk Here? Design and Policy Responses to Women's Fear of Victimization in Public Places." *Research on Women's Issues in Transportation Conference Proceedings* (Vol. 2). Washington, DC: Transportation Research Board.

Loukaitou-Sideris, Anastasia. 2006. "Is It Safe to Walk? Neighborhood Safety and Security Considerations and Their Effects on Walking." *Journal of Planning Literature* 20(3): 219–232.

Loukaitou-Sideris, Anastasia, and Tridib Banerjee. 1993. "The Negotiated Plaza: Design and Development of Corporate Open Space in Downtown Los Angeles and San Francisco." *Journal of Planning Education and Research* 13: 1–12.

Loukaitou-Sideris, Anastasia, and Tridib Banerjee. 1998. *Urban Design Downtown: Poetics and Politics of Form.* Los Angeles: University of California Press.

Loukaitou-Sideris, Anastasia, Evelyn Blumenberg, and Renia Ehrenfeucht. 2005. "Sidewalk Democracy: Municipalities and the Regulation of Public Space." In Eran Ben-Joseph and Terry S. Szold, eds., *Regulating Place: Standards and the Shaping of Urban America* (141–166). New York: Routledge.

Low, Setha. 2003. *Behind the Gates: Life, Security, and the Pursuit of Happiness in Fortress America.* New York: Routledge.

Low, Setha, Dana Taplin, and Suzanne Scheld. 2005. *Rethinking Urban Parks: Public Space and Cultural Diversity.* Austin: University of Texas Press.

Lumsden, Linda J. 1997. *Rampant Women Suffragists and the Right of Assembly.* Knoxville: University of Tennessee Press.

Maco, Scott E., and E. Gregory McPherson. 2003. "A Practical Approach to Assessing Structure, Function, and Value of Street Tree Populations in Small Communities." *Journal of Arboriculture* 29(2): 84–97.

Maher, Adrian. 1995. "Venice: Firm Picked for Boardwalk Project to Seek Public Input." *Los Angeles Times*, January 5, J8.

"A Market Place." 1890. *Los Angeles Times*, May 5, 4.

Marston, S. A. 2002. "Making Difference: Conflict over Irish Identity in the New York City St. Patrick's Parade." *Political Geography* 21: 373–392.

Martinez, Ruben. 1991. "Sidewalk Wars: Why LA Street Vendors Won't Be Swept Away." *Los Angeles Weekly*, December 6–12, 20, 24.

McCammon, Holly J. 2003. "'Out of the Parlors and into the Streets': The Changing Tactical Repertoire of the U.S. Women's Suffrage Movements." *Social Forces* 81(3): 787–818.

McGerr, Michael. 1990. "Political Style and Women's Power, 1830–1930." *Journal of American History* 77(3): 864–885.

McPherson, E. Gregory. 2000. "Expenditures Associated with Conflicts between Street Tree Root Growth Hardscape in California." *Journal of Arboriculture* 26(6): 289–297.

McPherson, E. Gregory, and Jules Muchnick. 2005. "Effects of Street Tree Shade on Asphalt Concrete Pavement Performance." *Journal of Arboriculture* 31(6): 303–310.

McShane, Clay. 1979. "Transforming the Use of Urban Space: A Look at the Revolution in Street Pavements." *Journal of Urban History* 5: 279–307.

McShane, Clay. 1994. *Down the Asphalt Path: The Automobile and the American City.* New York: Columbia University.

Medrich, E., J. Roisen, V. Rubin, and S. Buckley. 1982. *The Serious Business of Growing Up.* Berkeley: University of California Press.

"Merchants Amendable for Allowing Boxes and Bales to Obstruct the Sidewalks." 1881. *Los Angeles Times*, December 22, 3.

"The Merry War." 1890. *Los Angeles Times*, January 9, 3.

Meyer, Jeremy P. 2006. "Planners Hope to Put Denver in the Shade." *Denver Post*, October 20, B1.

Meyerowitz, Joanne J. 1988. *Women Adrift: Independent Wage Earners in Chicago, 1880–1930. Women in Culture and Society.* Chicago: University of Chicago Press.

Miami. 2004. "State of the City Address." Available at http://www.ci.miami.fl.us/cms/mayor/1285.htm. Accessed on April 18, 2006.

Miami-Dade County Department of Environmental Resources Management (DERM). n.d. "Welcome to Adopt-a-Tree!" Available at http://www.miamidade.gov/derm/adoptatreet.asp. Accessed on April 18, 2007.

Miethe, Terance D. 1995. "Fear and Withdrawal from Urban Life." *The Annals of the American Academy of Political and Social Science* 539: 14–27.

Miller, Grace. 1972. "The I.W.W. Free Speech Fight: San Diego, 1912." *Southern California Quarterly* 54(3): 211–233.

Miller, Martin. 1995. "Perspective: Cities Raring to Send Their Homeless Packing; Court Decisions May Inspire Rush of Tougher Laws." *Los Angeles Times*, July 17, B3.

Millich, Nacy A. 1994. "Compassion Fatigue and the First Amendment: Are the Homeless Constitutional Castaways?" *U.C. Davis Law Review* 27 (Winter): 255.

Million Trees LA. n.d. "About Million Trees LA." Available at http://www.milliontreesla.org/mtabout.htm. Accessed on August 31, 2006.

Mitchell, Don 1996. "Political Violence, Order, and the Legal Construction of Public Space: Power and the Public Forum Doctrine." *Urban Geography* 17(2): 152–178.

Mitchell, Don. 1998. "Anti-Homeless Laws and Public Space 1: Begging and the First Amendment." *Urban Geography* 19(1): 6–11.

Mitchell, Don. 2003. *The Right to the City: Social Justice and the Fight for Public Space*. New York: Guilford Press.

Mitchell, Don. 2004. "The Liberalization of Free Speech: Or How Protest in Public Space Is Silenced." *Stanford Agora* 4. Available at agora.stanford.edu. Accessed on March 3, 2006.

Mitchell, Don, and Lynn Staeheli. 2005. "Permitting Protests: Parsing the Fine Geography of Dissent in America." *International Journal of Urban and Regional Research* 29(4): 796–813.

Moehring, Eugene P. 1981. *Public Works and the Patterns of Urban Real Estate Growth in Manhattan, 1835–1894*. New York: Arno Press.

Monkkonen, Eric H. 1981. *Police in Urban America 1860–1920*. New York: Cambridge University Press.

Monkkonen, Eric H., eds. 1984. "Introduction." *Walking to Work: Tramps in America, 1790–1935*. Lincoln: University of Nebraska Press.

Moser, Sandra L. 2001. "Anti-Prostitution Zones: Justification for Abolition." *Journal of Criminal Law and Criminology* 91(4): 1101–1126.

Muller, Mike. 2006. "Business Improvement Districts." *Gotham Gazette*, October 19. Available at http://www.gothamgazette.com/article/communitydevelopment/20061019/20/2005. Accessed on July 24, 2008.

Mumford, Kevin J. 1997. *Interzones: Black/White Sex Districts in Chicago and New York in the Early Twentieth Century*. New York: Columbia University Press.

"Municipal Improvements for 1915." 1915. *Municipal Engineering* 43(4) (April): 252–263.

"Municipal Liability Concerning Streets." 1918. *The American City* 18(4) (April): 249.

Munt, Sally. 1995. "The Lesbian *Flâneur*." In David Bell and Gill Valentine, eds., *Mapping Desire: Geographies of Sexualities* (114–125). New York: Routledge.

"Murderous Assault." 1890. *Los Angeles Times*, December 7, 5.

Murphy, Alexandra K., and Sudhir Alladi Venkatesh. 2006. "Vice Careers: The Changing Contours of Sex Work in New York City." *Qualitative Sociology* 29: 129–154.

Nalick, Jon. 1995. "New Law Is a Tough Sell: Santa Ana Vendors Go to Court in Effort to Stop Enforcement of Restrictions on Their Trade." *Los Angeles Times*, May 2, B1.

National Law Center on Homelessness and Poverty (NLCHP). 1993. "The Right to Remain Nowhere: A Report on Anti-Homeless Laws and Litigation in Sixteen United States Cities." Available at www.nlchp.org. Accessed on May 14, 2005.

National Law Center on Homelessness and Poverty (NLCHP). 1994. "No Homeless People Allowed: A Report on Anti-Homeless Laws, Litigation and Alternatives in Forty-nine United States Cities." Washington, DC: NLCHP. Available at www.nlchp.org. Accessed on May 14, 2005.

National Law Center on Homelessness and Poverty (NLCHP). 2003. "Punishing Poverty: The Criminalization of Homelessness, Litigation, and Recommendations for Solutions." Washington, DC: NLCHP.

Neill, William J. V. 2001. "Marketing the Urban Experience: Reflections on the Place of Fear in the Promotional Strategies of Belfast, Detroit and Berlin." *Urban Studies* 38(5–6): 815–828.

Newman, Simon P. 1997. *Parades and the Politics of the Street*. Philadelphia: University of Philadelphia Press.

Newman, Tim. 2001. "The Commodification of Policing: Security Networks in the Late Modern City." *Urban Studies* 38(5–6): 829–848.

Nielsen, Kirk. 2003. "Headbangers Ball Claims That Police Didn't Aim at FTAA Protesters' Upper Bodies Get a Black Eye." *Miami New Times*, December 11, 1.

Novak, William J. 1996. *The People's Welfare: Law and Regulation in Nineteenth-Century America*. Chapel Hill: University of North Carolina Press.

"Obnoxious Class Legislation." 1897. *Los Angeles Times*, February 17, 6.

Oc, Taner, and Steven Tiesdell, eds. 1997. *Safer City Centres: Reviving the Public Realm.* London: Chapman.

Oldenburg, Ray. 1989. *The Great Good Place: Cafes, Coffee Shops, Community Centers, Beauty Parlors, General Stores, Bars, Hangouts, and How They Get through the Day.* New York: Paragon House.

Olsen, Donald J. 1986. *The City as a Work of Art.* New Haven, CT: Yale University Press.

O'Neill, Maggie, and Rosemary Barberet. 2000. "Victimization and the Social Organization of Prostitution in England and Spain." In Ronald Weitzer, ed., *Sex for Sale: Prostitution, Pornography, and the Sex Industry* (123–138). New York: Routledge.

O'Reilly, Kathleen, and Michael E. Crutcher. 2006. "Parallel Politics: The Spatial Power of New Orleans' Labor Day Parades." *Social and Cultural Geography* 7(2): 245–265.

Owens, P. E. 1999. *Recreation and Restrictions: Community Skateboard Parks in the United States.* Davis: University of California.

Pacenti, John. 2003b. "Miami Demonstrators Deflated Amid Massive Police Showing." *Palm Beach Post*, November 19, 2A.

Pacenti, John. 2003a. "Miami Fears Storm of Protest at Trade Talks." *Palm Beach Post*, November 3, 1A.

Pain, Rachel. 2001. "Gender, Race, Age and Fear in the City." *Urban Studies* 38(5–6): 899–913.

Pain, John. 2003. "Anti-Globalization Activists Begin Free-Trade Protests in Miami." *Associated Press State and Local Wire*, November 16.

"Pedestrians Who 'Bump' into Autos Held Liable." 1933. *Los Angeles Herald Examiner*, September 6.

Peiss, Kathy Lee. 1986. *Cheap Amusements: Working Women and Leisure in Turn-of-the-Century New York*. Philadelphia: Temple University Press.

Perrine, Aaron. 2001. "Notes and Comments: The First Amendment vs. the World Trade Organization: Emergency Powers and the Battle in Seattle." *Washington Law Review* 76(April): 635–668.

Peterson, Paul E. 1981. *City Limits*. Chicago: University of Chicago Press.

Phillips, Tim, and Philip Smith. 2003. "Everyday Incivility: Towards a Benchmark." *Sociological Review* 51(1): 85–108.

Phillips, Tim, and Philip Smith. 2004. "Emotional and Behavioral Responses to Everyday Incivility: Challenging the Fear/Avoidance Paradigm." *Journal of Sociology* 40(4): 378–399.

Phillips, Timothy, and Philip Smith. 2006. "Rethinking Urban Incivility Research: Strangers, Bodies and Circulations." *Urban Studies* 43(5–6): 879–901.

Podmore, Julie A. 2001. "Lesbians in the Crowd: Gender, Sexuality and Visibility along Montreal's Boul. St.-Laurent." *Gender, Place and Culture* 8(4): 333–355.

Polchin, James. 1997. "Having Something to Wear: The Landscape of Identity on Christopher Street." In Gordon Brent Ingram, Anne-Marie Bouthillette, and Yolanda Retter, eds., *Queers in Space*. Seattle: Bay Press.

"Police Matters." 1890. *Los Angeles Times*, January 8, 2.

Posner, Richard A., and Katharine B. Silbaugh. 1996. *A Guide to America's Sex Laws*. Chicago: University of Chicago Press.

"A Public Market and Its Benefits." 1890. *Los Angeles Times*, May 18, 6.

Purdum, Todd, S. 2000. "The Democrats: The Protesters; Los Angeles Keeps Its Eyes on Protesters and the Police." *New York Times*, August 16, A1.

Quillian, Lincoln, and Devah Pager. 2001. "Black Neighbors, Higher Crime? The Role of Racial Stereotypes in Evaluations of Neighborhood Crime." *Journal of American Sociology* 107(3): 717–767.

Rabban, David M. 1994. "The IWW Free Speech Fights and Popular Conceptions of Free Expression before World War I." *Virginia Law Review* 80(5) (August): 1055–1158.

Rabin, Jeffrey, and Shuster, Beth. 2000. "Judge Voids Convention Security Zone." *Los Angeles Times*, July 20, A1.

Reckdahl, Katy. 2008. "City Dismisses Second-Line Case: Memorial Procession Honored Tuba Player." *New Orleans Times-Picayune*, February 21, B1.

Regis, Helen A. 1999. "Second Lines, Minstreslsy, and the Contested Landscapes of New Orleans Afro-Creole Festivals." *Cultural Anthropology* 14(4): 472–504.

Rendell, Jane. 1998. "Displaying Sexuality: Gendered Identities and the Early Nineteenth-Century Street." In Nicholas Fyfe, ed., *Images of the Street: Planning, Identity and Control in Public Space* (75–91). London: Routledge.

Reynardus, Jorge E. 2004. "The Free Trade Area of the Americas Inquiry Report, Chairperson, Civilian Oversight of Miami-Dade Police and Corrections and Rehabilitation Departments." September 20. Available at www.Miami-fl.gov. Accessed on March 11, 2008.

Ricci, Lind. 1994. "Focus on Urban America: Hawking Neighborhood Justice: Unlicensed Vending in the Midtown Community Court." *Yale Law and Policy Review* 12: 231–278.

Ripston, Ramona. 2000. "Chicago's Lessons Remain Unlearned." *Los Angeles Times*, August 16, B11.

Rivera, Carla. 2002. "Crackdown Demanded on Skid Row Camps." *Los Angeles Times*, November 19, B1.

Roach, Joseph. 1993. "Carnival and the Law in New Orleans." *Drama Review* 37(3): 42–75.

Robertson, Kent. 1993. "Pedestrianization Strategies for Downtown Planners: Skywalks versus Pedestrian Malls." *Journal of the American Planning Association* 59(3): 361–370.

Rodino, Robert. 1998. "Urban Revitalization in an Ethnic Enclave: Huntington Park, CA 1965–1998." Working paper, Department of Urban Planning, University of California, Los Angeles.

Rojas, James. 1993. "The Enacted Environment of East Los Angeles." *Places* 8(3): 42–53.

Rothenberg, Tamar. 1995. "'And She Told Two Friends': Lesbians Creating Urban Social Space." In David Bell and Gill Valentine, eds., *Mapping Desire: Geographies of Sexualities* (165–181). New York: Routledge.

Rubin, Gayle S. 1998. "The Miracle Mile: South of Market and Gay Male Leather." In James Brook, Chris Carlsson, and Nancy L. Peters, eds., *Reclaiming San Francisco: History, Politics, Culture* (247–286). San Francisco: City Lights.

Ryan, Mary P. 1989. "The American Parade: Representations of the Nineteenth-Century Social Order." In Lynn Hunt, ed., *The New Cultural History* (131–153). Berkeley: University of California Press.

Ryan, Mary P. 1990. *Women in Public: Between Banners and Ballots, 1825–1880.* Baltimore: John Hopkins University Press.

Ryder, Andrew. 2004. "The Changing Nature of Adult Entertainment Districts: Between a Rock and a Hard Place or Going from Strength to Strength." *Urban Studies* 41(9): 1659–1686.

Salem. n.d. *History of Salem Sidewalks.* Available at http://www.cityofsalem.net/~sidewalk/history.htm. Accessed on July 27, 2001.

Sampson, Robert J., and Stephen W. Raudenbush. 2004. "Seeing Disorder: Neighborhood Stigma and the Social Construction of 'Broken Windows.'" *Social Psychology Quarterly* 67(4): 319–342.

San Diego. 2002. *The City of San Diego Street Design Manual.* San Diego, CA.

San Francisco. 1995. *The San Francisco General Plan*. San Francisco, CA.

Sanchez, Lisa E. 2004. "The Global Erotic Subject, the Ban, and the Prostitute-Free Zone: Sex Work and the Theory of Differential Exclusion." *Environment and Planning D: Society and Space* 22: 861–883.

Sandercock, Leonie. 2003. *Cosmopolis II: Mongrel Cities in the Twenty-first Century*. New York: Continuum.

Santino, Jack. 1999. "Public Protest and Popular Style: Resistance from the Right of Northern Island and South Boston." *American Anthropologist. New Series* 101(3): 515–528.

"Sauce: A Perambulator See the Sights about the City." 1882. *Los Angeles Times*, May 6, 1.

Schneider, Mary Beth, and George Stuteville. 2000. "Democrats and L.A. Won't Take Chances with Protesters; National Convention Has Special Security, Surroundings for Those Who Will Demonstrate." *Indianapolis Star*, August 14, 1A.

Schneider, Mike. 2003. "Security Tight as FTAA Protesters Gather for March." *Associated Press State and Local Wire*, November 20.

Schultz, S. K., and C. McShane. 1978. "To Engineer the Metropolis: Sewers, Sanitation, and City Planning in Late Nineteenth-Century America." *Journal of American History* 65: 389–411.

Schwada, John. 1990. "Crackdown Urgent on Illegal Street Vendors." *Los Angeles Times*, July 18, B3.

Seattle/King County Coalition for the Homeless. 2006. "One Night County for King County, Washington." January 27. Available at http://www.homelessinfo.org/onc.html. Accessed on November 4, 2006.

"Seattle Is Found Liable for WTO Protest Arrests." 2007. Associated Press, January 31. Available at http://findarticles.com/p/articles/mi_qn4188/is_20070131/ai_n17163151. Accessed on June 30, 2007.

"Seeing Stars: The Ultimate Guide to Celebrities and Hollywood." n.d. Available at http://www.seeing-stars.com/Shop/CityWalk.shtml. Accessed on February 21, 2007.

Sennett, Richard 1971. *The Uses of Disorder: Personal Identity and City Life*. Harmondsworth: Penguin.

Sennett, Richard. 1977. *The Fall of Public Man*. New York: Knopf.

"Setting Urban Tree Canopy Goals." n.d. American Forests. Available at http://www.americanforests.org/resources/urbanforests/treedeficit.php. Accessed on January 5, 2007.

Sewell, Jessica Ellen. 2000. *Gendering the Spaces of Modernity: Women and Public Space in San Francisco, 1890–1915*. Ph.D dissertation, University of California Berkeley.

Sewell, Jessica Ellen. 2003. "Sidewalks and Store Windows as Political Landscapes." In A. Hoagland and K. Breisch, eds., *Constructing Image, Identity, and Place: Perspectives in Vernacular Architecture IX* (85–98). Knoxville: University of Tennessee.

Shoup, Donald C. 1996. "Regulating Land Use at Sale: Public Improvement from Private Investment." *Journal of the American Planning Association* 62(3): 354–372.

Shuster, Beth, and Jim Newton. 2000. "Campaign 2000: LAPD's Response of Protests Shows Its Strength and, Critics Say, Its Faults." *Los Angeles Times*, August 16, A1.

Silverman, Eli B., and Jo-Anne Della-Giustina. 2001. "Urban Policing and the Fear of Crime." *Urban Studies* 38(5–6): 941–957.

Simmel, Georg. 1950. "Metropolis and Mental Life." In K. Wolff, ed., *The Sociology of Georg Simmel* (409–424). Glencoe, IL: Free Press.

Simon, Bryant. 2004. *Boardwalk of Dreams: Atlantic City and the Fate of Urban America*. New York: Oxford University Press.

Sinton, Peter. 1998. "Cleaning Up the Streets: Merchants Unite to Spruce Up Shopping Areas." *San Francisco Chronicle*, December 16, B1.

Skogan, Wesley. 1990. *Disorder and Decline*. New York: Free Press.

Slevin, Peter and Kari Lydersen. 2006. "Greening of Chicago Starts at the Top Floor." *Washington Post*, August 10, A3.

Smith, Michael P. 1994. "Behind the Lines: The Black Mardi Gras Indians and the New Orleans Second Line." *Black Music Research Journal* 14(1): 43–73.

Smith, Neil. 2001. "Global Social Cleansing: Postliberal Revanchism and the Export of Zero Tolerance." *Social Justice* 28(3): 68–74.

Smith, Neil, and Setha Low. 2006. "Introduction: The Imperative of Public Space." In Setha Low and Neil Smith, eds., *The Politics of Public Space* (1–16). New York: Routledge.

"Snow Removal Ordinances." 1918. *The American City* 19(4) (October): 329.

Soja, Edward. 1989. "The Reassertion of Space in Critical Social Theory." *Postmodern Geographies*. New York: Verso.

Soja, Edward, Rebecca Morales, and Goetz Wolfe. 1983. "Urban Restructuring: An Analysis of Social and Spatial Change in Los Angeles." *Economic Geography* 59(2): 195–230.

Sommer, Robert, Fred Learey, Joshua Summit, and Matthew Tirrell. 1994. "The Social Benefits of Resident Involvement in Tree Planting." *Journal of Arboriculture* 20(3): 170–175.

Sorkin, Michael, ed. 1992. *Variations on a Theme Park: The New American City and the End of Public Space*. New York: Hill and Wang.

Southworth, Michael, and Eran Ben-Joseph. 1995. "Street Standards and the Shaping of Suburbia." *Journal of the American Planning Association* 61(1): 65–81.

Southworth, Michael, and Eran Ben-Joseph. 1997. *Streets and the Shaping of Towns and Cities*. New York: McGraw Hill.

Staeheli, Lynn, and Albert Thompson. 1997. "Citizen, Community, and Struggles for Public Space." *Professional Geographer* 49(1): 28–38.

Stansell, Christine. 1986. *City of Women: Sex and Class in New York, 1789–1860*. Urban and Chicago: University of Illinois Press.

Starr, Roger. 1984. "The Motive behind Olmsted's Park." *Public Interest* 74: 66–76.

Steinhauer, Jennifer. 2006. "City Says Its Urban Jungle Has Little Room for Palms." *New York Times*, November 26, A8.

Stevens, Quentin. 2007. *The Ludic City: Exploring the Potential of Public Spaces*. London: Routledge.

Stoller, Paul. 1996. "Spaces, Places, and Fields." *American Anthropologist* 98(4): 776–788.

Street Vendor Project. n.d. "The Street Vendor Project." Available at http://streetvendor .org/public_html. Accessed on September 21, 2006.

Stychin, Carl. 1998. "Celebration and Consolidation: National Rituals and the Legal Construction of American Identities." *Oxford Journal of Legal Studies* 18: 265–291.

Takahashi, Lois M. 1998. *Homelessness, AIDS, and Stigmatization: The NIMBY Syndrome in the United States at the End of the Twentieth Century*. Oxford: Clarendon Press.

Taylor, Ralph B. 2001. *Breaking Away from Broken Windows: Baltimore Neighborhoods and the Nationwide Fight against Crime, Grime, Fear, and Decline*. Boulder: Westview.

Teachey, Lisa. 2000. "Democratic Convention Los Angeles 2000, Lots of Cops, Lots of Protesters, 3,500 March through Heart of Downtown." *Houston Chronicle*, August 14, 8A.

Teaford, J. C. 1984. *The Unheralded Triumph: City Government in America, 1870–1900*. Baltimore: Johns Hopkins University Press.

Teaford, Jon C. 1990. *The Rough Road to Renaissance*. Baltimore: Johns Hopkins University Press.

Teir, Rob. 1998. "Restoring Order in Urban Public Spaces." *Texas Review of Law and Politics* 2 (Spring): 256–291.

Tepper, Paul. 2004. "Homeless in Los Angeles: A Summary of Recent Research." Report available from the Institute for the Study of Homelessness and Poverty at the Weingart Center.

Tester, Keith, ed. 1994. *The Flâneur.* New York: Routledge.

"The Week." 1901. *Los Angeles Socialist,* November 9, 3.

"Thirty Thousand Homeless." 1908. *Los Angeles Times,* February 22, 15.

Tilly, C. 1986. *The Contentious French.* Cambridge: Cambridge University Press.

Tobar, Hector. 2000. "Convention 2000/The Democratic Convention; Protests Are Just a TV Show for Delegates." *Los Angeles Times,* August 16, A1.

Tuinstra, Rachel. 2005. "Tent-Cities Ordinance Approved." *Seattle Times,* May 3. Available at community.seattletimes.nwsource.com/archive. Accessed on July 26, 2008.

Ullman, William. 1937. "The Dumb Pedestrian Really Is Dumb." *Westways* 29 (October): 24–25.

Urban Justice Center. 2003. "Revolving Door: An Analysis of Street-Based Prostitution in New York City (report)." Available at http://www.urbanjustice.org/ujc/publications/sex.html. Accessed on June 13, 2006.

U.S. Conference of Mayors. n.d. "Miami Curbs Prostitution with Strategic Mapping Program." Available at http://www.usmayors.org/uscm/best_practices/usmayor03/Miami_BP.asp. Accessed on July 18, 2006.

U.S. Department of Health and Human Services. 1996. *Surgeon General's Report on Physical Activity and Health.* Report S/N 017-023-00196-5. Washington, DC: DHHS.

Valentine, Gil. 1996. "Children Should Be Seen and Not Heard: The Production and Transgression of Adults' Public Space." *Urban Geography* 17(3): 205–220.

Valentine, Gil. 1998. "Food and the Production of the Civilized Street." In Nicholas Fyfe, ed., *Images of the Street: Planning, Identity and Control in Public Space* (192–204). London: Routledge.

Valentine, Gil, and J. H. McKendrick. 1997. "Children's Outdoor Play: Exploring Parental Concerns about Children's Safety and the Changing Nature of Childhood." *Geoforum* 28: 219–235.

Venturi, Robert, Denise Scott Brown, and Steve Izenour. 1977. *Learning from Las Vegas*. Cambridge, MA: MIT Press.

Vidler, Anthony. 2001. "Aftermath: A City Transformed: Designing 'Defensible Space.'" *New York Times*, September 23, 4:6.

Wade, Richard. 1964. *Slavery in the Cities: The South 1820–1860*. Oxford: Oxford University Press.

Waldron, Jeremy. 1991. "Homelessness and the Issue of Freedom." *UCLA Law Review* 39 (December): 295–324.

Wallace, Amy. 1992. "Like It's So LA! Not Really." *Los Angeles Times*, February 29, A1.

Weitzer, Ronald. 1999. "Prostitution Control in America: Rethinking Public Policy." *Crime, Law and Social Change* 32: 83–102.

Weitzer, Ronald. 2000. "The Politics of Prostitution in America." In Ronald Weitzer, ed., *Sex for Sale: Prostitution, Pornography, and the Sex Industry* (159–180). New York: Routledge.

Whyte, William H. 1980. *The Social Life of Small Urban Spaces*. Washington, DC: Conservation Foundation.

Whyte, William H. 1988. *City: Rediscovering the Center*. New York: Doubleday.

Wilcox, Pamela, Neil Quisenberry, and Shayne Jones. 2003. "The Built Environment and Community Crime Risk Interpretation." *Journal of Research in Crime and Delinquency* 40(3): 322–345.

Wild, H. Mark. 2005. *Street Meeting: Multiethnic Neighborhoods in Early Twentieth-Century Los Angeles*. Berkeley: University of California Press.

Wilson, Elizabeth. 1991. *The Sphinx in the City: Urban Life, the Control of Disorder, and Women*. Berkeley: University of California Press.

Wilson, James Q., and George Kelling. 1982. "Broken Windows." *Atlantic Monthly* (March): 29–38.

Winter, James. 1993. *London's Teeming Streets: 1830–1914*. New York: Routledge.

Wolch, Jennifer, Michael Dear, Gary Blasi, Dab Flamig, Paul Tepper, and Paul Koegel. 2007. *Ending Homelessness in Los Angeles*. Los Angeles: USC Center for Sustainable Cities.

Wolf, Kathleen L. 1998. "Enterprising Landscapes: Business Districts and the Urban Forest." In C. Kollin, ed., *Cities by Nature's Design: Proceedings of the Eighth National Urban Forest Conference*. Washington, DC: American Forests.

Wolf, Kathleen L. 2003. "Public Response to the Urban Forest in Inner-City Business Districts." *Journal of Arboriculture* 29(3): 117–126.

Wolf, Kathleen L. 2004. "Trees and Business District Preferences: A Case Study of Athens, Georgia, U.S." *Journal of Arboriculture* 30(6): 336–346.

"Won't Disturb the Flower Vendors." 1908. *Los Angeles Record*, February 28, 7.

Woodyard, Chris, and Valerie Alvord. 2000. "Police, Protesters Clash in Los Angeles, Ten Activists Arrested Near Convention Hall." *USA Today*, August 15, 4A.

Wooley, Helen, and Ralph Johns. 2001. "Skateboarding: The City as a Playground." *Journal of Urban Design* 6(2): 211–230.

"WTO: Since Cops Were Outnumbered Resorted to Sheer Violence" (letter to the editor). 2000. *Seattle Times*, April 7, B5.

Young, Iris Marion. 1990. *Justice and the Politics of Difference*. Princeton, NJ: Princeton University Press.

Young, John H. 1882. *Our Department*. Springfield, MA: King.

INDEX

Series editor: Robert Gottlieb, Henry R. Luce Professor of Urban and Environmental Policy, Occidental College

Maureen Smith, *The U.S. Paper Industry and Sustainable Production: An Argument for Restructuring*

Keith Pezzoli, *Human Settlements and Planning for Ecological Sustainability: The Case of Mexico City*

Sarah Hammond Creighton, *Greening the Ivory Tower: Improving the Environmental Track Record of Universities, Colleges, and Other Institutions*

Jan Mazurek, *Making Microchips: Policy, Globalization, and Economic Restructuring in the Semiconductor Industry*

William A. Shutkin, *The Land That Could Be: Environmentalism and Democracy in the Twenty-First Century*

Richard Hofrichter, ed., *Reclaiming the Environmental Debate: The Politics of Health in a Toxic Culture*

Robert Gottlieb, *Environmentalism Unbound: Exploring New Pathways for Change*

Kenneth Geiser, *Materials Matter: Toward a Sustainable Materials Policy*

Thomas D. Beamish, *Silent Spill: The Organization of an Industrial Crisis*

Matthew Gandy, *Concrete and Clay: Reworking Nature in New York City*

David Naguib Pellow, *Garbage Wars: The Struggle for Environmental Justice in Chicago*

Julian Agyeman, Robert D. Bullard, and Bob Evans, eds., *Just Sustainabilities: Development in an Unequal World*

Barbara L. Allen, *Uneasy Alchemy: Citizens and Experts in Louisiana's Chemical Corridor Disputes*

Dara O'Rourke, *Community-Driven Regulation: Balancing Development and the Environment in Vietnam*

Brian K. Obach, *Labor and the Environmental Movement: The Quest for Common Ground*

Peggy F. Barlett and Geoffrey W. Chase, eds., *Sustainability on Campus: Stories and Strategies for Change*

Steve Lerner, *Diamond: A Struggle for Environmental Justice in Louisiana's Chemical Corridor*

Jason Corburn, *Street Science: Community Knowledge and Environmental Health Justice*

Peggy F. Barlett, ed., *Urban Place: Reconnecting with the Natural World*

David Naguib Pellow and Robert J. Brulle, eds., *Power, Justice, and the Environment: A Critical Appraisal of the Environmental Justice Movement*

Eran Ben-Joseph, *The Code of the City: Standards and the Hidden Language of Place Making*

Nancy J. Myers and Carolyn Raffensperger, eds., *Precautionary Tools for Reshaping Environmental Policy*

Kelly Sims Gallagher, *China Shifts Gears: Automakers, Oil, Pollution, and Development*

Kerry H. Whiteside, *Precautionary Politics: Principle and Practice in Confronting Environmental Risk*

Ronald Sandler and Phaedra C. Pezzullo, eds., *Environmental Justice and Environmentalism: The Social Justice Challenge to the Environmental Movement*

Julie Sze, *Noxious New York: The Racial Politics of Urban Health and Environmental Justice*

Robert D. Bullard, ed., *Growing Smarter: Achieving Livable Communities, Environmental Justice, and Regional Equity*

Ann Rappaport and Sarah Hammond Creighton, *Degrees That Matter: Climate Change and the University*

Michael Egan, *Barry Commoner and the Science of Survival: The Remaking of American Environmentalism*

David J. Hess, *Alternative Pathways in Science and Industry: Activism, Innovation, and the Environment in an Era of Globalization*

Peter F. Cannavò, *The Working Landscape: Founding, Preservation, and the Politics of Place*

Paul Stanton Kibel, ed., *Rivertown: Rethinking Urban Rivers*

Kevin P. Gallagher and Lyuba Zarsky, *The Enclave Economy: Foreign Investment and Sustainable Development in Mexico's Silicon Valley*

David N. Pellow, *Resisting Global Toxics: Transnational Movements for Environmental Justice*

Robert Gottlieb, *Reinventing Los Angeles: Nature and Community in the Global City*

David V. Carruthers, ed., *Environmental Justice in Latin America: Problems, Promise, and Practice*

Tom Angotti, *New York for Sale: Community Planning Confronts Global Real Estate*

Paloma Pavel, ed., *Sustainable Metropolitan Communities and Regional Equity: New Models for Change*

Anastasia Loukatou-Sideris and Renia Ehrenfeucht, *Sidewalks: Conflict and Negotiation over Public Space*